SIGNIFICANT DISABILITY

ABOUT THE EDITOR

E. Davis Martin, Jr., Ed.D., CRC, NCC: Professor, Department of Rehabilitation Counseling, School of Allied Health Professions (SAHP), Medical College of Virginia (MCV) of Virginia Commonwealth University (VCU), Richmond. Formerly, Interim Chair, Department of Rehabilitation Counseling, SAHP, MVC/VCU; Professor of Special Education, School of Education, VCU; Acting Dean, School of Community and Public Affairs (SCPA), VCU; Associate Dean and Assistant Dean, SCPA, VCU; Director of Continuing Studies, SAHP, MCV/VCU and various administrative and counseling positions in the state-federal rehabilitation program. Dr. Martin has co-authored/co-edited four major textbooks and has been a frequent contributor to rehabilitation literature. His primary research interests have focused on advocacy, leadership, inclusion, and empowerment for persons with disabilities. He has consulted with local, state, and federal agencies as well as with organizations in the private sector. Dr. Martin has been repeatedly recognized for his outstanding leadership and service by the receipt of many awards and commendations from professional, governmental, and private agencies including appointment to significant Boards and Councils by the past five Governors of the Commonwealth of Virginia. Considered to be a leading forensic disability expert, he has served as a Vocational Expert to the Office of Hearings and Appeals for more than 20 years and has provided Vocational Expert testimony in numerous civil suits involving occupational injury, accidental injury, disability retirement, and issues of product liability involving injury. He is a Licensed Professional Counselor (Virginia), Certified Rehabilitation Counselor, and National Certified Counselor.

SIGNIFICANT DISABILITY

Issues Affecting People with Significant Disabilities from a Historical, Policy, Leadership, and Systems Perspective

Edited By

E. DAVIS MARTIN, JR., ED.D., CRC, NCC
Professor of Rehabilitation Counseling
Virginia Commonwealth University

With a Foreward by

John S. Oehler, Ed.D
Dean, School of Education
Virginia Commonwealth University
Richmond, Virginia

Charles C Thomas
P U B L I S H E R • L T D.
SPRINGFIELD • ILLINOIS • U.S.A.

Published and Distributed Throughout the World by

CHARLES C THOMAS • PUBLISHER, LTD.
2600 South First Street
Springfield, Illinois 62704

ISBN 0-398-07192-6 (cloth)
ISBN 0-398-07193-4 (paper)

Library of Congress Catalog Card Number: 2001027143

With THOMAS BOOKS *careful attention is given to all details of
manufacturing and design. It is the Publisher's desire to present books that
are satisfactory as to their physical qualities and artistic possibilities and
appropriate for their particular use.* THOMAS BOOKS *will be true
to those laws of quality that assure a good name and good will.*

*Printed in the United States of America
RR-R-3*

Library of Congress Cataloging-in-Publication Data

Significant disability: issues affecting people with significant disablities
from a historical policy, leadership, and systems perspective/edited by E.
Davis Martin, Jr.; with a foreword by John S. Oehler.
p. cm.
Includes bibliographical references and index.
ISBN 0-398-07192-6 (cloth) – ISBN 0-398-07193-4 (pbk.)
1. Handicapped–Government policy–United States. 2.
Handicapped–Rehabilitation–United States. 3. Handicapped –Mental
health–united States. 4. Social work with the handicapped–United States.
5. Sociology of disability–United States. I. Martin, E. Davis.

HV1553.S555 2001
362.4'0973–dc21

2001027143

For

My Beloved Son, Richard David Martin, who has taught me much
about disability and hope;
and
My Mentors, Colleagues, and Good Friends
Gerald L. Gandy, Ph.D., Professor Emeritus
Richard E. Hardy, Ed.D., Professor and Chair Emeritus
George R. Jarrell, Ph.D., Professor Emeritus
Warren R. Rule, Ph.D., Professor Emeritus
Keith C. Wright, M.A., Professor Emeritus

CONTRIBUTORS

J. Dewey Brown, MS: Adjunct Professor, School of Continuing Studies, University of Richmond. Formerly Biology and Chemistry Teacher, Wheaton High School, Montgomery County Maryland Public Schools. Mr. Brown is an educational consultant with the National Institutes of Health, Office of Science Education, the Howard Hughes Medical Institute, and a faculty consultant for the Advanced Placement Board and the Educational Testing Service. He has been an advocate for inclusive schools and communities and has delivered numerous speeches to legislators, state, national, and international audiences on these topics.

Patricia Johnson Brown, Ed.D: Associate Dean and Director of Community and Professional Education, School of Continuing Studies, University of Richmond. Formerly an Assistant Dean and Associate Professor, School of Community and Public Affairs, Virginia Commonwealth University. She has been a 4-H youth extension agent and international staff associate. Dr. Brown has been an advocate for people with disabilities for more than 30 years. Throughout her career she has worked tirelessly to create inclusive environments for people with disabilities. She is the author of many journal articles and chapters as well as a frequent speaker and consultant on the topic of recreation and disability. Most recently, Dr. Brown was recognized by the University of Richmond with the Story Award for her outstanding contributions on behalf of people with disabilities.

John P. Coates, M.A.: Teacher, The Collegiate School. Formerly taught at St. Catherine's School, Richmond, Virginia and the University of Arizona. Mr. Coates teaches History and English. He was appointed by the Governor of Virginia to the Statewide Rehabilitation Council where he served two terms with distinction. Additionally, he has served on the Chesterfield County Disability Services Board. Mr. Coates has a special interest in the accessibility and availability of assistive technology.

Ann Tucker Durden, MS, CRC: Outreach Counselor, St. Paul's Episcopal Church Prison Ministry. She is a graduate of the Rehabilitation Counseling program at Virginia Commonwealth University where she was the recipient of the prestigious Stalnaker-Wright Award for outstanding academic and community service achievement. Ms. Durden is currently a doctoral student at Virginia Commonwealth University.

Robin Fischer Hoerber, MS: Customer Service Representative, J. C. Penny. Mrs. Hoerber is a graduate of the Rehabilitation Counseling program at East Carolina University. An active advocate for people with disabilities, she has been appointed by the past two Governors of Virginia to significant councils concerned with issues in independent living. She currently serves as Chair of the Chesterfield County Disability Services Board.

Ruth Mackey Martin, RN, BSN: Psychiatric Nurse, Chesterfield County Community Services Board.. Mrs. Martin has been a tireless advocate on the behalf of children and young people with disabilities focused on inclusive education, supported employment, recreation, and case management. She has volunteered her time and considerable energies in bringing an awareness to the everyday issues faced by persons with significant disabilities.

Michele Martin Murmer, AAS: Mrs. Murmer is presently pursuing a degree in psychology and education for a career in teaching at the elementary level. She has a special interest teaching in inclusive school settings. She is an effective advocate for persons with disabilities and for issues affecting siblings.

John S. Oehler, Ed.D: Professor and Dean, School of Education, Virginia Commonwealth University (VCU). Formerly Director of Continuing Professional Education (VCU) and Director of Continuing Education and Field Services (School of Education). Throughout his career, Dr. Oehler has worked to improve the preparation of teachers. He provided leadership for the development of an extended teacher preparation program at Virginia Commonwealth University. He is an advocate of inclusion, and the School of Education's teacher preparation programs reflect this commitment. Dr. Oehler supported the development of an internationally recognized Rehabilitation Research and Training Center in supported employment and the Virginia Institute for Developmental Disabilities, both affiliates of VCU's School of Education. His interest in high standards for teacher education programs is reflected in current service as a member of the Executive Board of the National Council for Accreditation of Teacher Education and Chair of the Committee on Accreditation of the American Association of Colleges for Teacher Education. He also is a member of the Board of Directors of the Association of Colleges and Schools of Education in Land Grant, State Universities, and Affiliated Private Universities.

Michael D. Payne, MS: Formerly an investment banker for various firms. Mr. Payne is a recent graduate of the Rehabilitation Counseling program at Virginia Commonwealth University. His current research interests are in alternative health and pain management related to persons who have experienced long-term or chronic pain. He is an effective advocate for persons with disabilities and often shares his experience and knowledge regarding Social Security Disability and Long-Term Disability insurance benefits.

James A. Rothrock, MS: President of Rothrock Group, Ltd., Richmond, Virginia, a consulting firm working with business and government on the Americans with Disabilities Act. Formerly, Director of the Department for the Rights of Virginians with Disabilities; Executive Director of Handicaps Unlimited of Virginia; served in positions in both the public and private sector of rehabilitation in Virginia; and was a rehabilitation counselor with the Woodrow Wilson Rehabilitation Center. Mr. Rothrock is quite active in community service, professional organizational activity, and legislative advocacy related to rehabilitation and independent living. He has contributed to the rehabilitation literature. Mr. Rothrock is a Licensed Professional Counselor (Virginia).

Justin S. Rybacki, BGS: Mr. Rybacki recently completed an innovative nontraditional bachelor's degree program at Virginia Commonwealth University in which he designed an academic program in disability studies. He is particularly interested in historical and social treatment of persons with disabilities.

Stanford J. Searl, Ph.D.: Dr. Searl lives in Los Angeles, California and teaches at the Union Institute Graduate College, a self-directed Ph.D. program with emphasis upon interdisciplinary, socially relevant doctoral work. Currently, his research focuses upon the connections between spirituality and social change, with particular references to the practices of contemporary Quakers. In the past, Dr. Searl founded a community-based home health care service, worked as a writer about disability issues at the Center on Human Policy at Syracuse University and taught in the English Department at the State University College at Buffalo.

Steven J. Taylor, Ph.D.: Professor of Cultural Foundations of Education, Coordinator of Disability Studies, and Director of the Center on Human Policy, a disability research and policy institute, at Syracuse University. He currently serves as Editor of the journal *Mental Retardation*, which is published by the American Association on Mental Retardation (AAMR), and was the recipient of the AAMR's Research Award in 1997. He is the author of numerous articles and books, including *Introduction to Qualitative Research Methods: A Guidebook and Resource; The Social Meaning of Mental Retardation: Two Life Stories; The Variety of Community Experience: Qualitative Studies of Family and Community Life; and Life in the Community: Case Studies of Organizations Supporting People with Disabilities.* He is also Co-Editor with Stephen Blatt of *The Collected Paper of Burton Blatt.*

Charles C. Wakefield, Jr., M.Ed.: Exceptional Education Teacher, Prince George County Public Schools, Virginia. Formerly, a Learning Disabilities Teacher, Richmond Public Schools, Virginia. Mr. Wakefield was a Dental Technician for 15 years prior to his subsequent educational pursuits. He is currently completing a second graduate degree in special education with the long-term goal of completing doctoral work advancing further in the field of advocacy.

FOREWORD

The concept of inclusion is a singularly American ideal. To exclude or separate persons on the basis of an attribute is antithetical to the American way of life. But, as a society, that is exactly what we have done from a historical perspective. At various times in our history we have excluded groups of persons because of an attribute that differed from the majority. The great hope of American society however is our capacity to do the right thing–to undertake a course of action that brings us together. And, in the end, a recognition that our diversity is our enduring strength.

Professor Martin provides the reader with a unique perspective of significant disability and what it means to have a disability. From the horrors of institutionalization to the contemporary stories of the text's contributors, several recommendations spring forth that we must heed:

1. We must insist and require that teachers, counselors, and other health service professionals receive the appropriate pre-service education and training that results in certification, licensure, or endorsement of their particular skill or area of expertness. While certification does not guarantee competency, it does assure a greater probability that services delivered by teachers, counselors, and others are consistent and effective and support schools and organizations in doing the right thing.

2. Our schools must continue to develop inclusive models that afford the best possible opportunities for children and youth to become a part of American society. Separation and stereotypical thinking as noted by Professor Martin, leads to a parallel existence of shadow within the larger community after exiting a school experience of separation.

3. "We must listen." Professor Martin concludes the text with these words. Indeed, we must listen, not only to the words of

the present but we must heed the lessons of the past.

This is a well-written and researched text. The inclusion of individuals' and families' life stories adds a dimension which enriches the education of teachers, counselors, and other health professionals.

JOHN S. OEHLER, ED.D.
Dean, School of Education
Virginia Commonwealth University
Richmond, Virginia

PREFACE

This text will provide the reader with a comprehensive overview of the issues that affect people with significant disabilities from a historical, policy, leadership, and systems perspective. The text will be particularly useful in either graduate or advanced undergraduate courses for prospective rehabilitation counselors, teachers, community mental health professionals, social workers, psychologists, case managers, or allied health professionals. A major goal of the text is to transmit the ideal of living, working, and playing in the community; an ideal that has often been denied to persons who have significant disabilities. The issues that parallel the typical progression of life such as education, employment, transportation, housing, health care, and leisure are often impeded in important ways for persons with significant disabilities. Some persons who, perhaps, were institutionalized for a part of their life, or were educated in segregated or self-contained classrooms, or were isolated from their peers–other people–as a result face a life of shadow when compared to the general population. An understanding of these issues hopefully will motivate us–persons with disabilities, parents, siblings, loved ones, and professionals–to become effective advocates for an inclusive society that allows all of its members to access the meaning and reality of the "American Dream." Additionally, the book should prove to be a useful and current source for the rehabilitation or community mental health practitioner or the educational professional.

An outstanding group of contributors was selected. They have achieved an excellent balance between their personal and professional experience, and service to the community of persons with disabilities. Considerable thought was put into the organization of this book to assure a consistent and integrated frame of reference as reflected in the following description of each section.

In Part 1 of the text, "Historical, Philosophical, and Public Policy Perspectives," issues relating to community living–education, employment, housing, transportation, health care, and leisure–are explored from a historical perspective that begins with the identification of issues affecting persons with significant disabilities that have impeded independence, productivity, and inclusion within the larger community. Professors Taylor and Searl overview the various social contexts and connections between social and economic forces–urbanization, industrialization, and immigration–that fostered the development of institutions as a means of dealing with the poor, deviant, and those with disabilities. Drs. Taylor and Searl chronicle the history of institutionalization as well as the key legal and constitutional challenges to segregation and exclusion of persons with disabilities. Much of the material they present, when judged by contemporary standards of care, reveal some particularly inhumane and depressing facts. Nonetheless, if we are to learn from the past, as the philosopher George Santayana has warned us, we must be aware of that past. This section of the text concludes with an analysis of the legislative response as well as implications for future trends.

In Part 2, "Portraits of Leadership," the perspectives of persons with significant disabilities, parents, and siblings focus on the issues of everyday life from the vantage point of life roles. Topics ranging from funding, inclusion, IEPs, related services, assistive technology, employment, stigma, spirituality, advocacy, case management, medication policies, education and training for human service professionals, and adaptation among others are presented in a passionate, personal, insightful, and meaningful manner. Sincere appreciation and warm thanks are extended to each person who shared their experiences, thoughts, and recommendations: Pat and Dewey Brown, Christopher Brown, John Coates, Ann Durden, Robin Hoerber, Ruth Martin, Michele Murmer, Michael Payne, Jim Rothrock, Justin Rybacki, and Charles Wakefield. Their insights will challenge the reader to truly understand the meaning and implications embedded in the values of independence, productivity, and inclusion.

The final part of the text concludes with an assessment and analysis of current policies and advocates that our educational and human service systems develop an infrastructure or foundation which allows for positive change and encourages inclusion. Specific recommendations of the text's contributors complete this section.

Special thanks and appreciation is extended to my graduate Rehabilitation Counseling Fall 2000 Semester class who read and discussed the final manuscript and provided me with many substantive suggestions: Linda Albrecht, Charles T. Blaine, Debra A. DeLorey, Kendra DelBalzo, Jessica Dotson, Karla Helbert, Elaine Platt, V. J. Petillo, Mimi Stoner, and Shona Whitfield-Sykes.

Finally, grateful appreciation is extended to Michele Martin Murmer, my much beloved daughter, who typed, contributed, and assisted me in editing this text. She is a person of keen intelligence, warmth, and humor. She has added much to my life and to that of her family.

E. DAVIS MARTIN, JR.

CONTENTS

Part 1
Historical, Philosophical, and
Public Policy Issues

Chapter

Part 2
Portraits of Leadership

Part 3
Leadership and Systems Change

SIGNIFICANT DISABILITY

Part 1

HISTORICAL, PHILOSOPHICAL, AND PUBLIC POLICY ISSUES

Chapter 1

SIGNIFICANT DISABILITY: AN OVERVIEW OF THE ISSUES

E. Davis Martin, Jr.

THE 1987 AMENDMENTS to the Developmental Disabilities Assistance and Bill of Rights Act signaled a major change in the perspective and attitudes held toward persons with developmental disabilities and similarly enhanced the concept of habilitation/rehabilitation by introducing into legislation the values of independence, productivity, and integration. The stated purpose of this legislation was to ". . .assure that all persons. . .receive the services and other assistance and opportunities necessary to enable such persons to achieve their potential through increased independence, productivity, and integration into the community." This legislation required the solicitation of consumer input into the planning process:

> Each State Planning Council shall conduct a review and analysis of the effectiveness of, and consumer satisfaction with. . .services. . .to all persons with developmental disabilities in the State. Such review and analysis shall be based upon a survey of a representative sample of persons with developmental disabilities receiving services and their families, if appropriate.

Each state planning council was mandated by this legislation to collect data, hold public forums, and develop a comprehensive report to be submitted to the Governor and State Legislature. Data from each state and territory was to be aggregated and forwarded to the Secretary of Health and Human Services and then to the Congress of the United States of America. The Consumer Satisfaction Survey, as it was to be called, collected data on six areas:

1. *Demographics*: Information relating to race, marital status, gender, education, living situation, and affiliation with advocacy groups.
2. *Eligibility*: Information regarding disability status vis-a-vis the definition of developmental disability regarding the seven areas of major life activity: self-care, receptive and expressive language, learning, mobility, self-direction, economic self-sufficiency, and the need for lifelong services.
3. *Independence*: Information regarding ability to function independently.
4. *Integration*: Information regarding ability to function in community activities and settings and interaction with persons without disabilities.
5. *Productivity*: Information regarding employment (income, fringe benefits, transportation, unpaid work in the home and community).
6. *Services and Satisfaction*: Information regarding availability of services, satisfaction with services received, and need for additional services.

The analysis of the data for each state could be undertaken in slightly different ways. In Virginia, we chose to relate findings to two major themes: (1) *Targets for Improving Services* and (2) *Targets for Improving Quality of Life.* This paralleled changes at the national level in terms of a move from categorical definitions of disability to a more functional definition of disability. This change related primarily to the seven areas of major life activity (as noted in PL 100-146) and toward a philosophically driven movement that inclusion in the work and play of a community promotes a higher quality of life for people with significant disabilities and conversely for all people. Additionally the issues of employment, housing, education, transportation, healthcare, and community living in the context of major life roles (e.g., child/youth, student, leisure and social person, worker, citizen, spouse, parent, homemaker, retiree) guided the analysis of data. Findings of the Virginia Consumer Satisfaction Survey revealed (Goalder, Martin, Heck, Gandy, & Jarrell, 1990, pp. v–xii):

Targets for Improving Services

1. Consumers with developmental disabilities were dissatisfied with sitting on the sidelines of life. They wanted services and supports that would allow them to be active and integrated members of their communities.

   Consumers gave high satisfaction ratings to all services aimed at increasing community participation. They indicated a high level of need for services and supports such as community living assistance or training, self-help or support groups, and community support services. This finding was not surprising since our data indicated limited social community integration among members of our sample despite the fact that more than 80% of adults rated community integration as important to their lives.

2. Services and supports related to financial welfare dominated perceptions of satisfaction and need.

   The most consistent perceptions of satisfaction and need were related to financial welfare. Thus, high levels of need were indicated for income assistance, food assistance, financial management assistance, private health insurance, payment for medication, and payment or provision of medical equipment. Why was this area of assistance of such importance? Because having adequate income allows independence, community integration and productivity, values strongly endorsed by consumers.

3. While satisfaction with Virginia's direct services was generally high, satisfaction with supports (that were often needed to use services effectively) was much lower.

   Assistance to Virginia's consumers comes in two forms: services (e.g., sheltered employment) that were provided to mitigate the effects of a consumer's disability and secondly, supports (e.g., job coach) that were provided to increase the effectiveness of the service and/or to contribute to the quality of life of the consumer. A decade ago, Virginia's service system offered virtually all persons in a category of disability the same service mix regardless of a consumer's uniqueness. Today, there is a gradual trend toward designing a unique set of services and supports around the specific needs of the consumer.

While this trend is commendable, there remained a consistent discrepancy between satisfaction with services and supports. For example, 72 percent of consumers receiving income assistance (i.e., SSI) were satisfied with that assistance, while only 55 percent were satisfied with the support(s) that helped them make the most out of their income (i.e., financial management assistance). Educationally, satisfaction with regular school classes and career and professional education was 75 percent and 77 percent respectively. In contrast, satisfaction with attendants and after school tutors was 55 percent and 50 percent respectively. Similar relationships held for services and supports for transportation and work. This pattern suggested a need for increased emphasis on improving supports in the service of major life roles and activities.

4. Virginia's service system often failed to target resources with appropriate differentiation across disability groups.

Results from the survey suggested that the satisfaction with and needs for services were often different for different disability groups. For example, there was a high need for transportation training for persons with physical disabilities, but not for other groups. Psychosocial rehabilitation was needed by persons with disabilities related to cognition and mental illness, but not other groups. Personal service attendants were needed at work by many persons with physical and cognitive disabilities, but by few with sensory or mental disabilities. Virginia's service system was set up to provide different services for different disabilities; unfortunately, it often failed to provide the services that were needed. When asked why they were not receiving needed services, a common response by consumers was "not eligible by type or degree of disability."

Targets for Improving Quality of Life

5. The unavailability of work was a major barrier to increasing productivity and quality of life for many persons with developmental disabilities.

Less than a third of the adults in our sample worked full-time; an additional 12 percent worked part-time. Yet only 25 percent of our sample rated themselves as unable to work or retired. That means that 31 percent, almost a third, were available for work but were not working. Is working important? Eight of every ten consumers rated productivity as important to them as a life value. Yet almost a third of the adult consumers felt generally unproductive. The practical implications of these statistics were stunning. Only 28 percent of adult consumers own their own home (compared with 65 % of home ownership of persons without disabilities). Over two-thirds of adult consumers reported continuing to live with relatives and over one-half described their primary caregiver as either a relative or service provider, strongly suggesting the daily implications of inadequate financial resources.

6. The social support networks of most consumers were extremely limited.

Psychological literature strongly suggests that social networks positively contribute to mental health and life satisfaction. Yet involvement in social networks by most persons with developmental disabilities was quite limited. The neighborhood social contacts of both children and adults with developmental disabilities appeared constricted when compared to those of peers without disabilities. Many life roles, which serve to establish social networks (e.g., parent, worker, student, etc.) were either less available or more isolated from the mainstream for consumers.

7. The commitment of Virginia's primary caregivers and service system to the independence of persons with developmental disabilities was limited by the vested interest of the caregivers and service systems.

Consumers demonstrated a very high level of independence in certain life activities (e.g., decorating one's room) but considerably less independence in other activities (e.g., handling personal finances). Lower levels of independence were often associated with the potential for inconvenience or liability on the part of caregivers or the service system. Only 24.1 percent of consumers whose primary caregiver was a service provider and 65.5 percent of consumers whose primary caregiver was a relative reported choosing their own jobs. Assistance to increase level of independence in such activities as choosing one's own attendant or service provider and handling personal finances was limited and sporadic for many.

8. While children and their parents were generally satisfied with their current service and family environments, this satisfaction often cloaked dependence, a potential barrier of importance to future life satisfaction.

Children and adolescents were, for the most part, satisfied with their lives. Most lived in loving and warm family settings and spend a great amount of their time in school. They were often given special assistance. For example, with 70 percent of youth in school, only 21 percent were in classrooms not providing special assistance–that we provide this for our children should comfort us. But how well do we ensure that children grow up believing they can be independent? Relatively few youth were members of consumer groups though over half of their parents had joined at least one group. On a majority of indices of independence, caregivers providing foster care allowed more freedom of choice to consumers than did either parents or institutional staff. These examples suggested a discrepancy between life values and reality. While eight of every ten consumers endorsed independence as an important life value, over half of these same consumers characterized themselves as dependent.

9. Many consumers remained isolated and limited in their involvement in "real world" roles and environments.

While children seemed to be fairly satisfied with their lives, adults appeared somewhat less so. How does such a change come about? Our results suggested that an answer may be found in considerations of life involvement. Children's lives revolve around the roles of child, student, and leisure person. In contrast, adults are traditionally engaged in additional roles. Many roles taken for granted by persons without disabilities are simply not available to persons with developmental disabilities. Seventy-nine percent of our sample of consumers had never married and, of those who had married, 40 percent had divorced (spouse role). Only 32 percent of adult consumers worked full time (worker role). Only 42 percent of adult consumers living in multi-family homes or institutions were allowed to choose their leisure activities on weekends and evenings (leisure role). The likelihood of having children if you have a developmental disability was so remote that no questions about the needs of consumer-parents were included in the survey (parent role). Yet pleas for participation in the "real world" abounded in the survey. More than 80 percent of adult respondents indicated that integration into community was important to their lives.

These findings, a decade later, still ring true for many if not most persons with significant or developmental disabilities whether in Virginia or America. What does it mean to have a disability, particularly a significant or developmental disability? The conclusions of the 300 persons interviewed in Virginia (and most probably for all persons regardless of geography) mean for the most part:

You are alone.
You are poor.
You are uninvolved, standing on the periphery of life.
You do not work.
You are treated with less respect and dignity than others.

To our credit we have tried, particularly over the course of the past 20 or so years, to develop programs that foster independence, productivity, and inclusion. Yet, these same programs designed to build self-esteem and facilitate meaningful work for persons with significant disabilities have been constrained by the following stereotypes (Gerry and Mirsky, 1992, p. 342):

1. *The medical/pathological stereotype,* in which persons with severe disabilities are viewed as sick or unmotivated individuals whom it is proper to regard as burdens of charity who should passively accept permanent social and economic dependence.
2. *The economic worth stereotype,* in which people with disabilities are discounted as economically worthless and excluded from the workforce on the basis of their perceived congenital unproductiveness.
3. *The needed professional stereotype,* in which the continued dependence of people with severe disabilities is assured by career structures of the helping professionals whose very jobs depend on retaining the power to distribute scarce resources to their

de-facto wards.

4. *The bureaucratic stereotype*, in which disability is characterized as a set of administrative problems to be solved by administrators rather than as a label signaling the restrictions on personal dignity and social freedom.

Gerry and Mirsky (1992) further noted that self-esteem, as an inherent component of one's identity, is diminished with the usage of labels which are affixed to persons through our categorical programs of supports and services (e.g., schools, service delivery agencies that affix labels that refer to the disability first and thus promote stereotypical thinking). The subtle effects of words can be especially devastating (Gandy, Martin, Hardy, 1999). For example, the following is a listing of commonly used words or phrases that are encountered in the print media, in our school systems, various human service delivery systems, and in our daily speech:

Disabled
Handicapped
Confined to a Wheelchair
Afflicted with . . .
Suffers with . . .
Victim of . . .
Cripple/crippled by . . .

Special Education labels: EMR (educable mentally retarded), TMR (trainable mentally retarded, ED (emotionally disturbed), SPH (severely and profoundly handicapped), etc.

Physically challenged, Mentally challenged
Able-bodied, nondisabled

Usage of such language is generally not intended to devalue the person, yet that is exactly what occurs. The rationale set forth for usage of such language is that it is quicker, easier, and more accurate to use these terms. Yes, it may be quicker and it's certainly easier to say these words rather than using *person first* language, but it is not more accurate. Quite to the contrary, the phrase "confined to a wheelchair," for example, is quite inaccurate. A wheelchair for a person who uses one represents freedom of movement, mobility not confinement. Euphemistic language such as "physically challenged" or "mentally challenged" should as well be avoided. What do these phrases really mean–are not most of us physically or mentally challenged? Should not we all strive to be mentally challenged? Physically challenged? The usage of words such as "able-bodied" or "nondisabled" to refer to people without disabilities is also a reference to people who are "disabled" and is often used gratuitously. Newspaper articles about a person with a disability, for example, will often distinguish other persons in the story who do not have a disability with a reference to being able-bodied or non disabled. What does this bit of information add to the story? What it does do, however, is to further separate or segregate people with disabilities from the mainstream of society. The perceived meaning of such words, phrases, or labels is not good for a person's sense of self or worth. Two questions should be asked when tempted to use language other than person first:

1. What effect does usage of language do to the self concept or image of the child or person who is repeatedly referred to in terms of their disability?
2. What effect does usage of language of this type have on the perceptions of the child's or person's parents, loved ones, peers, teachers, and human service workers?

Some persons–whether professionals, the general public, and/or aspiring professionals–will question the need to use person first language indicating that it has been inspired by the notion to be politically correct or by dismissing person first language because a person with a disability used the previously noted pejorative words, labels, or phrases to describe themselves or others who have a disability. Person first language is not inspired by a need to be politically correct; it is language that conveys information without the excess baggage of emotionally laden words and stereotypical images of, generally, what a person cannot do. People without disabilities, in general, do not refer to themselves in negative and limiting ways. Why should reference to people with disabilities be presented in such a manner? It does not make good sense. Because some persons refer to themselves in some pejorative manner does not give others' permission to use pejorative language to refer to other persons with similar attributes. If one person refers to him or herself in a derogatory or devaluing way (e.g., *bastard* or *bitch*) does that give others the right to call all males or females by these terms because of the attribute of birth or gender? Similarly, if a person who uses a wheelchair refers to him or herself as a *cripple* or *gimp*, does that legitimatize referring to other persons who use wheelchairs as cripples or gimps? Of course not! In the instance of using the words bastard or bitch, it is recognized by most persons as an exception that related to one particular person while the word cripple or gimp is generalized as a rule to all persons who may have a similar attribute. A major reason for this response may be due to our tendency as human beings to "pigeon hole" or to stereotype and to generalize situations that we are unfamiliar with or uncomfortable around.

It should be noted that some persons wish to be referred to in terms of their disability and not strict person first language. Most notable are persons with sensory disabilities. Some persons who are deaf wish to be referred to as "deaf" or "hard-of-hearing" or prefer all who have hearing disabilities to be collectively referred to as the "deaf community." Similarly, some persons who are blind prefer to be referred to as "blind" and not as visually impaired or as having a visual disability. When communicating with persons with disabilities, it is always a good idea to ascertain that person's preferences regarding language usage. In all situations, courtesy and tact are appropriate regardless of the presence or absence of a disability. Reference to the presence or absence of a disability when it adds nothing material to the conversation or written material is superfluous, and serves only to send a confused and perhaps erroneous message. In a very powerful cartoon, Morrie Turner (Field Enterprises, Inc., 1981) displayed in two scenes the essence of language usage and the effects words have on our self concept: In scene one, two young girls are asking a third young girl who is sitting in a wheelchair "Do we call you handicapped or disabled?" In the next scene, the young girl in the wheelchair says "Call me Charlotte." Perhaps we spend too much time trying to be too precise and correct that we miss the essence of the encounter. We need to pay attention to the person, not the disability.

Secondly, Gerry and Mirsky (1992) noted that meaningful work for persons with significant disabilities is limited when stereotypical thinking predominates the perspectives of professionals and of the philosophies human service programs are based upon. The last decade of the twentieth century witnessed the passage of the Americans With

Disabilities Act, important amendments to the historic 1973 Rehabilitation Act (1992 and 1998), the Workforce Investment Act of 1998, and the Ticket to Work and Work Incentives Act of 1999. Each of these legislative events had as its purpose the development of human service delivery systems to be more consumer or customer centered and directed. Is this occurring? The purpose of this text will be to explore the various dimensions of this basic question from a historical, policy, leadership, and systems perspective.

The issues referenced in this overview will be presented and analyzed in three sections of the text: In this first section, a historical perspective of the policies and trends related to persons with significant disabilities will be presented inclusive of the resulting debate and controversies as well as an analysis of the recent legislative response and implications for future trends. The second part of the text will present the perspectives of persons with significant disabilities and parents and siblings and will focus on the issues of life identified earlier in this chapter: education, employment, housing, health care, transportation, and community living from the vantage point of life roles. The third section of the text will focus on advocacy and leadership needed for future delivery systems based on the perspectives presented in Parts 1 and 2.

REFERENCES

Americans With Disabilities Act of 1990. Public Law 101-336.

Developmental Disabilities Assistance and Bill of Rights Act Amendments of 1987. Public Law 100-146.

Goalder, J.S., Martin, Jr., E. D., Heck, M. J., Gandy, G. L., & Jarrell, G. R. (1990). *Life patterns: A report on life and service satisfaction of Virginians with developmental disabilities.* Richmond: Virginia Commonwealth University.

Gandy, G. R., Martin, Jr., E. D.& Hardy, R. E. (1999). *Counseling in the rehabilitation process: Community services for mental and physical disabilities.* Springfield: Charles C Thomas.

Gerry, M. H., & Mirsky, A. J. (1992). "Guiding principles for public policy on natural supports" in Nisbet, J. (1992). *Natural supports in school, at work, and in the community for people with severe disabilities.* Baltimore: Paul H. Brookes Publishing Company.

Rehabilitation Act of 1993. Public Law 93-112.

Rehabilitation Act Amendment of 1992. Public Law 102-569.

Rehabilitation Act Amendments of 1998.

The Ticket to Work and Work Incentives Improvement Act of 1999.

Chapter 2

DISABILITY IN AMERICA: A HISTORY OF POLICIES AND TRENDS[1]

STEVEN J. TAYLOR AND STANFORD J. SEARL

DISABILITY MUST BE UNDERSTOOD in the context of broad social forces. If we are to understand disability, special education, or vocational rehabilitation, we must understand these forces.

If you are reading this book, you are likely to be preparing for a career in rehabilitation, special education or a related field. You are going to hear a lot about trends, philosophies, and controversies, and you might have heard something about them already.

INSTITUTIONS AND DEINSTITUTIONALIZATION. You probably know something about institutions. Chances are that you have read about bad conditions at institutions. Just the same, you might think that some people with severe disabilities will always have to live in institutions. Do you know *why* institutions were developed? Have you always assumed that our society developed institutions for the benefit of people with disabilities? Have you ever thought that maybe we developed institutions because we did not want certain people around?

Are you aware that many people today believe that all people with disabilities should be integrated into the community?

SCHOOLS, INTEGRATION, AND INCLUSION. Did you know that as

1. The preparation of this chapter was supported in part by the National Resource Center on Supported Living and Choice, Center on Human Policy, School of Education, Syracuse University, through the U.S. Department of Education, Office of Special Education and Rehabilitative Services, National Institute on Disability and Rehabilitation Research (NIDRR), through Contract No. H133A990001. Members of the Center are encouraged to express their opinions; however, these do not necessarily represent the official position of NIDRR and no endorsement should be inferred.

16

recently as the 1970s thousands of children with disabilities were excluded from America's schools? Do you know how that changed? Today, most children with disabilities receive some kind of an education. Where do you think these children should go to school? Have you considered that maybe children with disabilities should be educated alongside their peers in an inclusive setting? What would you say if you were told that this is happening at an increasing number of schools across the country?

CHARITY AND RIGHTS. You may be drawn to this field because you want to help other people. The field needs you—but be aware that people with disabilities and their families do not want charity or pity. They want their rights, just like anyone else. Did you ever hear about the disability rights movement? What do organizations of people with disabilities and their parents want? How has the government responded? What do you think the courts have said about the civil rights of people with disabilities? These and other issues are described in the pages that follow.

The field of disability today is characterized by new and controversial ideas that emerged during the 1960s, '70s, '80s, and '90s. Indeed, this period can be characterized as nothing less than a revolution in our thinking about people with disabilities and our treatment of them. Yet each of these ideas have deep historical roots. Thus, we start with a look at the history of disability in America.

A Look at History: Institutions and Education

The history of disability in eighteenth and ninteenth-century America is the history of institutions. It is only in the past 100 years that public schools had anything to do with students with significant disabilities. In fact, public school systems across the nation did not begin to accommodate students with a full range of disabilities until the mid-seventies.

The Origins of the Asylum

The segregation of children and adults with disabilities in special institutions is a relatively modern phenomenon. It was not until after 1820 that states began to develop separate institutions for a diverse range of deviant or dependent members of the population: insane asylums, orphanages and reformatories, penitentiaries, and asylums and schools for the so-called feebleminded.

The existence of large public state institutions is so taken for granted that it is difficult to imagine what happened to people with mental and physical disabilities in colonial America. Where were people with physical disabilities, mental retardation, and emotional problems? First of all, many people with severe disabilities simply did not survive. Indeed, it is only in recent years that medical advances have made possible lifesaving treatment for many infants born with serious disabilities.

Second, Americans in the colonial period cared for elderly, dependent, and family members with disabilities at home. As David Rothman (1971) has pointed out, the colonists left poor and dependent people in the care of relatives and neighbors. There were no orphan asylums, nursing homes, mental hospitals, institutions, or group homes for people with mental retardation.

Third, many people whom we would label mentally retarded or otherwise today blended into the community because participation in society did not require sophisticated technical or intellectual skills, such as the ability to read and write. Practically everyone could perform some useful social role in society. Many people who might not blend into today's society could have been easily accommodated in eighteenth-century America. They were not regarded as a problem and, for all practical purposes, were not mentally retarded.

Beginning in the eighteenth century and extending into the early nineteenth century, larger towns and cities began to build workhouses, poorhouses, or almshouses for the destitute and dependent (Rothman, 1971). These were repositories for people who could not support themselves; including orphans, widows, the elderly, and paupers as well as people labeled idiotic, insane, crippled, and epileptic. As we shall see, conditions in almshouses were wretched.

The Development of State Institutions

The development of separate institutions for discrete populations of people often has been characterized as progress in society's treatment of the so-called mentally retarded, mentally ill, and others. Yet, as Rothman (1971, p. xv) poignantly has asked, "Was an organization that would eventually turn into a snake pit a necessary step forward for mankind?" Rothman's question suggests the answer. The irony is that the first institutions were funded by social reformers who subscribed to humanitarian ideals.

Throughout the 1800s, and indeed extending into the 1960s, institutions were developed at a rapid pace. Almshouses for poor people proliferated. Rothman (1971) has reported that in Massachusetts 60 towns constructed new almshouses between 1820 and 1840; the number of people in New York almshouses grew from 4,500 in 1830 to roughly 10,000 in 1850; other states soon followed suit.

As almshouses flourished, states began to develop specialized institutions for other populations. New York and Pennsylvania led the way with the development of the first state penitentiaries for criminals. The Auburn system in New York, devised in 1819, stressed congregate activities and "the liberal use of the whip" (Erikson, 1966). The Pennsylvania system, developed in the 1820s and founded on Quaker ideals, stressed solitude and separate confinement (Erikson, 1966).

In 1773, the nation's first public mental hospital for the "insane" and "idiotic" was established in Williamsburg, Virginia (Szasz, 1970). For 50 years, however, no other state established a mental hospital until Kentucky did so in 1824 (Scheerenberger, 1983). In the next several decades, practically every state opened public asylums for the insane. "A cult of asylum . . .", wrote Rothman (1971, p. 130), "swept the country." By 1860, 28 of the 33 states had established public insane asylums.

The development of separate institutions for the "feebleminded" gradually followed the establishment of insane asylums. In 1848, Massachusetts opened the nation's first institution specifically for people with mental retardation. In 1851, Albany, New York established the second such institution, which was moved to Syracuse in 1854. Davies (1959, p. 22) has stated that by 1890, fourteen states had opened separate public institutions for the "mentally defective."

The institutional movement gripped other populations. Orphan asylums and reformatories for juvenile offenders flourished in the 1830s, 1840s, and 1850s. Similarly, institutions for people who are blind, such as Perkins Institute and Massachusetts School for the Blind, both opened in the 1830s, and those who are deaf, such as the American Institute for the Deaf and Dumb in Hartford, Connecticut, founded in 1818, were developed during the first half of the eighteenth century. Eventually, states and communities turned to asylums to care for the elderly, people with tuberculosis, and, in some places, people with epilepsy. By the end of the nineteenth century, some states had even established separate institutions for different categories of people labeled mentally retarded, including "feebleminded women" and "unreachable idiots." The founders and early proponents of the asylum may be characterized as what sociologist Howard Becker (1963) has called "moral entrepreneurs." They were social reformers who succeeded in gaining public acceptance of their definitions of social problems and their proposed solutions to those problems. Many reformers advocated for diverse populations: Dorothea Dix crusaded for the poor, "idiotic," and "epileptic," as well as for the "insane"; Samuel Gridley Howe was instrumental in the establishment of institutions for the blind and the mentally retarded; Benjamin Rush, regarded as the founder of American psychiatry, promoted asylums for the so-called mentally ill and mentally retarded in addition to a Quaker version of solitary confinement for criminals (Erikson, 1966, p. 199).

These moral entrepreneurs advocated for humane, if strict, treatment of people who were mentally retarded or mentally ill, and other populations. Dorothea Dix crusaded against the squalid conditions under which people were forced to live in the public almshouses. According to Scheerenberger (1983, pp. 105–106), Dix traveled over 10,000 miles in 1850, visiting jails, almshouses, and mental hospitals. She addressed the U.S. Congress and the legislatures of Massachusetts, New York, New Jersey, Pennsylvania, Kentucky, Tennessee, North Carolina, Mississippi, and Maryland, telling them what she had seen. In a famous address before the Legislature of Massachusetts, Dix (1843) made a plea for humane care:

> I come to present the strong claims of suffering humanity. I come to place before the Legislature of Massachusetts the condition of the miserable, the desolate, the outcast. I come as the advocate of helpless, forgotten, insane, and idiotic men and women: of beings shrunk to a condition from which the most unconcerned would start with real horror: of beings wretched in our prisons, and even more wretched in our almshouses. And I cannot suppose it needful to employ earnest persuasion, or stubborn argument, in order to arrest and fix attention upon a subject only the strongly pressing in its claims because it is revolting and disgusting in its details. . . .

I proceed, gentlemen, briefly to call your attention to the *present* state of insane persons confined within this Commonwealth, in *cages, closets, cellars, stalls, pens! Chained, naked, beaten with rods,* and *lashed* into obedience. (p. 32)

As Scheerenberger (1983) and Rothman (1971) have pointed out, Dix was joined by other reformers in exposing the institutions of her day. In 1857, a legislative committee in New York reported: "Common domestic animals are usually more humanely provided for than the paupers in some of these institutions" (Rothman, 1971, p. 198).

Dix exposed the asylums and pleaded for mental hospitals founded on humane principles for the insane and idiotic. Others advocated treatment based on scientific and educational grounds. Benjamin Rush's distinctive contribution to psychiatry was his claim that there was no difference between physical and mental illness. In a thought-provoking book on the history of mental illness, psychiatrist Thomas Szasz (1970) has attributed to Rush an ideological conversion from theology to science. What had been considered "sin" now had become "illness." The medical doctor replaced the priest, psychiatric treatment replaced religious ritual, and the asylum replaced the cathedral.

Rush offered the hope of curing mental illness. By placing the insane in mental institutions and subjecting them to various forms of treatment, including bloodletting, work, strict discipline, and a strange contraption known as a tranquilizing chair, the insane could be cured. "It will be necessary," wrote Rush, "to mention the means of establishing a complete government over patients afflicted with it (madness), and thus, by securing their obedience, respect, and affections, to enable a physician to apply his remedies with ease, certainty, and success" (Szasz, 1970, pp. 146–147).

In mental retardation, Edouard Seguin, Hervey B. Wilbur, and Samuel Gridley Howe played prominent roles in the establishment of the first institutions in America. Born in France, Seguin immigrated to the United States in 1848 and worked with Howe and Wilbur in developing institutions in Massachusetts and New York. He was a strong supporter of educationally-oriented asylums for "idiots."

Like Seguin, Howe and Wilbur advocated for the education of the idiotic or feebleminded. As superintendents of the Massachusetts and New York asylums respectively, they envisioned their institutions as small boarding schools where higher-functioning retarded people would receive the training necessary to perform useful roles in society.

The founders of the first institutions believed, however, that not all people labeled mentally retarded could be educated. They advocated for the exclusion of people with severe disabilities. Thus, in 1852, Howe wrote, "The institution is not intended for epileptic or insane children, nor for those who are incurably hydrocephalic or paralytic, and any such shall not be retained, to the exclusion of more improvable subjects" (quoted in Wolfensberger, 1975, p. 25).

Seguin, Howe, and Wilbur shared a deep distrust of large, segregated institutions. In 1866, in an address at the opening of a state institution for the blind in Batavia, New York, Howe seriously questioned the institution:

> As much as may be, surround insane and excitable persons with sane people, and ordinary influences; vicious children with virtuous people and virtuous influences; blind children with those who see; mute children with those who speak; and the like. People run counter to this principle for the sake of economy, and of some other good end, which they suppose cannot be had in any other way, as when they congregate the insane in hospitals, vicious children in reformatories, criminals in prisons, paupers in almshouses, orphans in asylums, blind children and mute children in boarding schools. Hence I begin to consider such establishments as evils which must be borne with, for the time, in order to obviate greater evils. I would take heed, however, against multiplying them unnecessarily. I would keep them as small as I could. I would take the most stringent measurements for guarding against those undesirable effects which lessen their usefulness: and for dispensing with as many of them as may be possible. (quoted in Wolfensberger, 1975, p. 65)

The ideals of these reformers were never realized. In fact, many of their worst fears came true. Conditions at new asylums soon deteriorated to the level of those at the almshouses and sometimes were worse. Large isolated institutions replaced smaller ones. Once asylums were firmly in place, society turned to them to deal with the casualties of the emerging social and economic order. The reformers of the early years of the asylum were replaced by a new generation of leaders whose ideals were not nearly as humane or progressive.

The Era of Institutional Expansion

The turn of the twentieth century was a period of rapid institutional expansion in American society. The number of prisons, mental hospitals, asylums for the feebleminded, and reformatories increased at a rapid pace during this period. In an exhaustive review of historical trends in institutions for the so-called mentally retarded, Lakin (n.d.) reported that the number of facilities increased from ten in 1880 to 20 in 1890, 28 in 1904, 35 in 1910, 40 in 1916, 66 in 1923, and 77 in 1926.

What were supposed to be small homelike facilities became large, overcrowded warehouses. Platt (1969) has noted that by 1899 an Elmira, New York juvenile reformatory, then considered a model institution, housed as many as 1,500 juveniles though it had been built with only 500 cells. Asylums for the feebleminded swelled in size. The number of people in these institutions grew from 2,429 in 1880 to 55,466 in 1926: the average size of the asylums expanded from 243 to 720 in that time (Lakin, n.d.). Further, while the number of almshouses stabilized around the turn of the century and the percentage of the population in almshouses actually decreased dramatically, the number of feebleminded in these institutions jumped from 7,811 in 1890 to 16,551 in 1904 (Lakin, n.d.). Not only did institutional populations soar during that period, but they also greatly outpaced the growth of the general population, which itself increased dramatically throughout the nineteenth and into the twentieth centuries. According to Lakin (n.d.), the number of residents of public institutions for people with mental retardation per 100,000 of the general population grew from 4.8 in 1880 to 47.8 in 1926.

During that period there also was a retreat from the optimism and idealism of the asylum's earlier proponents (Rothman, 1971; Wolfensberger, 1975). In the 1870s, Pliny Earle wrote a widely accepted article entitled *The Curability of Insanity,* in which he disputed the claims of successful treatment of the founders of mental hospitals (Rothman, 1971). In the field of "feeblemindedness," leaders, too, had their doubts about whether the lot of the feebleminded could be markedly improved. "Give them an asylum, with good and kind treatment," stated Governor Butler of Massachusetts, "but not a school" (quoted in Wolfensberger, 1975, p. 28).

As we shall see, the era of institutional expansion was marked not by a concern for people considered disabled or deviant, but by a conscious attempt to protect society by removing them altogether. In order to fully understand this era, we must look at what was happening in our society at the time.

ontext

nineteenth and early twentieth centuries were a time of major changes and disruptions in American society. What seemed to be a simple and stable society underwent tremendous social upheaval: yet, the changes that shook the nineteenth century did not occur overnight. They seemed, nevertheless, to have caught the attention of the social and political leaders of the time all at once and to have roused them to action.

Three major social trends confronted American society in the nineteenth century. The first was the growth of cities: *urbanization*. Throughout the century and extending well into the twentieth century, the American population moved out of rural communities and into cities and towns. During the latter half of the 1800s, the rural population doubled while the urban population increased by almost seven times (Platt, 1969). The percentage of the American population living in urban areas stood at 6.1 percent in 1800 (Stockwell, 1968). By 1870, the percentage had increased to 25.7 percent and by 1920 to 51.2 percent (Stockwell, 1968).

The second major trend, related to the first, was *industrialization*. It was the prospect of work in the industrial factory that lured people to urban areas. Not everyone could fit into the economic order, however. In an agricultural society, practically everyone can perform some useful social role: the elderly, the young, and those with disabilities– all can contribute to the household. In an urban industrialized society, one's social role, both job and social worth, is dependent upon the value of one's work in the competitive labor market. In the dog-eat-dog world of the marketplace, some people cannot compete on an equal footing.

The final trend, also related to the previous ones, was *immigration*. In the 1800s and early 1900s, millions of foreign-born persons migrated to American shores. Of course, America had been a nation of immigrants since its founding. Toward the latter half of the eighteenth century, though, the annual number of immigrants increased at an incredible pace. In the 1820s, a mere 151,000 people immigrated to the United States. In the next 100 years, over 38 million foreign-born persons came to America, reaching a peak of over 8 million in the period from 1900 to 1909, an average of over 800,000 per year (Stockwell, 1968). Just as significant as the number of immigrants was where they come from. Those who arrived in the late eighteenth and early nineteenth centuries did not share the cultural and ethnic ancestry of the established class, and they were greeted by suspicion, resentment, and hostility.

It is not a coincidence that by the mid-1800s mental hospitals and almshouses were filled with immigrants. According to Rothman (1971, p. 283), at the mental institution in Worcester, Massachusetts, over 40 percent of the inmates in the 1850s were foreign born: at Ohio's Longview asylum 67 percent of the inmates in 1861 were immigrants: at the state asylum in Wisconsin the figure reached 60 percent in 1872. In Massachusetts, state officials expressed grave concern over the number of poor immigrants filling the almshouses in 1857:

> Why has Massachusetts so many paupers? Because we have a larger proportion of foreigners from which they are made. . . . Our almshouses paupers are nearly all foreigners. . . . Aliens who have landed in this State and their children . . . embrace five-sixths of all those who become chargeable. (quoted in Rothman, 1971, p. 290)

The combined effects of urbanization, industrialization, and immigration resulted in the rise of the first large-scale social problems in American society: slums, unemployment, homeless children and adults, culture conflict, crime, delinquency, and, according to many, vice and immorality. The asylum became the solution to these problems, providing a way to deal with homeless and idle populations and a way to remove from society, those presumed responsible for causing the social problems. The political, social, and intellectual leaders of the time traced the roots of social problems to the victims of the emerging social and economic order: the poor, the deviant, and those with disabilities.

The Indictment: The Eugenics Movement

A new breed of moral entrepreneurs emerged in the latter part of the nineteenth century. Citing an equal concern for the preservation of society and the well-being of the feebleminded and other disability groups, they sought to prevent the spread of degeneracy and immorality throughout society. Included in their ranks were institutional superintendents like Fernald and Kerlin, leaders of charitable organizations like Lowell, researchers like Dugdale and Goddard, and intellectuals like Spencer and Sumner.

In attempting to understand and explain the social problems of their times, social theorists, beginning with Spencer (1851) and Galton (1869), began to apply evolutionary theory to the development of society. The cause of the spread of poverty, crime, immorality, and other social evils throughout society, they reasoned, was the proliferation of people with defective genes. The feebleminded gradually came to be singled out as especially dangerous carriers of social disease. These theories were translated into a program of social action known as the eugenics movement.

By the 1870s and 1880s politicians, institutional officials, and leaders of charitable organizations were sounding the eugenics alarm. Feeblemindedness, they warned, was a major peril to society; it was the cause of most of society's problems, crime, delinquency, pauperism, prostitution, and immorality.

For almost the next 50 years, these moral entrepreneurs carried on their crusade against the evils of feeblemindedness with fanatic zeal. In 1907, Butler wrote: "While there are many anti-social forces, I believe none demands more earnest thought, more immediate action than this. Feeblemindedness produces more pauperism, degeneracy and crime than any one other force" (quoted in Wolfensberger, 1975, p. 34). Several years later, Walter Fernald, recognized as an early leader in the field, expressed the same sentiments more strongly:

> Feebleminded women are almost invariably immoral, and if at large usually become carriers of venereal disease or give birth to children who are as defective as themselves. The feebleminded woman who marries is twice as prolific as the normal woman. . . . Every feebleminded person, especially the high-grade imbecile, is a potential criminal, needing expression of his criminal tendencies. The unrecognized imbecile is a most dangerous element in the community. . . . It has been truly said that feeblemindedness is the mother of crime, pauperism and degeneracy. It is certain that the feebleminded constitute one of the great social and economic burdens of modern times (quoted in Wolfensberger, 1975, pp. 35-36)

Supporting these outrageous claims was a series of studies of family histories that attempted to link crime, vice, insanity, and feeblemindedness, including *The Jukes* by Dugdale (1910), and *The Kallikak Family* by Goddard (1912). Goddard's study was especially well received in the field of feeblemindedness. In an attempt to prove the hereditary link between feeblemindedness and social evils, Goddard set out to study lines of descendants from a soldier in the Revolutionary War. One line descended from Martin Kallikak's illegitimate son from a sexual liaison with a feebleminded woman: the other came from Kallikak's marriage to a respectable woman from a good family after the war. Based on his fieldworker Elizabeth Kite's observations, interviews with family members, and whatever documents she could find, Goddard concluded that Martin Kallikak's illegitimate son yielded 480 descendants, of whom 143 were feebleminded, 36 were illegitimate, 133 were sexually immoral, 24 were alcoholic, 3 were epileptic, 3 were criminals, 8 kept houses of ill-repute and 82 died in infancy (Sarason & Doris, 1959). On the "good" side of the family, there were 496 descendants, all of whom were reportedly doctors, lawyers, educators, landholders, and other good citizens. Of that group, only 15 children lived to infancy; only 2 were alcoholics, 1 was insane, and 1 was a promiscuous male.

From this and other research, which has been thoroughly discredited (see Gould, 1981: Sarason & Doris, 1959), Goddard concluded that feeblemindedness was a hereditary condition that caused such social problems as crime, prostitution, poverty, and intemperance. In 1915, Goddard wrote:

> For many generations we have recognized and pitied the idiot. Of late we have recognized a higher type of defective, the moron, and have discovered that he is a burden; that he is a menace of society and civilization; that he is responsible to a large degree for many, if not all of our social problems. (quoted in Wolfensberger, 1975, p. 34)

As Wolfensberger (1975) and other commentators have noted, the indictment of the feebleminded and other groups waned toward the end of the 1920s. In fact, many of the leaders of the eugenics movement later recanted their earlier alarmist statements. Yet, the eugenics movement played a major role in shaping public policy toward people with disabilities for decades to come and so pervaded public and professional thinking that many of the views expressed during the period persist today.

Social Control

The leaders of the eugenics movement advocated a set of social politics designed to rid society of the alleged carriers of defective genes responsible for the spread of crime, vice, and degeneracy. In 1913, the American Breeders Association wrote:

> The following classes must generally be considered as socially unfit and their supply should if possible be eliminated from the human stock if we would maintain and raise the level of quality essential to the progress of the nation and our race: (1) the feebleminded, (2) paupers, (3) criminaloids, (4) epileptics, (5) the insane, (6) the constitutionally weak, (7) those predisposed to specific diseases, (8) the congenitally deformed, and (9) those having defective sense organs. (quoted in Scheerenberger, 1983, p. 154)

The eugenics cause was soon taken up by charitable organizations, the U.S. Congress and state legislatures, and a range of public figures. Beginning in the 1800s and extending well into the 1900s, the federal and state governments adopted a series of social control measures directed against people labeled mentally retarded, insane, epileptic, and otherwise stigmatized: segregation, sterilization, prevention of marriage and sexual relations, and restrictive immigration. Some leaders also considered a more drastic measure: euthanasia.

Segregation

By the 1870s, leaders in the field of "feeblemindedness" were promoting the asylum as an effective means of segregation. In stark contrast to earlier times, the purpose of the asylum was not to train the feebleminded to perform useful roles in society, but to remove them from society altogether. Johnson wrote in 1908 that "the only just and humane and civilized way of stopping the transmission of defectiveness is by segregation" (quoted in Wolfensberger, 1975, p. 43). Murdoch and Johnstone called for the quarantine of mental defectives, while Barr proposed the establishment of one or more national reservations (Wolfensberger, 1975).

The history of the establishment of an institution in Newark, New York, lends insight into the tenor of the times. In 1878, New York created an experimental "Custodial Asylum for Feebleminded Women" of childbearing age at Newark as a colony of the Syracuse asylum.

According to the state legislature, the purpose of the experiment "was to determine whether there are feebleminded women in county poorhouses or elsewhere who need care and protection to prevent them from multiplying their kind and so increasing the number of dependent classes in the state; also, could they be maintained without undue cost" (quoted in Newark State Custodial Asylum for Feebleminded Women, 1893). By the 1880s the experiment was declared a success and the legislature established a permanent location at Newark in 1885.

It was not until 1890 that the Newark Custodial, as it was called, was officially dedicated. The proceedings contain several speeches by members of the board of trustees, one a state legislator, one a member of women's charities, and one a member of the clergy. Each speech, while testifying to the humaneness of the asylum, points out the need to control the spread of "feeblemindedness" and immorality. The dedicatory address by the Reverend M. S. Hard, cloaked in humanitarian concern, carried an underlying theme of social control:

> And here let me say, *that it is the duty of the State to be humane.* It is not possible that all who make a commonwealth should be equal in brainforce, in power to construct wealth, or in purity of purpose. The encouragement offered every boy to strive for the presidency is a sophistry. Inequality in mind creates grades in morals. When morals come to minds of low grade, there comes promptly the need of security to society. . . . For those who cannot elect success: who are not responsible for their infirmities; who enter the census-count because they have the form of beings that are human, who are the impersonation of social wrongs, and carry in face and speech and form the tenderest pleadings for protection; toward these, we maintain, the State should exercise the most pronounced humanity. (Newark State Custodial Asylum for Feebleminded Women, 1893, p. 24)

The establishment of the Newark asylum, and similar ones in New Jersey and Pennsylvania, was a blatant effort to prevent so-called feebleminded women from having children by segregating them during their childbearing years. While most institutions were designed to serve both sexes, men and women were separated within the institutions. Cornell warned in 1915, "The institution that places . . . boys and girls anywhere near each other will never do its part in the work of preventing feeblemindedness in the community" (quoted in Wolfensberger, 1975, p. 43). It was common practice up until the

1980s for men and women to be segregated on different units or wards at institutions.

Sterilization

Sterilization was viewed by some political and social leaders as an effective means of preventing the transmission of "defectiveness." By the early 1900s officials of leading charitable organizations were actively advocating sterilization or "asexualization" for the so-called feebleminded, epileptic, and insane. Barr wrote in 1902:

> Knowing the certain transmission of such taint, how can one fail to appreciate the advantage of prevention over penalty, or to recognize as the most beneficent instrument of law the surgeon's knife preventing increase. And why not? We guard against all epidemics, are quick to quarantine smallpox, and we exclude the Chinese: but we take no steps to eliminate this evil from the body social. (quoted in Wolfensberger, 1975, p. 40)

Indiana was the first state to enact a sterilization law directed at people with disabilities and deviant populations (Sarason & Doris, 1959, p. 287). By 1912 eight states had passed laws that required sterilization or made sterilization a condition for institutional release for disparate groups such as the "feebleminded," "insane," "epileptic," "confirmed criminals," "syphilitics," and others (Scheerenberger, 1983, p. 155). Other states soon followed suit, and by 1926 similar laws existed in 23 states (Scheerenberger, 1983, p. 191).

Courts gradually began to hear cases involving the constitutionality of the sterilization laws. In several states, including Nevada, Indiana, New Jersey, and New York, courts overturned sterilization statutes; courts in other states upheld these laws. In 1927, a famous case, *Buck vs. Bell,* wound its way to the U.S. Supreme Court. This case involved a Virginia statute that applied to inmates of the state's institutions for the so-called feebleminded, insane, and epileptic and, in contrast to some of the laws overturned by courts, provided appeal procedures for people who were to be sterilized. The case was generated on behalf of Carrie Buck, an 18-year-old woman committed to the State Colony for Epileptic and Feebleminded of Virginia; she was the daughter of another inmate at the institution and the mother of an allegedly illegitimate, feebleminded child (Scheerenberger, 1983, pp.

191-192). In a resounding victory for the proponents of social control, the Supreme Court upheld the practice of forced sterilization. Writing on behalf of the Supreme Court, Justice Holmes commented:

> We have seen more than once that the public welfare may call upon the best citizens for their lives. It would be strange if it could not call upon those who already had the strength of the State for these lesser sacrifices, often not felt to be such by those concerned, in order to prevent our being swamped with incompetents. It is better for all the world, if instead of waiting to execute degenerative offspring for crime, or let them starve for their imbecility, society can prevent those who are manifestly unfit from continuing their kind. The principle that sustains compulsory vaccination is broad enough to cover the cutting of the Fallopian tubes . . . three generations of imbeciles are enough! (quoted in Scheerenberger, 1983, p. 192)

With the endorsement of the nation's highest court of law, sterilization of the feebleminded and other groups continued on a broad scale up until at least the 1950s and 1960s. Davies (1959) reported that by 1958 twenty-eight states had enacted sterilization laws and 31,038 persons labeled as mentally retarded had been sterilized nationally.

Some leaders in the field of feeblemindedness questioned the practice of sterilization on the grounds that this would encourage promiscuity. Fernald (1912, pp. 95-96) warned:

> The presence of these sterile people in the community, with unimpaired sexual desire and capacity would be direct encouragement of vice and a prolific source of venereal disease. Sterilization would not be a safe and effective substitute for permanent segregation and control. (quoted in Wolfensberger, 1975, p. 41)

Prevention of Marriage and Sexual Relations

In line with the practice of forced sterilization, professional and political leaders around the turn of the century advocated restrictions on the rights of people labeled feebleminded, insane, epileptic, and so on to marry and have sexual relations. Speaking at a convention of what is now the American Association on Mental Deficiency in 1911, Diller stated:

> There is a very widespread notion that the marriage between two persons is a matter of their affair and their affair only and that the next door neighbor

should not in any way meddle in the matter. I believe none of us here would subscribe to this doctrine. We have a right not only to take an interest in the subject of marriage, but I believe it is our duty to do so. (quoted in Scheerenberger, 1983, p. 154)

According to Scheerenberger, 39 states eventually outlawed marriage among people with mental retardation or established mental retardation as a ground for annulment.

States also enacted laws imposing stiff penalties for anyone having sexual relations with an "epileptic," "insane," or "feebleminded" person. Wolfensberger (1975, p. 40) reported that Connecticut passed a law containing the following language around 1895:

> Every man who shall carnally know any female under the age of forty-five years who is epileptic, imbecile, feebleminded, or a pauper, shall be imprisoned in the State prison not less than three years. Every man who is epileptic who shall carnally know any female under the age of forty-five years, and every female under the age of forty-five years who shall consent to be carnally known by any man who is epileptic, imbecile, or feebleminded, shall be imprisoned in the State prison not less than three years.

These laws are strikingly reminiscent of the Nuremberg Laws of 1933 that outlawed sexual relations between Jews and Gentiles and marked the beginning of the Nazi era in Germany. As we shall see, parallels between the eugenics movement in America and the Nazi reign of terror do not end here.

Restrictive Immigration

In United States immigration policies around the turn of the century, we find the clearest expression of what Sarason and Doris (1959, p. 289) called "the alliance of racism with eugenics." As noted earlier, the majority of immigrants during the latter half of the nineteenth and early part of the twentieth centuries did not share the Anglo-Saxon heritage of their forebears. They came to America with different customs, religions, and languages.

The professional and political establishment at that time viewed the new waves of immigrants as a severe threat to the purity of the American people. One after the other, political, civil, and professional leaders stood up to denounce the many "defective" among the "immigrant stock." In a study reported in 1917, Goddard reported that between 40 and 80 percent of the immigrants were feebleminded based on intelligence tests (Sarason & Doris, 1959, p. 293).

As early as 1891, the U.S. Congress amended the immigration law to exclude "idiots," "insane persons," and "paupers," among other groups. As the eugenics movement gathered steam, immigration laws became more strict and were more rigorously enforced. In the Immigration Act of 1917, Congress added provisions to exclude Orientals from admission into the United States, established Ellis Island as a clearinghouse for Europeans, and enacted a literacy test to ban illiterates from entering the country (Stockwell, 1968, p. 140). In 1924 Congress expanded the definition of undesirable groups and set firm quotas for immigrants from different nations.

According to Scheerenberger (1983), immigrants passing through Ellis Island were examined by two physicians, one to examine their physical condition and the other to test their mentality. Based on these examinations, "undesirables" were prevented from entering this country. In 1904, one immigrant out of every 5,300 was deported because of mental retardation. By 1927 the number had increased to one out of every 234.

Elimination

The policies of the eugenics era stopped short of turning to elimination—mass murder—of people with mental retardation and other disabilities. Yet the eugenics movement came dangerously close to this. In 1901, Johnson, who had been president of the National Conference of Charities and Correction and what is now the American Association on Mental Deficiency, wrote: "I do not think that, to prevent the propagation of this class it is necessary to kill them off or to resort to the knife; but, if it is necessary, it should be done" (quoted in Wolfensberger, 1975, p. 37).

The sentiments that spawned segregation, asexualization, restrictive marriage, and selective immigration in America reached their logical extension in the so-called euthanasia program in Nazi Germany. The mass murder of millions of Jews, gypsies, and intellectuals in Nazi Germany is widely known. What is less known is that the Nazis first practiced their mass murder techniques on the inmates of Germany's institutions for the mentally ill and mentally retarded (Werthman, 1978). Cloaked in euphemisms such as "mercy deaths" and "destruction of life devoid of value," the Nazi "euthanasia program" resulted in the deaths of as many as 275,000 inmates of institutions through starvation, poisoning, and gassing beginning in 1939. In fact, the Nazis perfected the mass murder techniques associated with Auschwitz and Buchenwald in Germany's mental institutions. In a haunting book on the subject, Werthman (1978) has made a convincing case that Germany's physicians and professionals played a central role in legitimating and carrying out the mass murders. He provided a chilling account of how psychiatrists developed questionnaires to distinguish between those "not worthy to live" and those "worthy to be helped." The Nazi experience serves as a grim reminder of what can happen when any group of people is singled out as lacking basic human rights.

Institutional Momentum

The 1920s saw the waning of the eugenics movement, although it has resurged on occasion even until today. Intellectuals such as Walter Lippman and G. K. Chesterton first stood up to denounce the outrageous claims of the eugenics movement, and in 1922 the latter published a book entitled *Eugenics and Other Evils.* Gradually, leaders in the field of mental retardation, such as Goddard and Fernald, began to recant their earlier views. By 1924, Fernald was forced to admit, "We have begun to recognize the fact that there are good morons and bad morons" (quoted in Wolfensberger, 1975, p. 54).

Wolfensberger (1975) has described the period from around 1920 to the 1950s as an era of institutional "momentum without rationales." That is to say, institutions continued to expand from the 1920s through the 1950s and into the 1960s in the absence of clear-cut rationales such as those provided in earlier periods. The belief that certain people belong in institutions came to be taken for granted. Of course, this view is held by many even today. Between 1930 and 1970, the number of public institutions for the mentally retarded increased from 77 to 190, while their populations grew from 68,035 to 186,743 (Lakin, n.d.). The populations of public institutions for the mentally retarded peaked in 1967 with 194,650 and have continued downward ever since. These figures do not include the number of people labeled mentally retarded in other kinds of institutions, including poorhouses, mental hospitals, jails, and nursing homes. Scheerenberger (1983, p. 199) indicated that many people with mental retardation were in almshouses as late as 1936. Lakin (n.d., p. 62) has reported that the number of people labeled mentally retarded in institutions for the so-called mentally ill peaked at 41,823 in 1961.

The populations of public institutions for other categories of dependent and deviant people similarly grew from the late 1920s into the 1950s and 1960s. Mental hospitals, nursing homes, detention centers, and institutions for persons with physical disabilities experienced significant expansion. The populations of state mental hospitals reached their peak in 1955 at 558,922.

While the populations of public institutions steadily increased during the first half of the twentieth century, that period also was marked by efforts to develop community alternatives to institutionalization. In the late 1920s and 1930s especially, progressive leaders in mental health and mental retardation, equally cost conscious and disillusioned with institutions, explored a series of arrangements to care for and supervise former inmates in the community. Alternatives included parole, colony care, and family care.

The history of mental retardation in the United States has been described as a pendulum swinging back and forth between institutions and the community. The period of the 1920s and 1930s is often described as a swing toward the community. Colonies, family care, and the parole system are cited as evidence of that trend.

The sad truth, however, is that the community was never really given a fair chance. David Rothman (1980) has argued that in the field of mental health, community programs never received wholehearted acceptance and support. In the field of mental retardation, the ideas that guided the colony and family care programs were never broadly endorsed. Scheerenberger (1983, p. 196) has reported that a survey conducted by the Committee on Research of the American Association on Mental Deficiency in 1937 revealed that over 50 percent of the responding institutions had less than 10 percent of their residents on parole, 87 percent had not placed any residents in a boarding home, 84 percent had no residents in a colony, and only 23 percent had residents in training for community placement. Similarly, the statistics of Lakin (n.d., p. 87) show that the percentage of people on the books of public institutions (presumably those in family care and parole) living outside the institution did not change significantly from 1927 to the 1950s and mid-1960s (between 13 and 14%).

From the late 1840s to the late 1960s, institutions for the so-called mentally retarded and persons labeled as developmentally disabled developed and flourished. The institutional model essentially went unchallenged for over 100 years. But the 1950s through the 1970s ushered in a new day, and the institution struggled for its very existence.

The Emergence of Special Education in the Public Schools

In the early history of America, education was the privilege of the upper classes. It was not until the nineteenth and early twentieth century that states began to pass and enforce compulsory education laws.

Of course, the rise of compulsory education in America can be attributed to many of the same social forces that led to the widespread development of institutions. Like institutions, the schools were a response to the changes occurring in American society at the time. In the context of the social dislocations brought about by urbanization, industrialization, and immigration, the schools were to perform an important social function: what Michael Katz (1983, p. 373) has called "cultural standardization."

From the perspective of early proponents of compulsory education such as Horace Mann, the schools were to provide a way to socialize the young and train them to be better, more productive workers. Katz and others have argued that schools were designed not only to teach students the skills necessary to function in the workplace, but also to inculcate the values and beliefs necessary for the maintenance of an urban working class. Further, according to Katz and others, schools have played a more insidious role in teaching students to blame themselves for failure.

The spread of compulsory education meant that schools had to begin to deal with students with disabilities. Prior to the latter part of the nineteenth century, of course, the only places at which children who were labeled as mentally retarded, blind, or deaf could receive an education were institutions. As we have seen, the first institutions established in the mid-eighteenth century were designed to be small boarding schools.

Toward the end of the nineteenth century, the public schools were first confronted with a large number of "backward" students. Many educators at the time expressed alarm at the disruptive influence of children who were disruptive, slow in learning, or otherwise different. In 1908, the superintendent of the Baltimore public schools, James Van Sickle, stated:

> The presence in a class of one or two mentally or morally defective children so absorbs the energies of teacher and makes so imperative a claim upon her attention that she cannot under these circumstances properly instruct the number commonly enrolled in a class. School authorities must therefore, greatly reduce this number, employ many more teachers, and build many more school rooms to accommodate a given number of pupils, or else they must withdraw into small classes these unfortunates who impede the progress of normal children. The plan of segregation is now fairly well established in large cities, and superintendents and teachers are working on the problem of classification, so that they may make the best of this imperfect material. (quoted in Sarason & Doris, 1979, p. 263)

As Van Sickle's remarks make clear, school systems began to segregate those children with disabilities and otherwise "deviant" students who were forced on them through compulsory education (Sarason & Doris, 1979, p. 267). Separate schools and special classes were established throughout the country. According to LaVor (1976), Boston established the first public day school for the deaf in 1869. New York City first initiated special education classes in 1874. Most commentators argue that Providence, Rhode Island schools were the first to establish special classes for students labeled as mentally retarded in 1896. Scheerenberger (1983, pp. 129–130), however, has stated that there is evidence that Cleveland initiated a special class for so-called mentally retarded students in 1875, although this class was disbanded at the end of the school year. In any case, many large cities had started special education classes for those persons labeled as mentally retarded by the turn of the century: Chicago in 1898, Boston in 1899, Philadelphia in 1899, and New York in 1899 (Scheerenberger, 1983, p. 130).

Many of the first special education classes served as a dumping grounds for a broad range of students who did not fit into typical school classes. Sarason and Doris (1979, p. 267) have written that these classes might include "slow learners, the mentally subnormal, epileptics, learning disabilities, chronic truants, behavior problem children, physically handicapped or immigrant children suffering from language or cultural handicaps." Sarason and Doris (1979, p. 266) have quoted Johnstone, then superintendent of an institution for the "feebleminded" in Vineland, New Jersey. "The special class must become a clearinghouse. To it will not only be sent the slightly blind and partially deaf, but also the incorrigibles, the mentally deficients, and cripples." Similarly, Scheerenberger (1983, p. 130) quoted Elizabeth Farrell, then inspector with the New York City schools who later was elected the first president of the Council for Exceptional Children as having reported:

> The first class was made up of the odds and ends of a large school. There were overage children, so-called naughty children, and the dull and stupid children. The ages ranged from eight to sixteen years. They were the children who could not get along in school.

Throughout the twentieth century, special education grew at a steady pace. Scheerenberger (1983, p. 166) has written that by 1922, 133 cities in 23 states had enrollments of 23,252 pupils in special education classes of all types. States began to enact special education laws. New Jersey passed a law mandating special education for students with mental retardation in 1911 (Sarason & Doris, 1979, p. 309; Scheerenberger, 1983, p. 166). Within the next 10 to 15 years, a large number of states passed laws mandating special education, providing state aid for special education, and requiring local school districts to identify students with disabilities.

Despite the gradual expansion of special education programs, students with severe disabilities were largely excluded from public education up until the 1970s. Sarason and Doris (1979, p. 312) have stated that a national survey found that there were no children labeled "trainable mentally retarded" in public schools in 1940, although they also cite other evidence indicating that at least some programs were in operation by that time. Scheerenberger (1983) has quoted a number of leading educators in the 1920s who advocated the exclusion of "low grade" cases from public programs. Finally, Lakin (n.d., p. 67) has reported that it was not until the mid-1950s that special education programs were serving more persons with mental retardation than were public institutions.

The period from around 1920 to 1950 was a relatively quiet one in special education. To be sure, the populations of public institutions as well as public special education programs gradually expanded.

Further, the federal government initiated a number of programs designed to benefit people with disabilities during that period. In the aftermath of World Wars I and II, federal vocational programs directed at veterans who sustained disabilities as a result of their war time experiences were initiated. As part of President Roosevelt's New Deal, the Social Security Act, which has become a basic income maintenance program for people with severe disabilities, was passed in 1935. Yet, compared to the decades either before or after, the 1920s through the 1940s were marked by maintenance of the status quo and the absence of major controversies about what people with disabilities are like and how they should be treated. The forces for change grew steadily throughout the 1950s and exploded in the field in the 1960s and 1970s.

A Time of Change

The 1950s and 1960s marked a new era in the history of society's treatment of people with disabilities. Tentatively at first, and then with increased conviction, professionals, parents, and people with disabilities began to question the legitimacy of traditional practices. The era started with pleas for modest reforms. By the late 1960s and 1970s, however, parent and professional leaders and disability rights advocates demanded fundamental changes in educational and social service systems.

New philosophies emerged during that period, but the seeds of those philosophies had been planted in earlier times. As we have seen, leaders like Seguin and Howe in the mid-nineteenth century expressed distrust of "abnormal environments" such as large institutions. Beginning in the 1950s, a new generation of leaders, allied with parent groups, directly challenged prevailing practices and attitudes toward people with disabilities. They waged their battles in public forums, courts, and legislatures.

The Rights Movement

In the 1950s, parents began uniting to form strong local, state, and national organizations. The first national organization for persons with mental retardation, what is now The Arc, was founded in 1950. Gradually, parents of children with other kinds of disabilities organized to form organizations such as the National Society for Children with Autism, the Spina Bifida Association, and the Association for Children with Learning Disabilities.

Over time, parent groups have grown increasingly aggressive in advocating for their children's rights. Initially, parents came together to provide each other mutual support, to share information, to sponsor fund-raising events, and even to operate schools and day programs. In the 1960s and 1970s, however, parent groups started to demand quality services from school districts and other service providers. Parent groups took their demands to the nation's courts and legislatures.

The development of organizations composed of people with disabilities occurred during the 1970s, just as African Americans, Latinos, women organized to confront societal prejudice and discrimination, adults with disabilities joined together to form groups like Disabled in Action and the American Coalition of Citizens with Disabilities. Like other groups, national organizations of persons with disabilities challenged those who presumed to speak and act on their behalf. "You gave us your dimes," said many people with disabilities, "now we want our rights."

In recent years, national and international organizations of people labeled mentally retarded formed to speak on their own behalf. One of the most notable of these is People First, which, as the name implies, has demanded that people with mental retardation be afforded the same rights and privileges enjoyed by other members of society. In the early 1980s, a group of mentally retarded adults from Austria presented a moving and forceful statement at the United Nations:

> We are people first and only secondly handicapped.
> We wish to speak for our rights and let other people know we exist.
> We want to explain to our fellow human beings that we can live and
>   work in a community.
> We want to show that we have rights and responsibilities like other
>   people.
> Our voice is new.
> We must first learn to speak.
> And we ask everyone to learn to understand our voices.
> We need people who teach us to speak. People who believe in us.
> Mentally retarded persons do not want to live in terrible institutions.

We want to live in the community.

Exposés

The 1960s ushered in an era of exposés of society's shameful treatment of people with disabilities. Of course, scandals and exposés were not new to the field of services for people with disabilities. Throughout the nineteenth and twentieth centuries, reformers like Beers (1908) had occasionally exposed deplorable conditions at institutions. Yet not since Dorothea Dix's crusades against the wretched conditions in almshouses did exposés so stir America's conscience as those that started in the 1960s.

"There is a hell on earth, and in America, there is a special inferno," wrote Burton Blatt (Blatt & Kaplan, 1966, p. v). "We were visitors there during Christmas, 1965." A respected educator and researcher in the field of mental retardation, Blatt closely followed the reactions of professionals and politicians to Robert Kennedy's unannounced tours of institutions in New York State in 1965. After visits to Willowbrook and Rome state schools, Kennedy had commented to the *New York Times*: "I was shocked and saddened by what I saw there. . . . There were children slipping into blankness and lifelong dependence." Blatt knew the truth of what Kennedy had reported. He, too, had been to institutions and had found the same filth and deprivation that Kennedy had decried. As Blatt listened to Governor Rockefeller, state legislators, and institutional administrators severely criticize Kennedy's "whirlwind" tours, he decided to follow through on what he termed a "seemingly bizarre venture." That Christmas, Blatt, together with a photographer named Fred Kaplan, secretly photographed the "back wards" at five institutions in the eastern United States. Their book, *Christmas in Purgatory*, and a subsequent article in *Look* magazine, shocked America and fueled the growing disenchantment with the institutional model.

It is difficult to put into words the conditions that Blatt and Kaplan found. Indeed, pictures do not fully capture the horror. They found locked wards, isolation cells, broken toilets, and incredible overcrowding:

> Beds are so arranged–side by side and head to head–that *it is impossible, in some dormitories, to cross parts of the room without actually walking over beds.*

Often the beds are without pillows. We have seen mattresses so sagged by
the weight of bodies that they were scraping the floor. (Blatt & Kaplan, 1966,
p. 1)

Blatt and Kaplan went on to describe the areas where people spent
their waking hours:

In each of the dormitories for severely retarded residents, there is what is
euphemistically called day room or recreation room. The odor in each of
these rooms is overpowering. . . . Most day rooms have a series of bench-
es on which sit unclad residents, jammed together, without purposeful activity, communication, or any interaction. In each day room is an attendant or
two, whose main function seems to be to "stand around" and, on occasion,
hose down the floor "driving" excretions into a sewer conveniently located
in the center of the room. (p. 22)

It was the infant wards, however, that Blatt and Kaplan found most
distressing:

The infant dormitories depressed us the most. Here, cribs were placed–as
in the other dormitories–side by side and head to head. Very young children, one and two years of age, were living in cribs, without any interaction
with any adult, without playthings, without any apparent stimulation. In
one dormitory, that had over 100 infants and was connected to 9 other dormitories that totaled 1,000 infants, we experienced a heartbreaking
encounter. As we entered, we heard a muffled sound emanating from the
"blind" side of a doorway. A young child seemed to be calling, "Come.
Come play with me. Touch me." We walked to the door. On the other side
were forty or more unkempt infants crawling around a bare floor. (p. 34)

The Kennedy and Blatt discoveries were merely the first of a long
set of exposés that received widespread public attention. Reporter
Geraldo Rivera's exposé of Willowbrook in Staten Island, New York,
in the early 1970s documented the same conditions found by Blatt and
Kaplan five years earlier (Rivera, 1972). The artful documentary of
Frederick Wiseman (1969), *Titticut Follies,* filmed at Bridgewater State
Hospital in Massachusetts, and the book by Kenneth Wooden (1974),
Weeping in the Playtime of Others, focused attention on mental hospitals
and juvenile institutions, respectively.

In the late 1970s, Blatt, McNally, and Ozolins (1979) returned to the
institutions depicted in *Christmas in Purgatory.* Institutional populations
had declined: the budgets had soared–yet Blatt and his colleagues

concluded that little else had changed:

> A decade or so we went to five state institutions for the mentally retarded. . . . Then, we found little to give us hope but, we were reluctant to admit that the concept of "institution" is hopeless. Today we find much to give us hope, but we are now unable to see a way to save the institutions. . . . We must evacuate the institutions for the mentally retarded. The quicker we accomplish that goal the quicker we will be able to repair the damage done to generations of innocent inmates. (Blatt, McNally, & Ozolins, 1979, p. 143)

Exposés of institutions have occurred in practically every state. In 1982, the Gannett newspapers undertook a major investigation of Oklahoma's institutions for juveniles and those labeled as mentally retarded. Hardly an institution in the nation has gone unscathed over the past two decades.

As professionals, reporters, and politicians exposed the shameful conditions in America's institutions, child advocacy groups began to focus public attention on the exclusion of children with disabilities and minority children from public schools. In 1970, the Task Force on Children Out of School published a scathing indictment of school exclusion in Boston entitled *The Way We Go to School.* "At a time when the public schools must take giant strides to prepare children for today's world" the report's introduction read: "Some children are being excluded from school, others discouraged from attending, and still others placed in special classes designed for the 'inferior.'" The task force concluded that large numbers of culturally, physically, mentally, and behaviorally different children were denied the right to equal educational opportunity. Other task forces and reports documented school exclusion throughout the nation. A report issued by the Children's Defense Fund in 1973 estimated that as many as two million children with disabilities were denied the right to a public education.

Social Science Perspectives

Traditionally, the fields of special education and disabilities have been dominated by medical and psychological perspectives that focus on the defects or deficiencies of people with disabilities. In the 1950s and 1960s, social science perspectives began to play an important role.

In contrast to traditional medical and psychological perspectives, these perspectives directed attention to how society treats persons with disabilities.

Sociologist Erving Goffman, in the classic study *Asylums*, was one of the first researchers to document the devastating effects on the identity and self-esteem of inmates of a broad range of institutions, including mental hospitals, nursing homes, tuberculosis sanatoriums, prisons, and concentration camps. Goffman (1961, p. xiii) coined the phrase "total institution" to refer generally to these facilities: "A total institution is a place of residence and work where a large number of like-situated persons, cut off from the wider society for an appreciable period of time, together lead an enclosed, formally administered round of life." Following in Goffman's footsteps, Vail (1966), Braginsky and Braginsky (1971), Morris (1969), Perrucci (1974) and others have studied the dehumanizing effects of institutions.

Social scientists also have focused attention on the social stigma that accompanies disabilities (Edgerton, 1967; Bogdan & Taylor, 1982; Scott, 1969; Hobbs, 1975; Mercer, 1973). Mental retardation, mental illness, and other such terms are labels or social constructs that demean those to whom they are attached. As Hobbs (1975) has written:

> The categorization of exceptional children involves much negatively loaded terminology: crippled, handicapped, limited, impaired, disturbed, disabled. Each of these labels also has pejorative, slang, or colloquial counterparts used casually by children's peers. . . it is widely accepted that such negative labels create a unique atmosphere around the children, complicating their lives in significant though unmeasured ways. A very important consequence of labeling is the tendency to stereotype. (p. 24)

If we abandon labels—that is, if we focus on people's humanity rather than their deficits—then we must abandon a whole set of discriminatory actions against those that are called "disabled."

In a wonderfully entertaining article first published in 1959, Louis Dexter (1994) illustrated the relative nature of labels such as mental retardation. Dexter described a mythical society in which people value grace the way people in our society value intelligence. He pointed out that everything in this society would be designed in such a way as to require grace for the performance of everyday tasks, just like our society requires intelligence.

Dexter explained that clumsy people, whom he calls the "gawkies," would be a major target of societal discrimination in this society. He speculated on what would happen to the gawkies. All school children would be ranked by grace quotient (GQ). Some clumsy people would present an embarrassment to those around them and would be sent to special schools and institutions. Professional organizations like the National Association on Clumsiness would be formed. Dexter even went as far as to suggest that professionals would be engaged in major debates over whether all clumsy people should live in the community.

Out of social science perspectives such as these has come the principle of normalization. First developed in Scandinavia, the principle of normalization is an alternative philosophy to social exclusion and segregation of people with disabilities. As Perske (1980) has pointed out, the principle of normalization has had many definitions. Two Swedish leaders, Karl Grunewald and Bengt Nirje, defined normalization as follows: "Making available to all mentally retarded people patterns of life and conditions of everyday living which are as close as possible to the regular circumstances and ways of life of their society." Gunnar and Rosemary Dybwad and Wolf Wolfensberger first popularized the concept in the United Sates. *Normalization*, by Wolfensberger (1972), provides the most comprehensive statement of this concept.

The concept of normalization has been subject to misunderstandings and misinterpretations. Some critics charge that normalization means that people's individual clinical or instructional needs should be ignored. Nothing in the concept implies this. Normalization simply means that we should stop treating people in abnormal ways; in the words of Perske (1980, p. 21): "Although the normalization principle is extremely positive, its strongest function lies in its power to uncover conditions and practices which for centuries had *denormalized* people with handicaps, and to which little attention had been paid."

Litigation

Toward the end of the 1960s, public interest and civil rights attorneys began to direct their attention to the plight of adults and children with disabilities. Their efforts resulted in a long series of smashing victories throughout the 1970s.

When the Supreme Court issued its landmark decision outlawing racial segregation in schools in the 1954 case *Brown* v. *Board of Education* ("Separate but equal is inherently unequal."), few could have predicted that the logic underlying this decision would be incorporated by federal judges ruling on the educational rights of students with disabilities. Yet this is precisely what happened in a series of major class action law suits on behalf of children with disabilities in the early 1970s. The PARC (*Pennsylvania Association for Retarded Children, Nancy Beth Bowman et al.* v. *Commonwealth of Pennsylvania and Mills (Mills* v. *Board of Education of the District of Columbia)* cases upheld the constitutional rights of children with disabilities to a free public education in the "least restrictive" (most integrated) setting possible.

Filed on behalf of all school-aged children labeled as mentally retarded in Pennsylvania, the *PARC* case challenged traditional school practices such as exclusion and segregation. In October 1971, the plaintiffs (PARC) and defendants (the Commonwealth of Pennsylvania) settled the case through what is called a consent agreement (a court-approved and implemented settlement). The *PARC* consent agreement supported the right to education in clear and unequivocal terms:

> It is the Commonwealth's obligation to place each mentally retarded child in a free, public program of education and training appropriate to the child's capacity, within the context of the presumption that, among the alternative programs of education and training required by statute to be available, placement in a regular public school class is preferable to placement in a special public school class and placement in a special public school class is preferable to placement in any other type of program of education and training.

Less than one year after the signing of the consent agreement in the *PARC* case, a federal judge in the *Mills* case challenged the exclusion of children identified as "mentally retarded, emotionally disturbed, learning disabled, hearing or speech-impaired, visually impaired, or physically handicapped" from Washington, D.C. schools. Rejecting the Board of Education's excuses for failing to provide an appropriate education for all children with disabilities, federal judge Joseph Waddy issued a far-reaching set of orders upholding the rights of children to a "free and suitable publicly-supported education regardless of the degree of the child's mental, physical or emotional disability or impairment."

Both the *Mills* and the *PARC* cases had repercussions throughout the nation. By 1973 thirty-one similar cases had been filed throughout the nation (Weintraub & Ballard, 1982, p. 3). Also, as we shall see, the orders in these cases served as a model for Public Law 94-142, the Education for All Handicapped Children's Act (now the IDEA or Individuals with Disabilities Education Act), passed by Congress in 1975.

ᵴ Just as parents turned to federal courts to enforce their children's educational rights, they, together with inmates themselves, began to challenge institutional abuse and neglect in lawsuits brought against state institutions across the country. From the 1960s to the 1980s, federal and state courts ruled on a broad range of institutional practices, including institutional peonage or forced labor (*Souder* v. *Brennan*), commitment procedures for adults (*Addington* v. *Texas*) and children (*Parham* v. *Institutionalized Juveniles*), involuntary administration of drugs and other "treatments" (*Rogers* v. *Okin*), the due process rights of juveniles in delinquency proceedings (In re *Gault*), and a host of other issues. In a major decision handed down in 1975, the U.S. Supreme Court ruled on the constitutional rights of "nondangerous mental patients" in *O'Connor* v. *Donaldson.*

In an unanimous decision in this case the Supreme Court ruled that Kenneth Donaldson, a "nondangerous" mental patient, had a constitutional right to liberty. Writing for the Supreme Court, Justice Stewart stated:

> A finding of "mental illness" alone cannot justify a State's locking up a person against his will and keeping him indefinitely in simple custodial confinement. Assuming that that term can be given a reasonably precise content and that the "mentally ill" can be identified with reasonable accuracy, there is still no constitutional basis for confining such persons involuntarily if they are dangerous to no one and can live safely in freedom.

Stewart went on to write: "In short, a State cannot constitutionally confine *without more* [emphasis added] a nondangerous individual who is capable of surviving safely in freedom by himself or with the help of willing and responsible family members or friends."

The *Donaldson* case resulted in the release of thousands of inmates from the nation's institutions. No longer could states warehouse people who harmed no one else and could live very well on their own.

Clearly, this was an important case. Yet it was a series of class action lawsuits directed at institutional conditions and the very nature of institutions that had the most profound effects on services for people labeled mentally retarded, mentally ill, and developmentally disabled. These suits sent shock waves through institutions across the country.

In less than a 15-year span of time, major lawsuits were filed against (and in most cases won) mental retardation and mental health institutions in Alabama, Connecticut, Vermont, New Hampshire, North Dakota, New York, Massachusetts, Florida, New Jersey, Pennsylvania, Tennessee, Kentucky, Texas, Louisiana, Virginia, West Virginia, Michigan, Washington, the District of Columbia, and other states. Three cases during this period received special notoriety and set forth the legal principles on which other cases were based: *Wyatt* v. *Stickney* in Alabama (the *Wyatt* case), *New York State Association for Retarded Children* v. *Rockefeller* in New York (the *Willowbrook* case), and *Halderman* v. *Pennhurst State School and Hospital* in Pennsylvania (the *Pennhurst* case).

Filed initially on behalf of inmates of Bryce Hospital for the mentally ill in 1970 and expanded to include Searcy Hospital and Partlow State School and Hospital for the mentally retarded in 1971, *Wyatt* was the first case to receive widespread public and professional attention. Conditions at Alabama's institutions were atrocious, although certainly not unique at the time. Based on evidence presented regarding the Partlow institution, federal District Judge Frank Johnson was later to find:

> The evidence . . . has vividly and undisputedly portrayed Partlow State School and Hospital as a warehousing institution which, because of its atmosphere of psychological and physical deprivation, is wholly incapable of furnishing (habilitation) to the mentally retarded and is conducive only to the deterioration and the debilitation of the residents.

Johnson also commented on "atrocities" that "occur daily":

> A few of the atrocious incidents cited at the hearing in this case include the following: (a) a resident was scalded to death by hydrant water; (b) a resident was restrained in a strait jacket for nine years in order to prevent hand and finger sucking; (c) a resident was inappropriately confined in seclusion for a period of years; and (d) a resident died from the insertion by another resident of a running water hose into his rectum.

Judge Johnson was not a timid judge. Well-respected for his legal opinions, he had taken on controversial civil rights cases before. It was Judge Johnson who had ordered Governor George Wallace to integrate the University of Alabama in the 1960s and who had employed federal marshals to make sure his orders were followed.

In rulings handed down in 1971 and 1972, Judge Johnson had ruled that mentally ill and mentally retarded persons committed to institutions had a right to treatment (in the case of mental illness) and habilitation (in the case of mental retardation). Basing his decision on a ruling handed down in *Rouse* v. *Cameron* in the District of Columbia in 1966 and similar decisions, Johnson reasoned that the only possible justification for committing a person labeled as mentally ill or mentally retarded to an institution, which represents a significant curtailment of one's civil liberties, is treatment or habilitation and, once committed, that person has an "inviolable constitutional right" to treatment or habilitation.

Johnson also ruled that people committed to Alabama's institutions had a right to treatment or habilitation under the *least restrictive circumstances*.

In his decisions, Judge Johnson made it clear that Alabama and other states were not under any obligation to maintain institutions for persons labeled as mentally ill and mentally retarded: however, once they had decided to do so, they were obliged to operate the institutions in a "constitutionally permissible" fashion.

Based on these legal principles, Johnson ordered far-sweeping changes in Alabama's mental health and mental retardation system. He ordered the institutions to comply with what he termed "Minimum Constitutional Standards," with separate standards for institutions for the so-called mentally ill and the mentally retarded. The standards were incredibly specific and covered almost every aspect of inmates' lives at the institutions. The 49 standards for the habilitation of those labeled as mentally retarded included the following:

> Each resident has a right to a habilitation program which will maximize his human abilities and enhance his ability to cope with his environment. The institution shall recognize that each resident, regardless of ability or status, is entitled to develop and realize his fullest potential. The institution shall implement the principles of normalization so that each resident may live as normally as possible.

In the *Willowbrook* case, Judge Judd was faced with a similar situation as that which confronted Judge Johnson (for a history of the case, see Rothman and Rothman, 1984). Certainly, Willowbrook was no better than Partlow or the other Alabama institutions: it simply was larger. In fact, several years prior to the filing of the suit, in 1969, Willowbrook, with 6,200 inmates, was the largest institution for those labeled as mentally retarded in the world. By the time the suit was filed, it had 5,700; by the time Judd issued his initial ruling in December 1972, Willowbrook's population stood at 4,727.

Presumably, Willowbrook had undergone reform. The population had declined and the state of New York assured the judge that major improvements were under way. Yet Judge Judd found the same deplorable and dehumanizing conditions and the same atrocities as Judge Johnson found at Partlow:

> Testimony of ten parents, plus affidavits of others, showed failure to protect the physical safety of their children and deterioration rather than improvement after they were placed in Willowbrook School. The loss of an eye, the breaking of teeth, the loss of part of an ear bitten off by another resident, and frequent bruises and scale wounds were typical of the testimony. During eight months of 1972 there were over 1,300 reported incidents of injury, patient assaults, or patient fights.

In contrast to Johnson, Judd argued that the failure of the state to accomplish its purpose in institutionalizing residents–to provide care and treatment–would only give them and their families the right to demand release from the institution. Judd thus rejected the constitutional right to treatment or habilitation for Willowbrook residents.

Judd ruled, however, that Willowbrook residents had another constitutional right: *the right to protection from harm.* Noting that federal courts had ruled that criminals in prisons had a right to be free from cruel and unusual punishment based on the Eighth Amendment of the Constitution, Judd reasoned that people labeled as mentally retarded confined to Willowbrook must be entitled to at least the same rights.

For Judd, the right to protection from harm entitled residents to safety, a tolerable living environment, medical care, "civilized standards of human decency," and freedom from conditions that "shock the conscience." He ordered New York to implement nine immediate steps to rectify some of Willowbrook's more blatant abuses, including a prohibition against seclusion and the hiring of additional ward attendants, nurses, physical therapy personnel, and 15 physicians.

After his initial ruling, Judd encouraged the two sides in the case, the plaintiffs and the defendants, to negotiate a final resolution to the problems of Willowbrook. From 1973, when the decision was handed down, until 1975, the plaintiffs and the defendants were involved in protracted negotiations. In 1975, soon after Governor Carey, who had made Willowbrook an issue in his election campaign, had taken office, the state and the plaintiffs entered into a binding consent agreement with Judge Judd's approval.

Ironically, the Willowbrook consent agreement contained many of the same provisions incorporated by Judge Johnson in his 1972 standards for the Partlow institution in Alabama. The consent agreement endorsed both the right to treatment and the principle of the least restrictive alternative. It also went much further than Johnson's order in mandating deinstitutionalization of Willowbrook. The consent agreement provided for Willowbrook to be reduced to a population of no more than 250 residents by 1981 and contained numerous standards for the operation of community programs.

Both the *Wyatt* and the *Willowbrook* cases were brought as institutional reform cases. In both cases, the plaintiffs advocated for massive improvements in institutional conditions. While both cases resulted in significant deinstitutionalization, it was not until the Pennhurst case, filed in 1974, that the institution itself was placed on trial. In the words of one of the attorneys who brought the case, Pennhurst represented a shift from institutional reform with deinstitutionalization to "anti-institutionalization" (Ferleger & Boyd, 1979).

In writing his opinion in the case in 1977, Federal District Judge Raymond Broderick, who happened to have been one of three federal judges in the *PARC* education case, noted some of the same conditions and atrocities found by his legal predecessors. Broderick, however, paid closer attention to the nature of institutional life. Broderick wrote:

> At its best, Pennhurst is typical of large residential state institutions for the retarded. These institutions are the most isolated and restrictive settings in which to treat the retarded. . . . Pennhurst is almost totally impersonal. . . . Its residents have no privacy, . . . they sleep in large, overcrowded wards . . . spend their waking hours together in large day rooms and eat in a large group setting.

Broderick proceeded to speak forcefully about the importance of the principle of normalization:

> Since the early 1960s there has been a distinct humanistic renaissance, replete with the acceptance of the theory of normalization for the habilitation of the retarded. . . . The environment at Pennhurst is not conducive to normalization. It does not reflect society. It is separate and isolated from society and represents group rather than family living.

Broderick could have been describing any institution in the nation.

Judge Broderick next turned to a consideration of the legal issues at stake. He ruled that the residents of Pennhurst had the same rights as those found by Johnson in Alabama and Judd in *Willowbrook*, and more. Citing Johnson's decision, among others, he ruled that Pennhurst residents had a constitutional right to minimally adequate habilitation. He cited Judd and others to uphold a constitutional right to be free from harm. And he cited a Pennsylvania state judge to support a right to minimally adequate habilitation based on state law.

The judge then considered other rights based on the Constitution and Section 504 of the Rehabilitation Act, which was enacted in 1973 to prohibit discrimination against the people with disabilities. Broderick ruled that both the equal protection clause of the Fourteenth Amendment of the Constitution and Section 504 provided for a *right to nondiscriminatory habilitation*. "In this record," wrote Broderick, ". . . we find that the confinement and isolation of the retarded in the institution called Pennhurst is segregation in a facility that clearly is separate and not equal" (*Halderman et al.* v. *Pennhurst*, 1977, p. 203). Broderick was using the Supreme Court's language in *Brown* v. *Board of Education* to suggest that the segregation of people with mental retardation in institutions, like racial segregation in schools, is illegal and unconscionable.

In a memorandum of March 1978, Judge Broderick issued the farthest-reaching orders ever handed down in a case involving an institution. He ordered Pennsylvania to provide "suitable community living arrangements for the retarded residents of Pennhurst" and, in essence, to close the Pennhurst institution.

Broderick's decision, it seemed, sounded the death knell for institutions. Calling Pennhurst, and by implication all such institutions, a "monumental example of unconstitutionality," his orders for the evacuation of Pennhurst were clear and unequivocal. Yet Broderick was only a district-level judge. His orders could be appealed to the Circuit Court of Appeals and then to the Supreme Court—and they were. As we shall see, in rulings on the *Pennhurst* case and on another case known as *Romeo*, the U.S. Supreme Court severely limited the role of federal courts redressing injustices at the nation's institutions.

The *Wyatt*, *Willowbrook*, and *Pennhurst* cases had profound effects, some real and some symbolic, far beyond the institutions named in the suits. For a time, at least, these lawsuits put state officials on notice that institutional abuse and dehumanization would no longer be tolerated and thus moved entrenched bureaucracies to develop community programs. They received widespread publicity, especially in the case of Willowbrook in New York City, and educated parents, the public, politicians, and even professionals on the evil of institutions. They also spurred Congress and state legislatures to enact laws to protect the rights of people with disabilities.

The Federal Response: Legislation

It was not until the 1960s that the federal government began to define a national policy on disability. Starting with President Kennedy whose sister happened to have mental retardation, five successive presidents endorsed the policy of deinstitutionalization (Herr, 1979). "We as a Nation," spoke Kennedy in an address to Congress in 1963, "have long neglected the mentally ill and mentally retarded." Kennedy went on to say: "We must act now . . . to reduce, over a number of years, and by hundreds of thousands, the persons confined to these institutions." Years later, in 1971, President Nixon announced a national goal to enable "one third of the more than 200,000 retarded persons in institutions to return to useful lives."

Throughout the 1960s, Congress expanded grant programs for people with disabilities in the areas of education, rehabilitation, research, housing, and social services. In 1963, Congress passed the Mental Retardation Facilities and Community Mental Health Centers Act, a grant program that was increased again in 1967.

In the 1970s, federal involvement in services for people with disabilities increased dramatically. Spurred by exposés of institutional life and countless lawsuits filed on behalf of children and adults with disabilities, Congress passed a series of laws designed both to protect the rights of people with disabilities and to provide federal financial support for a broad range of services.

In 1971, Congress amended Title XIX of the Social Security Act, Medicaid, to create the Intermediate Care Facility for the Mentally Retarded (ICF/MR). Under the ICF/MR program, a state is eligible to receive 50 to 78 percent reimbursement for the costs of services in facilities that have as the primary purpose the provision of health and rehabilitation services, provide Medicaid-eligible clients with "active treatment," and meet the standards developed by the secretary of Health, Education and Welfare (now Health and Human Services).

The federal government issued regulations for the ICF/MR program in January 1974. The regulations included detailed standards for facilities, which were in many ways similar to Judge Johnson's "minimum constitutional standards" for Partlow in the *Wyatt* case.

States seized the opportunity to pass on the costs for expensive institutional reforms to the ICF/MR programs in the 1970s. By 1978, 41 states received federal funds for institutions under the ICF/MR program. In 1978 the ICF/MR program cost a total of $1,337,846,369 nationally, almost all of which went to support institutions. New York State's ICF/MR program alone cost $214,148,442.

The ICF/MR program represented a mixed blessing. The influx of federal dollars to institutions certainly contributed to improved conditions at ICF/MR-certified facilities. However, in order to continue to receive federal funds, states invested heavily in institutional staffing and capital construction. In the period 1977 to 1980 alone, states spent $821,456,000 in the construction or renovation of institutional facilities (National Association of State Mental Retardation Program Directors, 1980). This not only drained funds from community programs, but also, once states had invested massive sums in institutional buildings, served as a strong disincentive for deinstitutionalization in future years. Despite vast expenditures for staff and facilities, programming and conditions at ICF/MR-certified institutions remained woefully inadequate. In a review of federally mandated survey reports at 44 institutions nationally (Taylor et al., 1981), major violations of the standards were found at each of the institutions, ranging from a lack of programming and activities to seclusion, unsanitary conditions, lack of privacy, and inappropriate use of restraints and drugs.

Toward the middle part of the 1970s, some states began to develop small community settings with ICF/MR funds. By 1978, 17 states had established ICFs/MR for 15 or fewer persons. At Michigan's Macomb-Oakland Regional Center, nationally known as a model community-based service system, officials developed small settings for six or fewer persons, including the so-called severely and profoundly retarded, using ICF/MR funds. In other states, however, officials established ICF/MR-certified "mini-institutions" containing as many as 100 or more people.

By the late 1970s, the ICF/MR program, like Medicaid, generally had generated strong criticism for encouraging costly, inappropriate, and restrictive institutional care. In 1981, as part of the "Omnibus Reconciliation Act of 1981," Congress passed the "Medicaid waiver" program. The thrust of the program was to encourage states to serve people in their natural families and home communities as opposed to placing them in institutions. Under the Medicaid waiver, states were allowed to receive federal reimbursement for a broad array of community services, including, among others, home health aid services, respite care, case management, homemaker services, day programs, and medical care. Two years after the passage of the 1971 Medicaid amendments, Congress totally revamped federal rehabilitation legislation that had originally been passed in 1920 and amended on over a dozen occasions. The Rehabilitation Act of 1973 expanded the scope of vocational rehabilitation services, provided additional federal funds for rehabilitation, and included additional provisions to assure the appropriateness of rehabilitation services. This act also contained the much-heralded Section 504, the civil rights bill for persons with disabilities (note Chapter 4 for a discussion of this legislation as well):

> Section 504. No otherwise qualified handicapped individual in the United States . . . shall, solely by reason of his handicap, be excluded from the participation in, be denied the benefits of, or be subjected to discrimination under any program or activity receiving federal financial assistance or under any program or activity conducted by any Executive agency, or by the United States Postal Service.

Section 504 called for the end of discrimination and the participation of people with disabilities into American life.

The federal government dragged its heels in developing regulations to implement Section 504. Without regulations, it was difficult to interpret 504 and, hence, end discrimination. It took a lawsuit and finally a sit-in by people with disabilities in the offices of then

Secretary of Health, Education and Welfare Joseph Califano for the federal government to issue regulations for Section 504. In May, 1977, the Department of Health, Education and Welfare published broad regulations that prohibited discrimination against the persons with disabilities in employment, program accessibility, preschool, elementary, secondary education, postsecondary education, and health, welfare, and social services.

As explained in the regulations, discrimination is a complex issue. In order to ensure equal opportunity, it is not enough simply to forbid exclusion of people with disabilities. The preface to the regulations states that "it is meaningless to 'admit' a handicapped person in a wheelchair to a program if the program is offered only on the third floor of a walk-up building." Recipients of federal funds thus are required to make "reasonable accommodations" for people with disabilities, including special aids, modified job or school requirements, and accessible facilities. While the regulations stop short of requiring accommodations that would result in an "undue hardship" on recipients of federal funds, they make it clear that ending discrimination may impose some costs and burdens:

> These problems have been compounded by the fact that ending discrimination, practices and providing equal access to program may involve major burdens on some recipients. Those burdens and costs, to be sure, provide no basis for exemption from Section 504 of this regulation: Congress's mandate to end discrimination is clear. But it is also clear that factors of burden and cost had to be taken into account in the regulation in prescribing the actions necessary to end discrimination and to bring handicapped persons into full participation in federally financed programs and activities.

In the 1978 amendments to the Rehabilitation Act, Congress authorized federal funds for "Centers for Independent Living." Modeled on the Berkeley Center for Independent Living established in 1972 as a self-help and self-advocacy organization, independent living centers provide a broad range of consumer-oriented services to enable people with disabilities to live as independently as possible, including advocacy, referral, housing assistance, peer counseling, community group living arrangements, attendant care, and others. Central to the concept of independent living centers is consumer self-determination. The 1978 amendments to the Rehabilitation Act mandate that "handicapped individuals will be substantially involved in policy direction and management . . . and will be employed." For the most part, independent living centers have been oriented toward people with physical disabilities, although many have begun to involve people with mental, cognitive, and sensory disabilities.

The year 1975 ranks with 1973 as the most important in the history of people with disabilities in America. In that year, both the Education for All Handicapped Children Act, popularly known as Public Law 94-142, and the Developmentally Disabled Assistance and Bill of Rights Act, the DD Act, were passed.

An amendment to the Mental Retardation Facilities and Community Mental Health Centers Act of 1963, the DD Act provided modest funds for grants for research and services for people with developmental disabilities. States accepting funds under the act were required to put into place a "protection and advocacy" system to protect the rights of persons with developmental disabilities.

The DD Act also contained a "bill of rights" (which the Supreme Court subsequently ruled in the Pennhurst case represented "national policy" but did not impose any obligations on the states):

SEC. 111. Congress makes the following findings respecting the rights of persons with developmental disabilities:

1. Persons with developmental disabilities have a right to appropriate treatment, services, and habilitation for such disabilities.
2. The treatment, services, and habilitation for a person with developmental disabilities should be designed to maximize the developmental potential of the person and should be provided in the setting that is least restrictive of the person's personal liberty.

The DD Act goes on to state that "The Federal Government and the States both have an obligation to assure that public funds are not provided to any institution or other residential program for persons with developmental disabilities that . . . does not provide treatment, services, and habilitation which is appropriate to the needs of such persons."

On November 29, 1975, President Gerald Ford signed into law Public Law 94-142, the Education for All Handicapped Children Act, approved some months earlier by a vast majority of both the U.S. Senate and House of Representatives. Public Law 94-142 guaranteed the right to education for all school-aged children with handicapping conditions, including those with the most severe disabilities.

As Zettel and Ballard (1982) have indicated, Public Law 94-142 was not a revolutionary piece of legislation. For some years previously the federal government had enacted laws designed to encourage the education of children with disabilities. Federal courts, too, had begun to mandate that children with disabilities be provided with "equal protection" under the law based on the U.S. Constitution. Yet Public Law 94-142 was the first law to define the educational rights of children with disabilities in clear and specific terms.

"It is the purpose of this Act," reads Public Law 94-142, "to assure that all handicapped children have available to them. . . a free appropriate public education which emphasizes special education and related services designed to meet their unique needs, to assure that the rights of handicapped children and their parents and guardians are protected, to assist States and localities to provide for the education of all handicapped children, and to assess and assure the effectiveness of efforts to educate handicapped children." The law itself and regulations issued by the Department of Health, Education and Welfare (now Department of Education) in 1977 define the meaning of "free appropriate public education":

- "Zero-reject." *All* children with disabilities are entitled to a public education under Public Law 94-142. The law specifically provides for the education of children ages five through 18, or the ages at which typical children are educated in a state.
- Least restrictive environment. Public Law 94-142 endorses the principle of "least restrictive environment" as outlined in prior court cases. The federal regulations elaborate on the meaning of "least restrictive environment": "That to the maximum extent appropriate, handicapped children, including children in public or private institutions or other child care facilities, are educated with children who are not handicapped." The regulations further state that removal of a child with a disability from the regular educational environment occurs only when the child's disability precludes education in regular classes with the use of supplementary services.
- Individualized education program. Each child must have an individualized written educational program, which must be reviewed at least annually.
- Due process procedures. Children with disabilities and their

parents are guaranteed "due process" in educational classification and placement. This includes notification prior to changes in a child's classification or placement and procedures whereby educational decisions can be challenged through an impartial hearing.

- Protection in evaluation. The law and regulations contain provisions to ensure that educational tests and procedures used to evaluate children are free of race and cultural bias and that educators do not rely on a single procedure to determine the appropriate educational program for the child.

In enacting Public Law 94-142 Congress also appropriated funds to assist states in educating children with disabilities and authorized increased levels of funding over the next seven years. Public Law 94-142 is what is termed a "funding statute." That is to say, states are mandated to meet the requirements of Public Law 94-142 only if they accept funds under the act. The federal government thus adopted a "carrot on a stick" approach to the education of children with disabilities. It was not until 1984 that the last state, New Mexico, finally applied for funds under Public Law 94-142, and hence became obligated to meet its provisions. Although funding under Public Law 94-142 has gradually increased since 1975, the federal government has never provided the level of funding authorized when the act was passed.

With the passage of Public Law 94-142, thousands of children with disabilities entered public school programs for the first time. Many thousands more began to have their educational needs met. Yet it would be naïve to assume that this law has resolved the many problems confronting children with disabilities and their families—it has not.

It is safe to say that most students with disabilities receive some form of education, although some, especially those in institutions, clearly do not (see Lakin, Hill, Hauber, & Bruininks, 1983). Once children with disabilities have gotten through the school door, however, attention has turned to the quality and appropriateness of the education they receive. What does "appropriate" really mean? What is the meaning of "least restrictive environment" in practice? These are controversial issues, ones on which parents and educators often disagree. Many parents lack the stamina and resources to tackle them, and those who are willing to tackle them have found courts and other bodies increasingly reluctant to take a stand on them.

By the mid-1980s, the federal government had enacted a diverse and often confusing range of laws directed at people with disabilities. Scheerenberger (1983, p. 250) reports that between 1963 and 1983, Congress passed 166 acts or amendments that provided support to people with mental retardation and their families.

The activities of the federal government in the 1970s and 1980s at times seemed contradictory. The government's posture on deinstitutionalization illustrates this. Section 504 and the DD Act call for participation in community life. Yet the ICF/MR program, the largest single source of funding for programs for persons with developmental disabilities, encourages institutionalization.

In 1977, the U.S. General Accounting Office, Congress's "watchdog" over the Executive branch, issued a critical report on the federal government's role in deinstitutionalization entitled *Returning the Mentally Disabled to the Community: Government Needs to Do More.* That report documented the failure of federal government to adopt a coordinated and consistent approach to deinstitutionalization. Yet, government not only has to do more, but also must do things differently.

REFERENCES

Beers, C. W. (1908). A mind that found itself. New York: Longmans, Green.

Biklen, D., Bogdan, R., Ferguson, D. L., Searl, S. J., & Taylor, S. J. (1985). *Achieving the complete school: Strategies for effective mainstreaming.* New York: Teachers College Press.

Blatt, B., & Kaplan, F. (1966). *Christmas in purgatory: A photographic essay on mental retardation.* Boston: Allyn & Bacon.

Blatt, B., Bogdan, R., Biklen, D., & Taylor, S. (1977). From institution to community: A conversion model. In E. Sontag (Ed.), *Educational programming for the severely and profoundly handicapped.* Reston, VA: Council for Exceptional Children.

Blatt, B., McNally, J., & Ozolins, A. (1979). *The family papers: A return to purgatory.* New York: Longman.

Bogdan, R., & Taylor, S. J. (1982). *Inside out: The social meaning of mental retardation.* Toronto: University of Toronto Press.

Braginsky, D., & Braginsky, B. (1971). *Hansels and Gretels: Studies of children in institutions for the mentally retarded.* New York: Holt, Rinehart, & Winston.

Center on Human Policy. (1979). *The community imperative.* Syracuse: Center on Human Policy, Syracuse University.

Chesterton, G. K. (1922). *Eugenics and other evils.* London: Cassell.

Davies, S. P. (1959). *The mentally retarded in society.* New York: Columbia University Press.

Dexter, L. A. (1994). On the politics and sociology of stupidity in our society. *Mental Retardation,* 32(2), 152-155.

Dugdale, R. L. (1910). *The Jukes.* New York: Putnam.

Edgerton, R. (1967). *The cloak of competence.* Berkeley: University of California Press.

Erikson, K. T. (1966). *Wayward Puritans.* New York: John Wiley & Sons.

Ferleger, D., & Boyd, P. A. (1979). Anti-institutionalization: The promise of the Pennhurst case. *Stanford Law Review,* 4(31), 717-752.

Fernald, W. E. (1912). The burden of feeble-mindedness. *Journal of Psycho-aesthetics,* 17, 87-111.

Galton, F. (1869). *Hereditary genius.* London: MacMillan.

Goddard, H. H. (1912). *The Kallikak family: A study in the heredity of feeble-mindedness.* New York: Macmillan.

Goffman, E. (1961). *Asylums: Notes on the management of a spoiled identity.* Boston: Prentice-Hall.

Greenleigh Associates, Inc. (1975). *The role of sheltered workshops in the rehabilitation of the severely handicapped.* New York: Author.

Herr, S. S. (1979). The new clients: Legal services for mentally retarded persons. *Stanford Law Review,* 31(4), 553-611.

Hobbs, N. (Ed.). (1975). *Issues in the classification of children, Vol II.* San Francisco: Jossey-Bass.

Katz, M. B. (1983). *Policy and poverty in American history.* New York: Academic Press.

Lakin, K. C. (n.d.). *Demographic studies of residential facilities for the mentally retarded.* Minneapolis: University of Minnesota, Department of Psychoeducational Studies.

Lakin, K. C., Hill, B, K., Hauber, F. A., & Bruininks, R. H. (1983). A response to the GAO report Disparities still exist in who gets special education. *Exceptional Children,* 50(1), 30-34.

Lam, C. S. (1986). Comparison of sheltered and supported work programs: A pilot study. *Rehabilitation Counseling Bulletin,* 30, 66-82.

Landesman-Dwyer, S. (1981). Living in the community. *American Journal of Mental Deficiency,* 86(3), 223-234.

LaVor, M. L. (1976). Federal legislation for exceptional persons: A history. In F. J. Weintraub, A., Abeson, J., Ballard, & M. L. LaVor (Eds.), *Public policy and the education of exceptional children.* Washington, DC: Council for Exceptional Children.

Mercer, J. R. (1973). *Labeling the mentally retarded: Clinical and social system perspectives on mental retardation.* Berkeley: University of California Press.

Morris, P. (1969). *Put away.* New York: Atherton.

National Association of State Mental Retardation Program Directors, Inc. (1980). *Trends in capital expenditures for mental retardation facilities.* Arlington, VA: Author.

Newark State Custodial Asylum for Feebleminded Women. (1893). *Dedication services.* Newark, NY: Burgess Printers.

Perrucci, R. (1974). *Circle of madness.* Englewood Cliffs, NJ: Prentice-Hall.

Perske, R. (1980). *New life in the neighborhood.* Nashville: Abingdon.

Platt, A. M. (1969). *The child savers.* Chicago: University of Chicago Press.

Rivera, G. (1972). *Willowbrook: A report on how it is and why it doesn't have to be that way.* New York: Vintage.

Rothman, D. (1971). *The discovery of the asylum: Social order and disorder in the new republic.* Boston: Little, Brown.

Rothman, D. (1980). *Conscience and convenience: The asylum and its alternatives in progressive America.* Boston: Little, Brown.

Rothman, D. J., & Rothman, S. M. (1984). *The Willowbrook wars.* New York: Harper & Row.

Santiestevan, H. (1979). *Out of their beds and into the streets.* Washington, DC: American Federation of State, County, and Municipal Employees.

Sarason, S. B., & Doris, J. (1959). *Psychological problems in mental deficiency.* New York: Harper & Row.

Sarason, S. B., & Doris, J. (1979). *Educational handicap, public policy and social history.* New York: Free Press.

Scheerenberger, R. C. (1983). *A history of mental retardation.* Baltimore: Paul H. Brookes Publishing Co.

Scott, R. (1969). *The making of blind men.* New York: Russell Sage.

Spencer, H. (1851). *Social statistics.* London: John Chapman.

Stockwell, E. G. (1968). *Population and people.* Chicago: Quadrangle.

Szasz, T. S. (1970). *The manufacture of madness.* New York: Dell.

Taylor, S. J. (1982). From segregation to integration: Strategies for integrating severely handicapped students in normal school and community settings. *The Journal of The Association for the Severely Handicapped,* 8(3), 42-49.

Taylor, S., Brown, K., McCord, W., Giambetti, A., Searl, S., Mlinarcik, S., Atkinson, T., & Lichter, S. (1981). *Title XIX and deinstitutionalization: The issue for the 80s.* Syracuse: Center on Human Policy, Syracuse University.

U.S. Comptroller General. (1977, January 7). *Report to Congress: Returning the mentally disabled to the community: Government needs to do more.* Washington, DC: GAO.

Vail, D. (1966). *Dehumanization and the institutional career.* Springfield, IL: Charles C Thomas.

Van der Klift, E., & Kunc, N. (1994). Friendships and the politics of help. In J. S. Thousand, R. A. Villa, & A. I. Nevin (Eds.), *Creativity and collaborative learning: A practical guide to empowering students* (pp. 391-401). Baltimore: Paul H. Brookes Publishing Co.

Weintraub, F. J., & Ballard, J. (1982). Introduction: Bridging the decades. In J. Ballard, B. A. Ramirez, & F. J. Weintraub (Eds.), *Special education in America.* Washington, DC: Council for Exceptional Children.

Werthman, F. (1978). *The German euthanasia program.* Cincinnati: Hayes.

Wiseman, F. (1969). *Titticut Follies* [film]. New York: Grove Press.

Wolfensberger, W. (1972). *The principle of normalization in human services.* Toronto: National Institute of Mental Retardation.

Wolfensberger, W. (1975). *The origin and nature of our institutional models.* Syracuse: Human Policy Press.

Wooden, K. (1974). *Weeping in the playtime of others.* New York: McGraw-Hill.

Zettel, J. J., & Ballard, J. (1982). The Education for All Handicapped Children Act of 1975 (P.L. 94-142): Its history, origins, and concepts. In J. Ballard, B. A. Ramirez, & F. J. Weintraub (Eds.), *Special education in America* Washington, DC: Council for Exceptional Children.

Chapter 3

DISABILITY IN AMERICA: CONTROVERSY, DEBATE, AND BACKLASH[2]

Steven J. Taylor and Stanford J. Searl

Throughout the 1960s and 1970s, all trends in the field of disabilities seemed to move in one direction–toward expanded rights, increased social acceptance, fuller integration, and increased funds for programs and services. Yet, beginning in the latter part of the 1970s and extending into the 1980s, people with disabilities and their families began to experience serious challenges to the progress they had made in the preceding years. Deinstitutionalization, mainstreaming, integration, and civil rights became topics of bitter debate and controversy among parents, professionals, human service workers, politicians, and even members of the general public.

The Federal Mood

It is important to understand the social, economic, and political climate of the late 1970s and the 1980s. The previous decades had witnessed an expansion of civil rights and social programs designed to benefit poor people, members of racial minority groups,

2. The preparation of this chapter was supported in part by the National Resource Center on Supported Living and Choice, Center on Human Policy, School of Education, Syracuse University, through the U.S. Department of Education, Office of Special Education and Rehabilitative Services, National Institute on Disability and Rehabilitation Research (NIDRR), through Contract No. H133A990001. Members of the Center are encouraged to express their opinions; however, these do not necessarily represent the official position of NIDRR and no endorsement should be inferred.

women, the elderly, and, of course, people with disabilities. Toward the end of the 1970s, political sentiments seemed to turn against minorities of all kinds.

In the early 1980s, a newly elected administration in Washington proposed major cutbacks in social programs and repeals of civil rights laws and regulations. Public Law 94-142 and Section 504 were among the laws targeted for repeal or "deregulation," although this was unsuccessful.

Just as attempts were made to weaken the rights protections contained in federal laws and regulations, the federal government proposed major cuts in funding for programs benefitting people with disabilities in the early 1980s. Thus, the Department of Education proposed a 25 percent cut in state Public Law 94-142 monies for 1982, a figure amounting to $230.5 million. These budget cuts, too, were rejected by Congress.

Repeated attempts to change federal protections and funds for people with disabilities failed in the early 1980s. Yet the 1980s represented a new era in the federal government's relationship to citizens with disabilities. No new major federal rights laws or programs were established. Further, the federal government withdrew from aggressive enforcement of laws such as Section 504 and Public Law 94-142 (with the exception of federal involvement in the so-called Baby Doe case, as described later in this chapter). More than anything else, the federal government's posture helped create a political climate in which the rights of persons with disabilities, and other groups, were pitted against the presumed general welfare of the society. It became acceptable to question the cost-effectiveness of social justice.

The Judicial Retreat

Since 1954, when the *Brown* v. *Board of Education* racial desegregation case was handed down, the Supreme Court had been a strong supporter of civil rights. In the 1970s, however, justices appointed for "strict constructionism" and "judicial restraint" came into the majority on the Supreme Court. The Supreme Court pulled back from handing down far-reaching rulings on civil rights. Just as the disability rights movement had ridden on the waves of the civil rights movement, it was dragged down by a judicial backlash to civil rights.

In the late 1970s and early 1980s, major court cases filed on behalf of people with disabilities gradually wound their way up to the U.S. Supreme Court. Not all these cases resulted in unfavorable decisions for people with disabilities. Yet, in ruling on these cases, the Supreme Court issued a warning to lower federal courts to refrain from ordering major reforms in the areas of institutions and deinstitutionalization, nondiscrimination, and special education.

Nondiscrimination: Section 504 and the Davis Case

Frances Davis was a licensed practical nurse with a hearing impairment who desired to become a registered nurse. When she applied for admission into a nursing program operated by Southeastern Community College in North Carolina, however, she was turned down based solely on her disability. Southeastern Community College argued that it would be impossible for Davis to participate safely in its nurse training program. Davis subsequently filed suit in federal court alleging a violation of Section 504, which prohibits discrimination based on disability. While a federal district court sided with the community college, the Court of Appeals for the Fourth Circuit overturned the district court ruling. The Court of Appeals ruled that Section 504 required Southeastern Community College to make modifications in its program to accommodate Davis. Southeastern Community College petitioned the Supreme Court to hear the case. In June, 1979, the Supreme Court issued a unanimous decision siding with Southeastern.

The Supreme Court's ruling in *Southeastern Community College* v. *Davis* centered on the meanings of the concepts of "otherwise qualified handicapped individual" and "reasonable accommodation" contained in Section 504 of its regulations. Davis argued that she was "otherwise qualified" to participate in the nursing program. An accomplished lipreader, she maintained that she met the academic and technical qualifications for admission into the training program. She further argued that Section 504 required "reasonable accommodations" for her handicap. These might include modifications in program requirements (for example, waiving certain clinical requirements), the provision of a sign language interpreter, or individual clinical supervision. The Supreme Court was unpersuaded.

According to the Supreme Court, a "qualified handicapped" person is one who meets all the requirements for participation in a program *in spite of* his or her handicap. Southeastern required nursing students to participate in clinical situations in which medical personnel wore surgical masks. Because Davis obviously would not be able to read lips in these situations, according to the Supreme Court she was not able to meet all program requirements.

The Supreme Court also rejected Davis' arguments that Southeastern was required to make accommodations in its training program to enable Davis to participate. According to the court, Section 504 did not require a program to undertake "affirmative action" or make "substantial modifications" to accommodate people with disabilities.

In analyzing the *Davis* case, it is important to point out that it involved admission to a training program and not employment for a specific nursing job. There are many nursing functions that an individual with a significant hearing impairment could easily perform—for example, private duty nursing or school nursing. Further, as the Appeals Court had noted, Davis would have been superbly qualified to serve as a nurse for other persons with hearing impairments. Indeed, many hearing-impaired persons currently function as nurses or physicians. Yet one obviously cannot practice nursing unless one has received the appropriate training. Would admission of Davis into Southeastern's program have required a lowering of standards, substantial accommodations, or undue financial burdens? Probably not.

Disability rights groups greeted the *Davis* case with dismay and anger. Many saw the Supreme Court's ruling as reflective of long-standing prejudice against persons with disabilities. Like all cases, the *Davis* case merely applied to the specific facts in the case (a hearing-impaired individual's admission to a nursing program). However, the case signaled to other recipients of federal funds, such as universities, public transportation agencies, and employers, that Section 504 was not the powerful civil rights law that disability groups had hoped and claimed.

Institutions and Deinstitutionalization: Pennhurst and Romeo

As we have seen, in the early 1970s federal courts started handing down far-reaching orders in cases involving the rights of persons with developmental disabilities and persons labeled as mentally retarded in institutions. The *Willowbrook, Wyatt,* and *Pennhurst* cases called for major reforms. In its 1975 *Donaldson* decision, the Supreme Court ruled that states could not simply warehouse "nondangerous" mental patients who could live safely on their own.

In a series of cases decided in the 1980s, the Supreme Court took an extremely narrow view of the rights of people with mental retardation confined to institutions. The court first considered the *Pennhurst* case. Judge Broderick's original decision in the case ordered the placement of all Pennhurst residents into community living arrangements. On appeal, the Third Circuit upheld the general thrust of Broderick's ruling. While Broderick had based his decision largely on Section 504 and the U.S. Constitution, the Court of Appeals looked to the Developmentally Disabled Assistance and Bill of Rights Act (the DD Act) to uphold Broderick. The state of Pennsylvania petitioned the Supreme Court to hear the case. In April, 1981, the Supreme Court handed down its decision.

In a six-to-three decision, the Supreme Court overturned the Third Circuit's decision on Pennhurst. The decision focused narrowly on the DD Act and thus left unresolved the constitutional and statutory (specifically, Section 504) issues initially raised by Judge Broderick. Delivering the majority's opinion, Justice Rehnquist, known for his reluctance to impose obligations on the states, concluded that the DD Act, which includes a specific bill of rights, did not impose a mandate on states to provide treatment or habilitation in the least restrictive environment. According to Rehnquist, the DD Act's Bill of Rights was not a statement of rights at all. It merely expressed a nonbinding congressional preference for certain kinds of treatment.

The Supreme Court sent the case back to the Third Circuit Court of Appeals for consideration of the constitutional and statutory issues initially raised by Judge Broderick in light of its opinion on the DD Act. In 1982, the Third Circuit ruled that it could affirm Broderick's decision on the basis of Pennsylvania state law alone. Once more, the state petitioned the Supreme Court to hear the case and, in 1983 the court accepted it for review. In yet another narrow decision, the Supreme Court ruled that a federal judge cannot order a state to take any action on the basis of state law; in other words, federal courts cannot enforce state law. Once more, the Supreme Court sent the case back to the Third Circuit for further consideration.

Shortly after the Supreme Court issued its original Pennhurst decision, another institutional case reached the court. This case, too, concerned the Pennhurst institution. In contrast to the preceding case, however, this one, *Youngberg* v. *Romeo*, involved a damages action filed by the mother of Nicholas Romeo, a Pennhurst resident, against the Pennhurst superintendent and other officials. Romeo's mother claimed that her son had been repeatedly injured, restrained, and denied treatment while at Pennhurst and requested a federal district court to award damages from Pennhurst officials.

In June 1982, the Supreme Court issued another cautious decision, Justice Powell wrote the opinion for an eight-member majority of the court. After noting that Romeo had a right to "adequate food, shelter, and medical care," which the state conceded, Powell considered whether Romeo had constitutional rights to safety, freedom from undue restraints, and treatment, which the state contested. Powell dispensed quickly with the rights to safety and freedom from restraint. Citing prison cases, Powell concluded that Romeo had rights to safe conditions and freedom from restraint based on his right to liberty under the Fourteenth Amendment of the Constitution.

Powell next turned to the right to treatment, which he described as more troubling. Treading cautiously, Powell ruled that Romeo at least had a right to training or habilitation that would be necessary to avoid "unconstitutional infringement" of his other rights. Romeo's "liberty interests," Powell wrote, "require the State to provide minimally adequate or reasonable training to ensure safety and freedom from undue restraint." Thus the majority left unresolved the issue of whether Romeo had an absolute right to treatment, although concurring opinions addressed this.

The Supreme Court thus ruled in the Romeo case that people with mental retardation committed to institutions have constitutional rights to safety, freedom from undue restraint, and treatment related to the preceding two rights. The court next considered the legal standard for determining whether these rights had been violated. Here the justices made it clear that courts should show deference to professional decisions. Powell wrote:

> Courts must show deference to the judgment exercised by a qualified professional. By so limiting judicial review of challenges to conditions in state institutions, interference by the federal judiciary with the internal operations of these institutions should be minimized.

In other words, according to the Supreme Court, federal courts should stay out of cases unless there is evidence that professional decisions represent a "substantial departure" from accepted professional judgment.

By the mid-1980s the legal challenge to institutions had lost some of its momentum. After a series of smashing victories against institutions in the early and mid-1970s, civil rights attorneys and the people they represented found federal courts increasingly reluctant to order sweeping changes in state mental health and mental institutions. While the Supreme Court in the Romeo case ruled that people labeled as mentally retarded committed to institutions have certain constitutional rights, it showed tremendous deference to institutional officials and professionals, many of whom still subscribed to dehumanizing attitudes and had resisted the changes of the past two decades.

The *Wyatt, Willowbrook,* and *Pennhurst* cases continued in litigation throughout the 1980s. In the *Wyatt* case, the state of Alabama never complied with all Judge Johnson's standards for institutions and attempted to have the case dismissed on many occasions. In 1978, Alabama brought in its own experts to testify that many residents of Partlow could neither benefit from training nor be placed successfully in community settings. The *Willowbrook* case has been subject to recurring battles between the plaintiffs, defendants, and an appointed review panel to oversee the consent agreement, which was subsequently disbanded by the state of New York (Rothman & Rothman, 1984). The state successfully modified the *Willowbrook* consent agreement to waive some of the standards regarding the size of community settings. While Willowbrook has experienced significant deinstitutionalization, it never reached the projection of 250 residents by 1981. As late as 1983, over 1,000 people remained confined at Willowbrook in substandard, even squalid conditions.

An interesting footnote to the *Willowbrook* and *Pennhurst* cases is that both institutions are scheduled to be closed. In 1984, the governor of New York announced his decision to close the Willowbrook institution, while the state of Pennsylvania signed a consent agreement in which it agreed to close Pennhurst. It is indeed ironic that at a time at which the courts had retreated from ordering broad-scale reforms, states agreed to what the plaintiffs in these suits had wanted all along. This underscores the fact that lawsuits sometimes have profound effects far beyond judicial orders.

The Meaning of a Free Appropriate Public Education: Rowley an

It took until 1982 for Public Law 94-142 to be interpreted by Supreme Court. The case, known as *Board of Education of the Henrick Hudson Central School District* v. *Rowley*, involved a bright young girl named Amy Rowley who happened to be deaf. Mainstreamed into a regular elementary school class, Amy was doing quite well in school. She was performing better than the average child in her class and was advancing easily from grade to grade, but her parents thought she could be doing much better. While an excellent lip-reader, she could understand much less of what went on in the class than the other children. Amy's parents, who were also deaf, asked the school district to provide a sign language interpreter so that she would have the same opportunity as other children. The school district refused, and a hearing officer and the state commissioner of education upheld this decision. Amy's parents filed suit in federal court. Both the district court and Court of Appeals for the Second Circuit sided with the Rowleys. Petitioned by the school district, the Supreme Court agreed to hear the case. The *Rowley* case hinged on the meaning of "free appropriate public education" guaranteed to children with disabilities under Public Law 94-142. Does this not mean that children with disabilities have a right to equal opportunity? Isn't that what Congress intended when it referred to "full educational opportunity" to all children with disabilities? A majority of the Supreme Court said no.

Writing for the majority, Justice Rehnquist reasoned that Public Law 94-142 merely required that states provide students with disabilities with "access" to a public education program. The meaning of "free appropriate public education," according to the majority, is the requirement that "the education to which access is provided be sufficient to confer some educational benefit upon the handicapped child." Since Amy Rowley was advancing from grade to grade, she was receiving "some educational benefit." It was irrelevant that Amy would probably achieve much higher if she were provided with a sign language interpreter.

The majority went on to consider the role of the courts in deciding educational cases. The courts, wrote Rehnquist, should limit their involvement to reviewing whether states have complied with the procedures set forth in Public Law 94-142 (for example, due process procedures) and whether the individualized educational program is "reasonably calculated to enable the child to receive educational benefits." Consistent with the deference shown to professional decision making in the *Romeo* case, Rehnquist added, "Courts must be careful to avoid imposing their view of preferable educational methods upon the States."

Of course, the *Rowley* decision left many important questions unanswered. For example, would Amy have been entitled to a sign language interpreter had she been failing in school? What does "some educational benefit" mean for students with severe mental retardation? Further, some areas covered in Public Law 94-142 were not addressed in the *Rowley* case.

Many parents and disability rights groups were understandably concerned when the Supreme Court decided to hear a case filed under Public Law 94-142 and Section 504 known as *Irving Independent School District v. Tatro*. This case focused on school districts' obligation to provide related services to enable children with disabilities to participate in special education programs. Public Law 94-142 specifically mandates the provision of special education and related services for children with disabilities. Related services are defined as:

> Transportation, and such developmental, corrective, and other supportive services (including speech pathology and audiology, psychological services, physical and occupational therapy, recreation, and medical and counseling services, except that such medical services shall be for diagnostic and evaluation purposes only) as may be required to assist a handicapped child to benefit from special education, and includes the early identification and assessment of handicapping conditions in children.

A young child with spina bifida, Amber Tatro required a health-related procedure known as clean intermittent catheterization (CIC) to avoid injury to her kidneys. CIC is a fairly simple procedure that can be performed by a nonmedical person with minimal training. Amber's parents, babysitter, and teenage brother performed the CIC procedure for her.

When Amber was first admitted to school, the school district refused to include the provision of CIC in her individualized education program. CIC, the school district argued, was a medical service (other than for diagnostic purposes) and did not fall under the definition of related services in Public Law 94-142. Amber's parents argued that CIC was a necessary supportive service and should be provided as a related service. A failure to provide CIC to Amber was tantamount to excluding her from school. The case eventually wound its way to the Supreme Court.

In the first clear-cut Supreme Court victory for people with disabilities and their families in years, the Supreme Court ruled that CIC is a related service under Public Law 94-142. The court distinguished between medical services provided by a licensed physician, which schools are not required to provide, and health-related services provided by a school nurse or other qualified person, which were mandated by Public Law 94-142. Chief Justice Berger wrote: "Services like CIC that permit a child to remain at school during the day are no less related to the effort to educate than are services that enable the child to reach, enter, or exit the school."

The Tatro family did not get everything they had requested. Amber's parents had also asked the court to award attorneys' fees under Section 504 based on their costs in upholding their child's rights. A majority ruled that Section 504 did not apply when plaintiffs could obtain what they wanted under Public Law 94-142; thus they were not entitled to attorneys' fees, which are not provided for under Public Law 94-142.

By the mid-1980s, several clear trends had emerged in Supreme Court decisions on the rights of people with disabilities. The first is that the court was willing to grant only narrow rights to adults and children with disabilities. The era of far-reaching court orders on behalf of people with disabilities was over. The court seemed to be going out of the way to ignore even clear-cut mandates from Congress. The second trend is that the court was loath to let judges act as intermediaries in controversies among professionals and experts. The message was clear: show deference to institutional administrators, state policymakers, and school officials. The final trend relates to the costs of nondiscrimination. If it might require "undue" or significant financial resources, the Supreme Court seemed to be saying, then judges should not require it.

Unions

Many unions have a long history of supporting causes of civil rights and social justice. Indeed, early in their history, unions waged hard-fought battles for workers' basic rights. Yet, beginning in the 1970s, some public employee unions started to feel threatened by the changes that were occurring in the field of disabilities. Teacher unions, for example, sometimes express misgivings about educating students with disabilities in regular public school programs. In regard to deinstitutionalization, public employee unions have been among the most vocal opponents. Of course, the policy of deinstitutionalization does not have to result in the loss of jobs. However, deinstitutionalization poses the threat that jobs will be shifted from publicly operated institutions to privately operated community programs, resulting in a loss of public employee positions.

In 1975, the American Federation of State, County, and Municipal Employees (AFSCME), a public employee union representing 250,000 mental health workers nationally, released a scathing report that blasted the policy of deinstitutionalization. The report, entitled *Out of Their Beds and into the Streets*, presented deinstitutionalization as a sinister plot to relieve state governments of the responsibility for caring for the mentally ill, the elderly, and other groups and to put money in the pockets of private profiteers (Santiestevan, 1979). Jerry Wurf, the president of AFSCME, wrote in the introduction of the report:

> It seems to us that "deinstitutionalization," a lofty idea, has become something very ugly—a cold methodology by which government washes its hands of direct responsibility for the well-being of its most dependent citizens. . . . Institutional reform need not be disruptive, discomforting or deadly to the thousands who look to the state to guarantee their survival. . . . It's time we came together, to build a constituency that supports the right of every American to proper institutional care, and takes the responsibility for that care out of the hands of private profiteers.

Several years after AFSCME expressed opposition to deinstitutionalization, the Civil Service Employees Association (CSEA), New York State's public employee union, took up the cause. In 1978, CSEA sponsored a major public relations campaign to convince politicians and the public that deinstitutionalization meant "dumping." "The State Calls It Deinstitutionalization," read one advertisement, "We Call It Cruel." As part of its campaign, CSEA prepared a series of sixty-second radio advertisements that painted deinstitutionalization as a cruel ripoff:

> It's bad enough that we New Yorkers pay one of the highest per-capita tax

rates in the nation. But it becomes scandalous when the State of New York squanders our tax money by filling the pockets of private profiteers as part of a plan called deinstitutionalization. . . . State employees with many years service are being put on unemployment and welfare roles instead of being allowed to provide services that are desperately needed. That's not what deinstitutionalization was supposed to be. It was supposed to give patients a better life, it's just not working.

It is difficult to gauge the impact of public employee union opposition to deinstitutionalization. Certainly, the public relations campaigns waged by AFSCME, CSEA, and other groups have fed public cynicism over the motives of state governments (some of which is undoubtedly warranted) and encouraged community opposition to group homes and other community living arrangements. Their lobbying efforts probably have also scared away potential supporters of deinstitutionalization, including some politicians who depend on public employee union endorsements and campaign contributions.

The Public: Bad Neighbors

The general public seems supportive of people with disabilities as long as they are content to be on the receiving end of charity drives and annual telethons. But let them demand their share of the American dream and the mood of the public can change drastically. The hard-fought gains of the past two decades often came at the cost of public support.

"Sometimes equality just costs too much," wrote Roger Starr, a member of *The New York Times* editorial board, in an article published in *Harper's* in 1982. According to Starr, laws like Section 504 and Public Law 94-142 demand too much too fast. It's a matter of dollars: "No matter how savage it sounds, spending money on people with disabilities must be measured against the wealth produced by the nation's economy, and against other demands for help that similarly return a smaller amount of money to the national treasury than they cost" (Starr, 1982, p. 14). Even if one could accept Starr's values and sense of national priorities, his position could be countered on factual grounds. The programs Starr would presumably cut are enabling millions of people with disabilities to be productive and contributing members of society.

Many educational officials and school board members have joined the backlash against disability rights. "Special Education Carried Too Far" read the headline on an article written by Max Rafferty in 1981. Rafferty's complaints against people with disabilities range from exorbitant costs to a decline in educational standards to a breakdown in school discipline.

> I don't believe it. Today's courts are holding that handicapped students, despite disruptive or even dangerously violent behavior, cannot be expelled from school. And yes, that's what I said: if a kid is classified as handicapped, he can get away with—almost murder. (Rafferty, 1981, p. A4)

Perhaps the most vicious attacks on people with disabilities have come from community opposition to deinstitutionalization. One need only pick up a local newspaper to see this. The myths and stereotypes promulgated during the eugenics movement have never totally disappeared.

Community resistance to deinstitutionalization takes many forms. It is not uncommon to find local editorial writers, politicians, and civic leaders decrying the release of "dangerous" people from institutions. *The Catholic Sun*, a central New York paper, reported a bizarre story in July 1976. Alarmed by the number of former residents of local mental health and mental retardation institutions wandering around the city, Mayor Edward Hanna of Utica banned all former residents from entering a city park without supervision. The mayor charged that there had been instances of panhandling, disrobing, and assaults by former residents. Two local priests and two nuns protested the action. Mocking the mayor's decree, they set up an "IQ booth" at the entrance to the park and asked visitors: "Do you have all of your mental faculties?" The mayor's decree was withdrawn. Similar stories have continued to appear in both our print and electronic media to the present.

Group homes have encountered stiff opposition in many communities across the country. The prospect of having so-called mentally retarded or mentally ill people next door seems to bring out all the stereotypes and prejudices. In Washington, D.C., and Staten Island, New York, prospective group homes were actually fire-bombed by fearful neighbors. Robert Keating, a free-lance writer, wrote an excellent article entitled "The War Against the Mentally Retarded," which appeared in *The New York Times* in 1979. Keating wrote that "bomb threats, vandalism, violence, and phone threats have become our newest method of treatment for the mentally retarded." Quoting one prospective neighbor of a group home, he wrote, "We don't want them. Put them back in Willowbrook." Keating reported how local politicians and others stir up hostility at local public hearings on proposed group homes:

> Even though the politicians are doing an excellent job of stoking the fire of discontent, they could take a lesson in inflammatory rhetoric from a man not in their field per se. . . . "'My name is Felton King,' he begins in a slow, powerful voice. I'm the president of local 429 at the Staten Island Developmental Center (Willowbrook). I'd like to give you some facts. . . . Approximately 88 percent of the clients being placed out in the community. . . have a severely bad behavior problem. . . . It is a fact that these kids have communicable diseases.'" The audience reacts with ahs and scattered whispers. King pauses after each fact. "'They say they're not going to harm your kids. . . . That's a bunch of crap. . . .'" King leaves the microphone while the audience extends the enjoyment of its own disorder. It is clear the threat of losing union jobs when Willowbrook closes.

It is not necessary to go to New York City to find backward attitudes expressed toward those labeled as mentally retarded or mentally ill and strong opposition to proposed group homes. In Syracuse, a 1981 article in the *Herald-American* quoted one prospective neighbor of a group home planned for an upper-middle-class neighborhood:

> Mentally retarded people are impaired, they don't have the conscience we do to control our actions. They don't know right from wrong. . . . It's unfortunate. But they could start a fire. They could be sexually deviate.

Sentiments such as these continue to exist in today's time. Prospective neighbors often cloak their prejudice with fears about neighborhood deterioration, additional traffic, and a decline in property values. Studies have shown, however, that group homes have no adverse effects on residential neighborhoods or local property values (Wolpert, 1978). Further, Perske (1980) has reported that despite initial fears of resistance, most neighbors come to accept group homes and their residents over time.

Parents: Jet Lag

Like their children, parents of people with disabilities have been victims of societal prejudice and discrimination. Prior to the 1970s, parents were often faced with two choices as to what to do with children with disabilities: keep them 24 hours a day with no supports or institutionalize them. Many made the painful decision to place their children in institutions, often on the advice of physicians and other professionals. In many communities, parents banded together to advocate special education programs. Their efforts often resulted in the establishment of special schools for children with disabilities.

It should not be surprising that many parents regard current trends like mainstreaming or inclusive education and deinstitutionalization with suspicion and distrust. Indeed, one of the saddest legacies of institutions has been to pit parent groups against one another, with one group supporting institutions and the other deinstitutionalization. In some states, deinstitutionalization lawsuits have fractured the parent movement. For example, the Connecticut Association for Retarded Citizens' courageous decision to file suit to close the Mansfield Training School and have its residents placed into the community eventually led several of its chapters to withdraw from the association.

Institutional parent groups in some states have been active in litigation involving institutions and legislative hearings regarding institutions and deinstitutionalization. The decision by the Supreme Court to hear the *Pennhurst* case brought forth a brief from a number of parent groups across the country urging the court to mandate institutional reforms, but not community placement. In 1981, the U.S. Senate Subcommittee on the Handicapped (now the U.S. Senate Subcommittee on Disability) held hearings on deinstitutionalization in Hartford, Connecticut (U.S. Government Printing Office, 1982). The list of witnesses included many of the nation's foremost experts on services for people with developmental disabilities, in addition to various state officials and representatives of parent groups. The testimony of the parents was divided between those who spoke in favor of deinstitutionalization and those who spoke against it. One parent's testimony seemed to capture the feelings of those parents who oppose deinstitutionalization:

The national policy of deinstitutionalization has affected the mental health services by stopping improvements and/or growth in institutions, stopped hiring very badly needed personnel for the care and education of the retarded, stopped instituting new programs and thousands of dollars spent on lawsuits.

The severely and profoundly retarded need constant attention, care and direction Their best care is in an institution where they have around-the-clock care and continuity of care. All facilities are provided for them on the grounds: medical, educational and recreational. Their surroundings are always the same so that they do not have to make any adjustments. They are not frightened or frustrated. It is a safe and happy environment for them. . . . Their needs and wants are not like the normal. If they could have remained in the community not one parent would have experienced the pain and agony of placing their child in an institution. They will never be adults, even though they get to be 100 years old. Mainstreaming is wishful thinking and to place the severely and profoundly retarded in the community is cruel. Anyone who has a severely and profoundly retarded child suffers the accompanying agony of knowing that that child is a misfit in society geared for normal people.

Parental opposition to integration and deinstitutionalization is probably a temporary phenomenon. There is a new generation of parents today. With the passage of Public Law 94-142, parents are growing accustomed to having their children attend regular public schools and having them live in the community. With few exceptions, these parents will never accept institutionalization.

Good integrated programs create a demand among parents for more integrated programs. In a follow-up study of people placed in the community from the Pennhurst institutions, Conroy and Bradley (1985) have reported that the vast majority of parents support their children's placement in the community, despite initial opposition.

In 1977, the Albuquerque public schools closed their only segregated facility for children with severe disabilities (Taylor, 1982). Over 100 children and youth attended regular public schools for the first time. While some parents supported the move, others opposed it fiercely. Many feared that their children would not be safe in regular schools or would receive a substandard education. A parent group formed to fight the closing of the segregated school and organized a legal defense fund. By the end of the 1977-78 school year, however, parents originally opposed to the integration program had become strong supporters. They donated thousands of dollars collected through the defense fund to support integration at the high school.

The Professional Backlash

Early in the 1970s, there seemed to be professional consensus on the dramatic need to correct injustices against people with disabilities. America's institutions were overcrowded and understaffed, abusive and dehumanizing. Public schools excluded large numbers of students with disabilities. Yet professional consensus on issues confronting the field was nothing more than an illusion. Professionals, researchers, and educators always have and always will disagree on key policy issues. It simply took a while for the lines of controversy to be drawn.

As the disability rights movement gained momentum, a number of noted professionals and researchers began to speak out against community placement, normalization, mainstreaming, and other trends. In articles published in professional journals and papers presented at conventions, professionals claimed that the pendulum had swung too far. Not all people with disabilities could be trained, they asserted, and not all could benefit from community living. Many of these professionals eventually joined forces with states embroiled in litigation to attempt to reverse the tide of reform and change.

Defending itself against the plaintiffs' claims that it had not implemented Judge Johnson's 1972 minimum constitutional standards for mental health and mental retardation institutions, the state of Alabama turned to outside help in the *Wyatt* case in 1978. It enlisted ten professionals, called the Partlow Review Committee, to testify on its behalf. In a notorious memorandum introduced into court, the committee reached some startling conclusions:

1. Only a small number of the present Partlow residents can reasonably be expected to adjust to community living.
2. The potential for behavioral improvement in a substantial number of Partlow residents is very low and training programs seem inappropriate for them.
3. The 1972 court standards set unrealistic goals and are so restrictive that professional judgment is often precluded in the treatment of individual residents.

In short, according to the Partlow Review Committee, the so-called severely and profoundly retarded cannot learn and certainly cannot live in the community; those labeled mildly retarded may be dangerous; one mildly retarded resident, in fact, molested a child. As we have seen, these were not new ideas. They were first set forth nearly 100 years earlier.

The Partlow Review Committee proposed a program of "enriched living" for Partlow residents: "The new, emphasis will, for example, increase the need for staff to provide snacks at prescribed times, to take residents on field trips (movies, to town, fishing, sporting events, etc.), to insure quiet, restful music rooms, or TV viewing areas, or to insure that an older resident is comfortably seated and monitored outside." What they were recommending was a return to custodial care.

After the introduction of the Partlow Committee Report in the *Wyatt* case, other professionals lined up to testify in other major court cases or to express similar views in published articles (Thorne, 1979; Ellis et al., 1981). Most stopped short of endorsing the Partlow Committee's bald assertions. It was much more common for professionals and researchers to demand more "research" on the issue of institutions and deinstitutionalization (see Landesman-Dwyer, 1981). However, research seldom, if ever, answers major policy issues and dilemmas. Rather, deinstitutionalization is first and foremost a moral and ideological issue.

Some professionals have even gone as far as to question the value of Public Law 94-142. The "least restrictive environment" provisions of the law, more generally, the principle of mainstreaming, have been a favorite target. One article published by Vernon in the *Peabody Journal of Education* in 1981 refers to Public Law 94-142 as education's "three mile island." Vernon (1981, p. 24) wrote:

> In reality, P.L. 94-142 is an ill-conceived law embodying a 'Pollyanna-Horatio-Alger-like euphoria contrary to fact perception of reality.' It threatens the education of an entire generation of handicapped youth and squanders the limited educational funds available for both disabled and regular children.

Later in the article, Vernon elaborates on this theme:

> Under P.L. 94-142, we as a country will be making by far our heaviest per capita financial investments in those youths least able to contribute to society. In fact, large sums of education money, normally spent on gifted or average children, most all of whom will return a dividend to society, we must invest now in children with little or no probability, of ever being other

than wards of the state.

The backlash to disability rights was to be expected. Every social movement generates a counter movement. That is to say, periods of social change are marked by controversy, resistance, and attempts to restore the status quo. There was no Ku Klux Klan until *after* the slaves were freed; there was no antiwomen's movement until there was a strong women's movement; and there was no backlash to disability rights until there was a strong disability rights movement.

Current trends in the field of disabilities—deinstitutionalization, integration, mainstreaming, normalization—challenge traditional practices and policies and deeply held beliefs. If there were no backlash, there would have been no progress.

The Decade of the 1980s

For people with disabilities, the 1980s lacked the dramatic breakthroughs that characterized the preceding decades. It would be misleading, however, to describe this period as merely an era of retrenchment and backlash. The momentum has slowed, but progress has not come to a halt.

The late 1970s and 1980s have witnessed the steady development of integrated educational and community service systems across the country. The populations of public institutions for those labeled as mentally retarded continue to decline.

To be sure, in some states deinstitutionalization has meant "transinstitutionalization" and "dumping" (see Scull, 1981; Warren, 1981). That is to say people have been transferred from large public institutions to somewhat smaller but equally restrictive private ones (for example, nursing homes, private residential facilities) or left to fend for themselves in urban slums. In a study of boarding houses and similar facilities around Los Angeles, Bercovici (1983) found that many people with mental retardation were just as isolated and segregated as they were in institutions.

As early as 1977, Blatt, Bogdan, Biklen, and Taylor warned that unless deinstitutionalization were reconceptualized, it would fail, either by inertia or backlash.

Too often, deinstitutionalization has simply meant releasing people from state facilities by moving traditionally, institutionalized people into community institutions. These have usually been nursing homes, and boarding homes that sometimes provide little more than bed and board. However, the goal of deinstitutionalization should not be simply to move people from one building to another, from one location to another, from a total-care institution to a partial-care one, or from a custodial care facility to a non-care facility. The goal should be to transform a dehumanizing, segregated institutional model of services into a humanizing, integrated community model. (Blatt et al., 1977, p. 40)

Deinstitutionalization does not, or rather should not, mean simply opening up the doors to the institution. It means putting into place a system of humane and responsive support services in the community.

In a growing number of places across the country, people labeled mentally retarded and mentally ill are living and thriving in small community settings and participating in community life. In the 1970s, two prominent community-based service systems for people labeled as mentally retarded emerged in eastern Nebraska (ENCOR) and the Macomb-Oakland region of Michigan (see Perske, 1979). These service systems serve a large number of people with significant and multiple disabilities in small homes dispersed throughout the community. On a more modest scale, model community programs have been developed in Rhode Island, Pennsylvania, New York, Vermont, Kentucky, and a host of other states.

These models provide tangible evidence that people with mental retardation and other disabilities not only *can* live in community settings, but also *are* living successfully in the community throughout the nation. For every institutionalized person, no matter how significant the impediments may be, there is someone with the same level of disability thriving in a community environment.

The demands for total deinstitutionalization have grown louder and stronger. In 1979, the Center on Human Policy at Syracuse University issued The Community Imperative declaration (and reissued in 2000), which was subsequently endorsed by hundreds of leaders across the country.

In the domain of Human Rights:

> All people have fundamental moral and constitutional rights.
> These rights must not be abrogated merely because a person has a mental or physical disability.

Among these fundamental rights is the right to community living.

In the domain of Educational Programming and Human Service:

All people, as human beings, are inherently valuable.
All people can grow and develop.
All people are entitled to conditions which foster their development.
Such conditions are optimally provided in community settings.

Therefore:

In fulfillment of fundamental human rights and
In securing optimum developmental opportunities,
All people, regardless of the severity of their disabilities, are
entitled to community living.

Similar positions have been adopted by the Association for Retarded Citizens of the United States (now Arc), the National Society for Autistic Children and Adults, and the Association for Persons with Severe Handicaps.

How we view people structures how we treat them. If we regard people with disabilities as a separate category of humanity, we will treat them in ways in which we would not like to be treated. We see this in history and in our contemporary institutions. If, however, we view people with disabilities as people more or less like ourselves, with potentialities as well as limitations, then we are obliged to open up our communities to them and encourage their participation in social life:

The issue of institutionalization, like the issues of slavery and apartheid, strikes at the very core, the very essence of our common humanity. Just as the emergence of Jim Crowism, the Ku Klux Klan, and racist theories of black inferiority do not and cannot justify, the conclusion that black Americans were better off under slavery, neither can neighborhood resistance, exclusionary zoning codes, expert claims that some people cannot learn or even firebombing of prospective homes be combined to justify the conclusion that so-called mentally retarded people are better off in institutions. What is at issue here is fundamental human rights and the quality of the lives of human beings. To claim that some people cannot learn, to place those same people in isolated institutions, and then to suppose that the dignity and well being of those people can be protected, let alone enhanced, is to deny history. And to suggest that some people cannot and should not live amongst their fellow human beings is to deny our shared humanness. (Center on Human Policy, 1979)

Despite some setbacks, an increasing number of children with disabilities and their families have found America's schools receptive to their needs during the 1980s and 1990s.

The issue of mainstreaming or integration (inclusion) looms as a major one in special education today. Like deinstitutionalization, mainstreaming has often meant "dumping"; that is, the placement of children with disabilities in regular classes without special aids and supports. That is why many teachers, principals, and school district officials oppose the concept. Just as deinstitutionalization does not have to result in dumping, neither does mainstreaming. Here again, there are many successful integration models in schools across the country (Taylor, 1982; Biklen, Bogdan, Ferguson, Searl, & Taylor, 1985).

Current trends in special education today support the inclusion of students with significant disabilities (severe and profound mental retardation, severe multiple disabilities, autism, and others) in normal educational settings. States (Vermont, Hawaii, and, for autistic students, North Carolina); school districts (Madison, Wisconsin; Albuquerque, New Mexico, Tacoma, Washington, Portland and Bangor, Maine, Birmingham, Alabama; Urbana and DeKalb, Illinois); and individual schools in many states are engaged in major integration efforts for students with severe and multiple disabilities (Taylor, 1982; Thomason & Arkell, 1980). Separate schools for children with disabilities are slowly closing.

For students with significant disabilities, integration in most states and schools does not usually mean placement in classes with students without disabilities, although this also is happening (McCollum School in Albuquerque, New Mexico; Ed Smith School in Syracuse, New York). However, it does mean involvement in a broad range of extracurricular and nonacademic activities (cafeteria, assemblies, graduate exercises, field trips, music, art, physical education classes, and joint play sessions). In addition, a number of schools have developed elaborate buddy and tutoring systems for students with and without disabilities.

Integrating students with significant disabilities, and perhaps all students with disabilities, in regular school programs requires careful planning and preparation, the creation of specialized support positions, and development of facilitative policies and other carefully planned strategies. Yet it would be inaccurate to portray integration as simply a technical matter. What distinguishes successfully integrated programs is a strong commitment to the principle of integration.

The critical issue facing educators, administrators, and parents is not whether integration can work, but how to make it work. As Wilcox and Sailor (1980, p. 282) have stated:

> In light of the professional consensus and the various legal and programmatic arguments supporting it, the appropriate question is not: "Should we do it?" Now that the basic criterion has been articulated, it is time to focus, not on further consensus, but on implementation.

Deinstitutionalization (community integration) and mainstreaming (educational integration) are not the only issues that dominate the current scene in the field of disabilities. The promise of Section 504 has yet to be fulfilled. For a time it seemed that the much heralded Section 504 would bring an end to discrimination against people with disabilities in employment, education, and accessibility to public facilities such as transportation. As we have seen, Section 504 does not have the legal clout that disability leaders had hoped. How far must employers, educational institutions, and public facilities go to accommodate people with disabilities? Should people with disabilities be excluded from participation in normal life simply because the society is designed around the needs of people without disabilities? The federal government and the courts are providing conservative answers to these questions. Meanwhile, disability rights groups continue to press for the same rights and privileges enjoyed by other citizens.

The area of vocational rehabilitation is just now undergoing the revolution in thinking that occurred in residential services and education a decade or so ago. For the past 20 or more years, sheltered workshops have served as the primary site for vocational training for people with significant disabilities. In recent years, segregated day treatment and training programs have been established for people deemed too "disabled" to function even in sheltered workshops.

Just as integration is becoming a guiding principle in residential services and education, so too is it emerging as a principle in vocational rehabilitation. The shortcomings of sheltered workshops and other segregated day programs (low or no pay, meaningless activities, low expectations, little advancement or placement) are gradually being exposed. An increasing number of leaders in vocational rehabilitation are advocating integrated work stations and job sites in industry and competitive employment, with vocational supports, for people with significant disabilities (Brown et al., 1983; Wehman, 1981).

Perhaps no disability issue so grabbed the public spotlight in the mid-1980s as the situation of a young infant in New York referred to as "Baby Jane Doe." Born in October 1983, Baby Doe came into the world with spina bifida (an incompletely closed spine) and other disabilities. Baby Doe's parents were confronted with a confusing and painful decision. Without surgery, the infant would probably die within two years. With surgery, doctors told her parents, she might live to be 20 but would be severely retarded, paralyzed, and bedridden. Acting on their doctors' advice, Baby Doe's parents decided against the life-prolonging surgery. Their decision set into motion a flurry of lawsuits filed by a right-to-life attorney and then the U.S. Department of Health and Human Services based on Section 504 (discrimination on the basis of disability). The courts eventually struck down outside intervention in the case, siding with the parents' decision and upholding their right to privacy.

The Baby Doe issue, as it has come to be called, is not new to the medical profession. In an article in *Pediatrics*, a group of medical professionals in Oklahoma described a decision-making process for determining which children with myelomeningocele should live and which should die. Of 24 infants who received no treatment, all died, with an average life of 37 days (Gross, Cox, Tatyrek, Pollay & Barnes, 1983). Dr. Raymond Duff of the Yale-New Haven Hospital has been one of the principal advocates of withholding medical treatment from infants with significant disabilities. Duff (1981, p. 315) has decried what he refers to as an oppressive "medical Vietnam": "costly sometimes abusive, use of technology, to ensure biologic existence with little regard for quality of child and family life and competing interests."

The Baby Doe issue was surrounded with tremendous emotion, political controversy, and misinformation. Many individuals and groups, some of which had been supporters of the rights of people with disabilities in schools and institutions, viewed the federal government's intervention in the Baby Doe issue as a thinly veiled effort to impose a right-wing right-to-life agenda on prospective and actual parents. As evidence for this view, they pointed out that the Baby Doe case is the only one in which the federal government attempted to enforce Section 504 aggressively. In such personal life and death decisions, they reason, why not let the parents decide?

Yet many disability rights activists and organizations, including the Association for Retarded Citizens (now Arc) and the Association for Persons with Severe Handicaps, strongly supported federal intervention in Baby Doe cases and condemned the practice of withholding medical treatment from anyone based on disability. Some expressed extreme discomfort at the involvement of the "right-to-life" movement in this issue. "The Right," wrote Mary Johnson (1984, p. 11), "is the wrong group to plead our rights."

In discussing the Baby Doe issue, it is important to point out that no disability rights group argues that extraordinary or heroic treatments should be employed to prolong the life of a *dying* infant, child, or adult. The question is *not* whether society or the government should intervene when parents decide to decline medical treatments that have little likelihood of saving their infant's life. The question raised by the Baby Doe issue is quite different: Should society, or the government intervene when medical treatment is withheld solely because of an infant's disability or presumed future quality of life? The issue thus boils down to one of discrimination on the basis of disability, which is what Section 504 was intended to end.

When stripped to its essentials, then, the Baby Doe controversy had to do with the value we place on the lives of people with disabilities. While sometimes cloaked in terms of *hopeless medical cases*, the arguments in favor of withholding medical treatment from infants with significant disabilities reflect deeply ingrained beliefs and values about the humanity and worth of people with disabilities.

> The surviving child's life at home might have such a detrimental effect on the family that the child, too, would suffer excessively. Deprived of a loving home, the severely handicapped child's life in a series of foster homes or an institution would be too miserable. Choosing death sometimes is viewed as an act of love because some life can only be wrongful. (Duff, 1981, p. 316)

One theologian, Joseph Fletcher (1972), has even attempted to define "humanhood" based on IQ: "Any individual of the species homosapiens who falls below the IQ 40-mark in a standard Stanford Benet test, amplified, if you like, by other tests, is questionably a person, below the 20-mark, not a person." Of course, this was the same view put forth by the Nazis in their "euthanasia program": "the destruction of life devoid of value."

What about the parents of these infants? From our point of view, no one has the right to judge parents who, shocked by the unexpected birth of a child with significant disabilities, might wish to let their infant die. Yet, as a matter of public policy in our society, parents do not have absolute rights to decide the fate of their children. We have mandatory education and child abuse and neglect laws. It is also not uncommon for courts to order medical treatment for "normal" children even though their parents object to such care on religious grounds.

Do people with disabilities have the right to live in normal communities? Do they have the right to be educated alongside other children? Do they have the right to equal opportunities in employment, transportation and the use of public facilities? Do they have the right to lead meaningful and productive lives? Do they have a right to equal medical care? These seem like simple questions, but they are controversial ones. As we have seen, they have been answered differently by different people at different times. As uncomfortable as these questions may make us, they cannot be wished away.

Epilogue

Many things have happened in rehabilitation, special education, and the field of disability generally in the 1990s. Yet the trends identified in this and the preceding chapter that emerged during the 1970s and 1980s continue to exert influence on the delivery of services and the attitudes of professionals and the general public regarding the development of public policy affecting persons with significant disabilities.

The Law

Perhaps the most significant event affecting people with disabilities since the 1980s was the passage of the Americans with Disabilities Act (ADA) in 1990. The ADA outlawed discrimination against people with disabilities by businesses, employers, state and local governments, transportation authorities, and other entities. In contrast to Section 504 of the Rehabilitation Act, the ADA applies to all entities whether or not they receive federal funds.

As we have seen, laws are always ambiguous and open to different interpretations. Under the ADA, public and private entities must provide "reasonable accommodations" to "qualified individuals with disabilities" unless they impose an "undue hardship." None of these concepts is self-explanatory, and federal courts continue to interpret the provisions of the ADA.

In 1999, the U.S. Supreme Court handed down a series of cases on the ADA. In three employment discrimination cases (*Alberto's, Inc.* v. *Kirkingburg, Murphy* v. *United Parcel Service,* and *Sutton* v. *United Air Lines, Inc.*), the Court narrowed the range of persons covered by the ADA by eliminating those with impairments that do not "substantially limit" a major life activity or whose conditions are improved by corrective devices or medication.

Although the Court's decisions in these employment cases were viewed as a setback by disability rights advocates, its decision in *Olmstead* v. *L.C.* the same year was heralded as a victory for people with disabilities. The *Olmstead* case involved two women with mental retardation and psychiatric histories who sued the State of Georgia for the right to receive services in the community as opposed to a mental hospital. The Supreme Court ruled that under the ADA individuals with disabilities have the right to be served in the "most integrated setting appropriate" to their needs. As in the *Romeo* case years earlier, the Court left it to professionals to determine what is "appropriate" for any specific individual. In addition, the Court made it clear that states would not be required to "fundamentally alter" their programs to comply with the *Olmstead* decision. Thus, the *Olmstead* decision will undoubtedly benefit specific individuals who want to receive services in the community, but it stops short of requiring major changes in state service systems.

In 2000, the Court accepted for review a case challenging the constitutionality of Title II of the ADA, which applies to state governments, on the grounds that it violates states' rights. Barring a late settlement of the case, the Supreme Court will decide the issue in its 2000-2001 term. Depending on how the Court rules, states could be immune from lawsuits based on the ADA. This would be a devastating development for people with disabilities and would make the *Olmstead* decision moot.

Because courts cannot be depended upon to establish the right of all people with disabilities to community living, disability rights advocates, led by the national organization ADAPT, are promoting federal legislation, the Medicaid Community Services and Supports Act (MiCASSA), that would require states to offer persons eligible for Medicaid the choice between institutional placement and home and community supports. Introduced in the U.S. Senate by Senators Tom Harkin and Arlen Specter in late 1999, MiCASSA's prospects remain unclear at this time. The legislation faces stiff opposition from some states, the nursing home industry, and some public employee unions and institutional parent groups.

Inclusion

Integration—generally referred to as inclusion today—remains a strong trend in all disability services.

The populations of public institutions for people with developmental disabilities continue to decline at a steady pace. By mid-1999, the number of people in state institutions had decreased to 48,496, a decline of over 25 percent in just five years (Anderson, Prouty, & Lakin, 1999). Even more striking, eight states (Alaska, Hawaii, Maine, New Hampshire, New Mexico, Rhode Island, Vermont, and West Virginia) and the District of Columbia had closed their only state institutions by that time. From 1960 to 1999, a total of 153 public institutions for people with developmental disabilities had closed their doors (Anderson et al., 1999).

In special education, inclusion is increasingly endorsed by policymakers and disability and parent leaders. Of the 5,388,483 children ages 6 to 21 served under PL 94-142 (now called the Individuals with Disabilities Education Act or IDEA) in 1997-98, 45.75 percent were educated in regular classes (U.S. Department of Education, 1999). Less than 5 percent of students with disabilities were educated in totally separate public and private schools.

In contrast to the initial stages of the deinstitutionalization and integration movements, there is greater appreciation today that it is not sufficient for people with disabilities merely to be physically present in communities, schools, and workplaces. Current approaches emphasize the importance of social integration—the opportunity to form relationships with classmates, community members, and co-workers—and greater individual control over the services and supports people receive. Educators increasingly stress helping children with disabilities build friendships with other children in inclusive classrooms (Kliewer, 1998; Van der Klift & Kunc, 1994); vocational specialists are focusing attention on "natural supports" in workplaces (Butterworth, Hagner, Kiernan, & Schalock, 1996) and the "typicalness" of jobs held by people with significant disabilities (Mank, Cioffi, & Yovanoff, 1997). Trends in community living, support a movement away from group homes and agency controlled services in favor of housing owned or rented by individuals with disabilities (O'Brien, 1994), self-directed personal assistance and supports (Walker, Taylor, Searl, Shoultz, Hulgin, Harris, & Handley, 1996), and individual control over funding budgeted for services (Nerney, Crowley, & Kappel, 1997).

Continued Controversies

The controversies that dominated attention in earlier decades are still with us in some form today.

Despite increased support for the right of all people to live in the community and declining institutional populations, deinstitutionalization and community living remain controversial in some states and localities (Taylor, in press). In California and other states, real or imagined deficiencies in community service systems have been used by institutional parent groups and public employee unions to oppose further deinstitutionalization. Controversies over community living have captured the attention of the media and politicians in some localities, but have not halted the momentum in favor of the community on a national basis.

In special education, some educators and academicians (Chesley & Calaluce, 1997; Fuchs & Fuchs, 1994) continue to defend segregated placements and oppose the trend towards full inclusion of students with disabilities in regular classes. Similarly, some vocational rehabilitation specialists (Lam, 1996) argue for a continuum of vocational options, including sheltered workshops and other segregated settings.

Public controversies over the right to life of people with disabilities—represented by the Baby Doe issue in the 1980s—also continue today. In 1999, the appointment of Peter Singer, an Australian ethicist, to a prestigious appointment at Princeton University sparked demonstrations by people with disabilities and parents. Ironically an advocate of animal rights, Singer takes the position that it is ethically justified to kill infants with disabilities as well as people of any age with severe cognitive disabilities. Officials at Princeton and ethicists at other universities defend Singer on the grounds that he is a well-respected ethicist whose views are shared by many in his field.

The rapid advance of genetic technology has the potential to introduce new controversies that could not have been anticipated in earlier times. Newspaper headlines herald the progress of the Human Genome Project, an ambitious undertaking to map the entire set of human genes. This will make it possible to identify prenatally, and perhaps even before conception, individuals or potential individuals prone to genetic disabilities, illnesses, and conditions (Smith, 1994). The ethical implications of this undertaking are profound. Will persons with certain genetic make-ups be subject to discrimination in exercising reproductive rights, seeking employment, and obtaining health or life insurance?

The Future

The recent past can help us anticipate the issues and challenges of at least the near future. Legislatures and courts will sometimes support the causes of people with disabilities and their families, but will sometimes be disappointing. The inclusion of people with disabilities in America's schools, communities, and workplaces will be increasingly accepted as a philosophy and implemented in practice, but not without opposition from certain sectors. Old ideas and approaches die slowly. Technological advances will offer new benefits, but will also pose new dilemmas. The society and the public will pleasantly surprise us one day and then perplex and frustrate us the next.

REFERENCES

Anderson, L.L., Prouty, R. W., & Lakin, K. C. (1999). Trends and milestones: Closure of large state facilities and reductions of resident populations. *Mental Retardation,*37(6), 509-510.

Bellamy, G. T., Sheehan, M. R., Horner, R. H. & Boles, S. M. (1980). Community programs for severely handicapped adults: An analysis of vocational opportunities. *Journal of The Association for Persons with Severe Handicaps*, 5(4), 307-324.

Bercovici, S. (1983). *Barriers to normalization.* Baltimore: Paul H. Brookes Publishing Co.

Biklen, D., Bogdan, R., Ferguson, D. L., Searl, S. J., & Taylor, S. J. (1985). *Achieving the complete school: Strategies for effective mainstreaming.* New York: Teachers College Press.

Blatt, B., Bogdan, R., Biklen, D., & Taylor, S. (1977). From institution to community: A conversion model. In E. Sontag (Ed.), *Educational programming for the severely and profoundly handicapped.* Reston, VA: Council for Exceptional Children.

Brown, L., Shiraga, B., Ford, A., VanDeventer, P., Nisbet, J., Loomis, R., & Sweet, M. (1983). Teaching severely handicapped students to perform meaningful work in nonsheltered vocational environments. In L. Brown, J. Nisbet, A. Ford, M. Sweet, B. Shiraga, R. Loomis, & P. VanDeventer (Eds.), *Educational programs for severely handicapped students* (Vol. 13), (pp. 1-100). Madison, WI: Madison Metropolitan School District.

Butterworth, J., Hagner, D., Kiernan, W., & Schalock, R. (1996). Natural supports in the workplace: Defining an agenda for research and practice. *Journal of The Association for Persons with Severe Handicaps,* 21, 103-113.

Center on Human Policy. (1979). *The community imperative.* Syracuse: Center on Human Policy, Syracuse University.

Chesley, G. M., & Calaluce, Jr., P. D. (1997). "The deception of inclusion. *Mental Retardation,* 35(6), 488-490.

Conroy, J. W., & Bradley, V. J. (1985). *The Pennhurst longitudinal study: Combined report of five years of research and analysis.* Philadelphia: Temple University Press.

Dexter, L. A. (1994). On the politics and sociology of stupidity in our society. *Mental Retardation,* 32(2), 152-155.

Duff, R. S. (1981). Counseling families and deciding care of severely defective children: A way of coping with Medical Vietnam. *Pediatrics,* 67(3), 315-320.

Education of the Handicapped. (1984, July 25). *ED sets 1984 handicapped child count.* Education of the Handicapped.

Ellis, N. R., Balla, D., Estes, O., Warren, S. A., Meyers, C. E., Hollis, J., Isaacson, R. L., Palk, B. E., & Siegel, P. S. (1981). Common sense in the habilitation of mentally retarded persons: A reply to Menolascino and McGee. *Mental Retardation,* 19(5), 221-226.

Fletcher, J. (1972). *Indicators of humanhood—A tentative profile of man.* Hastings Center Report, 5(1).

Fuchs, D., & Fuchs, L. S. (1994). Inclusive schools movement and the radicalization of special education reform. *Exceptional Children,* 60(4), 294-309.

Gross, R. H., Cox, A., Tatyrek, R., Pollay, M., & Barnes, W. A. (1983). Early management decision making for the treatment of myelomeningocele. *Pediatrics,* 12(4), 450-458.

Hauber, F. A., Bruininks, R. H., Hill, B. K., Lakin, K. C. Scheerenberger, R. C., & White, C. C. (1984). National census of residential facilities: A 1982 profile of facilities and residents. *American Journal of Mental Deficiency,* 89(3), 236-245.

Johnson, M. (1984, February-March). The right is the wrong group to plead our rights. *The Disability Rag.*

Keating, R. (1979, September 17). *The war against the mentally retarded.* New York.

Kliewer, C. (1998). *Schooling children with Down syndrome: Toward an understanding of possibility.* New York: Teachers College Press.

Lam, C. S. (1996). Comparison of sheltered and supported work programs: A pilot study. *Rehabilitation Counseling Bulletin,* 30, 66-82.

Mank, D., Cioffi, A., & Yovanoff, P. (1997). Analysis of the typicalness of supported employment jobs, natural supports, and wage and integration outcomes. *Mental Retardation,* 35, 185-197.

Nerney, T., Crowley, R. F., & Kappel, B. (1997). *An affirmation of community, a revolution of vision and goals: Creating a community to support all people including those with disabilities.* Keene, NH: Monadnock Developmental Services.

O'Brien, J. (1994). Down stairs that are never your own: Supporting people with developmental disabilities in their own homes. *Mental Retardation,* 32(1), 1-6.

Perske, R. (1980). *New life in the neighborhood.* Nashville: Abingdon.

Rafferty, M. (1981, October 19). Special education carried too far. *Syracuse Post-Standard,* A4.

Scull, A. (1981). A new trade in lunacy: The remodification of the mental patient. *American Behavioral Scientist,* 24(6), 741-754.

Smith, J. D. (1994). "Reflections on mental retardation and eugenics, old and new: Mensa and the Human Genome Project. *Mental Retardation,* 32(3), 234-238.

Starr, R. (1982, January). Wheels of misfortune: Sometimes equality just costs too much. *Harper's,* 7-15.

Taylor, S. J. (1982). From segregation to integration: Strategies for integrating severely handicapped students in normal school and community settings. *The Journal of The Association for the Severely Handicapped,* 8(3), 42-49.

Taylor, S. J. (in press). The continuum and current controversies in the United States. *Journal of Intellectual & Developmental Disability.*

Thomason, J., & Arkell, C. (1980). Educating the severely/profoundly handicapped in the public schools: A side-by-side approach. *Exceptional Children,* 47(2), 114-122.

Thorne, J. M. (1979). Deinstitutionalization: Too wide a swath. *Mental Retardation,* 17, 171-175.

U.S. Department of Education. (1999). *Twenty-first annual report to Congress on the implementation of the Individuals with Disabilities Education Act.* Washington, DC: Author.

U.S. Government Printing Office. (1982). *Care for the retarded,* 1981. Washington, DC: Author.

Van der Klift, E., & Kunc, N. (1994). Friendships and the politics of help. In J. S. Thousand, R. A. Villa, & A. I. Nevin (Eds.), *Creativity and collaborative learning: A practical guide to empowering students* (pp. 391-401). Baltimore: Paul H. Brookes Publishing Co.

Vernon, M. (1981). Education's Three Mile Island: PL 94-142. *Peabody Journal of Education,* 214-229.

Walker, P., Taylor, S., Searl, J., Shoultz, B., Hulgin, K., Harris, P., & Handley, M. (1996, April). *Evaluation of the Self-Directed Personal Services Program operated through Enable.* Syracuse, NY: Center on Human Policy, Syracuse University.

Warren, C. A. B. (1981). New forms of social control: The myth of deinstitutional-
     ization. *American Behavioral Scientist,* 24(6), 724-740.

Wehman, P. (1981). *Competitive employment: New horizons for severely disabled individ-
     uals.* Baltimore: Paul H. Brookes Publishing Co.

Wilcox, B., & Sailor, W. (1980). Service delivery issues: Integrated educational sys-
     tems. In B. Wilcox & R. York (Eds.), *Quality education for the severely handicapped:
     The federal investment.* Washington, DC: U.S. Department of Education.

Wolpert, J. (1978). *Group homes for the mentally retarded: An investigation of neighbor-
     hood property impacts.* Albany: New York State Office of Mental Retardation and
     Developmental Disabilities.

Chapter 4

DISABILITY IN AMERICA: THE LEGISLATIVE RESPONSE

E. Davis Martin, Jr.

D ISABILITIES THAT ARE CLASSIFIED as significant and/or developmental have been given greater emphasis since the historic passage of the 1973 Rehabilitation Act and, in fact, selection priority in the delivery of rehabilitation services. Subsequent amendments to the Rehabilitation Act, particularly the 1992 and 1998 amendments, mandated services to persons with significant disabilities. The programs created by these legislative events have moved the delivery systems toward a client or customer perspective with greater control vested in the person with a disability regarding choice. The Americans with Disabilities Act (ADA), for example, mandated educators, employers, businesses, and governmental agencies to provide goods and services to persons with disabilities from a posture of antidiscrimination. The major difference articulated in the ADA when compared to Section 504 of the 1973 Rehabilitation Act is its effect on the private sector of the economy. The Individuals with Disabilities Act (IDEA) calls for greater coordination in the transition of youth with disabilities from secondary schools to that of further education, work, or vocational rehabilitation (habilitation).

The purpose of this chapter will be to build upon the preceding chapters and to review these historic legislative events that originated during the 1970s, most notably the 1973 Rehabilitation Act and its subsequent amendments, denoting the changes over the course of the past three decades. The human service delivery systems created as a result of these legislative events will be analyzed from the perspective of the customer or consumer of those services provided by the rehabilitation and educational systems. The decade of the 1970s produced three of the most significant legislative accomplishments of the twentieth century: The Developmental Disabilities Services and Facilities Construction Act (PL 91-517); The Rehabilitation Act of 1973 (PL 93-112); and the Education for All Handicapped Children Act (PL 94-142). Each of these legislative events and subsequent amendments continuing to the present represented a paradigm shift that signaled an increased voice and influence for persons with disabilities regarding vocational, educational, and independent living choices.

Developmental Disabilities Legislation

With the passage of PL 91-517, the Developmental Disabilities Services and Construction Act of 1970, the term *developmental disability* first came into use (Kiernan and Schalock, 1995). The term *developmental disability* was defined to include the following specific disabilities: mental retardation, epilepsy, and cerebral palsy. Onset of the development disability was to have occurred at birth or prior to age 18 and have imposed severe limitation in the child's or person's ability to function. The Act established a formula grant program in which the states were encouraged to develop coordinated services for persons labeled as having a developmental disability. Braddock, Hemp, Parish, and Westrich (1998) noted that the ". . . states were required to establish interagency 'councils' representing numerous state government agencies relevant to the delivery of developmental disabilities services . . . (that would develop) . . . (e)very three years . . . formal state plans to set goals and improve the delivery of services" (p. 7).

In 1975, amendments to the Developmental Disabilities Services and Construction Act retitle the act as the Developmental Disabilities Assistance and Bill of Rights Act (PL 94-103). Categorical groupings of disabilities were maintained and the disabilities of autism and dyslexia (with some qualifications) were added. The 1975 amendments also specified essential services that should be available as basic rights to persons defined as having a developmental disability. Those services specified, among others, were residential services, employment services, treatment, transportation, and leisure services. These services were basic rights. These amendments were greatly influenced by ". . . a series of class-action law suits in which the courts ruled that the mentally retarded [*sic*] in institutions had constitutional rights to treatment, services, and habilitation that 'maximize the developmental potential of the person and are provided in the setting that is least restrictive of the person's personal liberty'." (Berkowitz, 1987, p. 207) Most notable of these class-action suits were *Wyatt* v. *Stickney* (344 F. Supp. 378, M.D., Alabama, 1972) and *New York State ARC* v. *Rockefeller* (357 F. Supp. 752, 1973) often referred to as the *Willowbrook* case (discussed in Chapter 2).

The 1978 amendments now titled as the Rehabilitation, Comprehensive Services, and Developmental Disabilities Act (PL 95-602) broadened the definition of developmental disability from the existing categorical basis to a functional basis; that is, a definition which no longer specifically denoted a particular mental or physical condition (e.g., mental retardation, epilepsy, etc.) but as a chronic and lifelong mental or physical condition that impaired substantial functional limitations in the performance of major life activities. Of the seven characterized major life activities, at least three must present substantial limitations to the person:

1. Self-care
2. Receptive and Expressive Language
3. Learning
4. Mobility
5. Self-Direction
6. Capacity for Independent Living
7. Economic Self-sufficiency

Braddock et al. (1998, p. 7), moreover, reported that the 1978 amendments established the Protection and Advocacy Program ". . . thus completing the triad of Developmental Disabilities Act funded organizations: university affiliated programs (UAPs), state planning councils, and advocacy agencies."

The 1973 Rehabilitation Act and Amendments

The passage of the 1973 Rehabilitation Act (PL 93-112) was, perhaps, one of the most significant events of the twentieth century; in particular, the effect and impact that Section 504 would have upon American society and for the rights of persons with disabilities. The major focus of the 1973 Rehabilitation Act dealt with equality of opportunity through provisions relating to consumer involvement, emphasis on persons with severe disabilities, creation of the now named National Institute on Disability and Rehabilitation Research (NIDRR), emphasis on program evaluation, and the advancement of the civil rights of persons with disabilities. The 1973 Rehabilitation Act represented a mandate to serve persons with severe disabilities.

Emphasis on Persons with Severe Disabilities

While the emphasis was to serve persons with severe disabilities, the creation of independent living rehabilitation options in the 1973 Rehabilitation Act were omitted, in large part, because President Nixon had vetoed two previous rehabilitation bills in 1972 that contained a provision related to independent living (Rubin and Roessler, 1995). The Nixon administration, as noted by Rubin and Roessler (1995, p. 46), "... did, however, agree to a compromise–a Comprehensive Needs Study (CNS; Section 130 of the Act) to determine the rehabilitation needs of individuals who 'cannot reasonably be expected to be rehabilitated for employment but for whom a program of rehabilitation would improve their ability to live independently or function normally within their family and community'." It would not be until the 1978 amendments that the independent living rehabilitation program would be authorized.

Title VII of the 1978 amendments contained three parts which provided the basis for independent living rehabilitation options:

Part A–authorized comprehensive services that would enhance the person's ability to function in employment or the home.
Part B–authorized the state agency to make grants for the establishment of centers for independent living which would provide a wide range of services inclusive of peer counseling, independent living skills, assistance with housing and transportation, and per-

sonal assistance services.

Part C–authorized independent living services to older blind persons.

DeJong stated that for the first time in more than 50 years, the professional rehabilitation leaders were joined in these efforts by an increasingly visible and effective leadership from people with disabilities. People with severe disabilities were representing a growing and vigorous constituency: a most assertive and, at times, a more militant group who were insistent on change (DeJong, 1979).

Consumer Involvement

The essence of the rehabilitation process is the relationship between the counselor and the client or consumer. The 1973 Rehabilitation Act stressed the nature of this relationship as one of joint involvement and responsibility that should pervade the rehabilitation process from beginning to closure. Throughout the process, the consumer or client was to be informed of decisions that may have an impact (that may be perceived by the client as adverse) and given an opportunity to appeal those decisions. Eligibility, for example, was one area that may be subject to disagreement. Initially, no formal or organized programs were available to assist clients who questioned the decisions of counselors or supervisors. Client Assistance Projects were first authorized in the 1978 amendments, and ultimately Client Assistance Projects would be required in each state in order to assure due process (the 1984 amendments).

The Individual Written Rehabilitation Program (IWRP) represented a real opportunity for the client and counselor to mutually plan a sequence of services that would enable the client to enter into employment. The basic nature of such a planning process had at its core the mutual involvement and joint formulation of a program that would have the capability to change the client's (and his or her family's) life. Such a momentous event required nothing less than mutual respect and involvement in decision making.

Subsequent amendments to the 1973 Rehabilitation Act in 1978 and 1984 created the National Council on the Handicapped in 1978 and later renamed the National Council on Disability in 1984. This 15-person council appointed by the President of the United States and confirmed by the United States Senate is an independent federal agency whose overall purpose is ". . . to promote the policies, programs, practices, and procedures that guarantee equal opportunity for all individuals with disabilities, regardless of the nature of the severity of the disability; and to empower individuals with disabilities to achieve economic self-sufficiency, independent living, and inclusion and integration into all aspects of society" (National Council on Disability, 1996, p. 187). This Council represents, perhaps, the zenith in consumer involvement from a policy perspective.

Creation of the National Institute on Disability and Rehabilitation Research

The 1973 Rehabilitation Act provided for the continued funding of innovation and expansion grants, rehabilitation research and training centers, and other types of demonstration grants; however, the 1978 amendments established the, then named, National Institute of Handicapped Research (Rubin & Roessler, 1995). Rubin and Roessler (1995, p. 51) noted that the National Institute of Handicapped Research " . . . was established to direct the research thrust in rehabilitation, in particular, that of the Rehabilitation Research and Training Centers . . ." and to:

> (a) disseminate information on ways to increase the quality of life of individuals with disabilities;
>
> (b) educate the public about ways of providing for the rehabilitation of individuals with disabilities;
>
> (c) conduct conferences concerning research and engineering advances in rehabilitation; and
>
> (d) produce and disseminate statistical reports and studies on the employment, health, and income of individuals with disabilities. (pp. 51-52)

Emphasis on Program Evaluation

Meaningful consumer involvement in the rehabilitation process also required that the outcomes of that process be assessed as well. Program evaluation to be undertaken by state agencies, as noted by Rubin and Roessler (1995), ". . . meant that state rehabilitation agencies would be held accountable for providing information on:

(a) the percentage of the existing target population being served;

(b) the timeliness and adequacy of their services,

(c) the suitability of the employment in which clients are placed and the sustention of that employment, and

(d) client satisfaction with rehabilitation services. (p. 51)

Needs assessments occurring on a three-year cycle (CFR 361.29) and client/consumer satisfaction surveys are now a defined component of the state rehabilitation agency.

Advancement of the Civil Rights of Persons with Disabilities

Sections 501, 502, 503, and 504 of Title V of the 1973 Rehabilitation Act addressed the following areas of concern respectively: nondiscriminatory federal hiring, accessability (creation of the Architectural and Transportation Barriers Compliance Board), affirmative action and prohibition of discrimination against persons with disabilities in terms of programmatic and physical accessability in schools, institutions of higher education, hospitals, and other institutions which receive federal financial assistance.

Increased awareness of persons with disabilities and of the environmental and attitudinal barriers encountered by persons with disabilities is generally credited as a major impetus for the passage of the 1973 Rehabilitation Act and the subsequent 1978 amendments. These legislative events signaled a change in public policy patterned largely after the Civil Rights Act. No longer were employers or potential employers asked on the basis of moral grounds to hire persons with a disability but to take affirmative action in hiring and, as well as, to assume a posture of nondiscrimination. Admission to schools and institutions of higher education, likewise, was addressed by Section 504 of Title V. This section noted:

No otherwise qualified handicapped [*sic*] individual in the United States, as defined in section 7 (7), shall, solely by reason of his handicap [*sic*] , be excluded from the participation in, be denied the benefits of or be subjected to discrimination under any program or activity receiving Federal financial assistance or under any program or activity conducted by any Executive agency or by the United States Postal Service.

Section 504 was originally envisioned as an antidiscrimination provision that would have more impact as a symbolic statement and not necessarily as a mandate (Percy, 1989). The origins of 504, as noted by Percy (1989, pp. 225-226) can be:

. . . traced to Senator Hubert Humphrey and Representative Charles Vanik, who introduced bills in Congress to amend the Civil Rights Act to include protections for persons with disabilities. While this strategy produced little result, it set the groundwork for Section 504 to be included, quietly and without fanfare, in the Rehabilitation Act as the legislation was being marked up by staff members from the Senate Committee on Labor and Public Welfare and the House Committee on Education and Labor.

Senator Humphrey's advocacy for what ultimately became Section 504 stemmed, in part, from his experiences as a grandparent of a child with a disability.

Another powerful reason for inclusion of Section 504 in the 1973 Rehabilitation Act, as noted by Scotch (1984) and reported in Percy (1989, p. 53) was:

Staff members were concerned that, when disabled [*sic*] individuals completed their training in the VR [vocational rehabilitation] system and were ready to enter the workplace, many employers appeared reluctant to hire them. Staff members felt the final goal of the VR program, getting disabled [*sic*] people into the mainstream of society, was being blocked by negative attitudes and discrimination on the part of employers and others.

The definition of disability and by extension who is protected by Section 504 was changed by the 1974 amendments to be much broader and inclusive than the original definition which was employment based (Percy, 1989). Broadening the definition allowed for inclusion of children with disabilities, older persons with disabilities, and persons with severe disabilities. A person with a disability according to this definition was defined as a person who:

1. has a physical or mental impairment that substantially limits one or more of such a person's major life activities;
2. has a record of such impairment;
3. or is regarded as having such an impairment.

One other concept that originated from Section 504 (and was applicable to Section 503 as well) was that of reasonable accommodation. Reasonable accommodation was defined ". . . with reference to examples that included making employee facilities readily accessible to and usable(,) . . . job restructuring, modifications in work schedules, changes in equipment, and provision of readers and interpreters. A limitation on mandated accommodations was included through the modifier "reasonable" (Percy, 1989, p. 76) An employer did not have to make an accommodation if it was deemed to create an "undue economic hardship." Little guidance was provided in the interpretation of what was reasonable or unreasonable. Because of this lack of specificity and the nature of individualized accommodations, compliance became a case-by-case situation that sometimes was confusing and controversial. Perhaps most notable was *Davis* v. *Southeastern Community College* (442 U.S. 397, 1979) in which the Supreme Court reversed an earlier favorable decision by the 4th U. S. Circuit Court of Appeals. *Davis* was the first real test of Section 504. Davis, a licensed practical nurse had applied for admission to the college's nursing program and had requested accommodations on the basis of her hearing impairment. The college denied her admission on the basis of safety (that Davis would not be able to lip read in clinical situations where masks were worn) and that to admit her would force the college to lower its standards. The Supreme Court found in favor of Southeastern Community College noting that this was a case about affirmative action, not an antidiscrimination case. Consequently, the issue of equality of opportunity and reasonable accommodation was sidestepped. Many regarded this decision as a continuing pattern of bias and prejudice against people with disabilities. In any event, it noted that the effectiveness and powerfulness of Section 504 may not be what was envisioned, particularly by persons with disabilities and other advocates.

Prior to the 1978 amendments, persons who pursued a legal course of action were not allowed to collect attorneys' fees in litigation in which they prevailed. Section 505 was added to the 1978 amendments which corrected this situation as well as allowing for the same rights, procedures, and remedies as outlined in Title VII of the Civil Rights Act of 1964 (Percy, 1989).

Toward the end of the decade of the 1980s, the National Council on Disability observed that the current status of existing nondiscrimination laws, such as Section 504, were (Percy, 1989, p. 224):

> . . . extremely important and have engendered much progress. (But) (i)n an overall context, however, our Nation's laws provide inadequate protection from discrimination for people with disabilities. Current statutes are not comparable in their scope of protection against discrimination afforded racial, ethnic, and religious minorities and women under civil rights laws.

As a result of this finding, the National Council on Disability championed the development and passage of new legislation in 1990, the Americans with Disabilities Act (ADA). The ADA, it was thought, would bring together and strengthen nondiscrimination policies for all persons with disabilities.

Individuals with Disabilities Education Act (IDEA)

Prior to the passage of PL 94-142, the Education for All Handicapped Children Act of 1975, children with disabilities–particularly those with significant disabilities–had few programs that were designed to accommodate instructional needs that differed from the mainstream. Parents and parent-based groups, the National Association of Retarded Children, and the Council for Exceptional Children lobbied the federal government for programs to educate children with disabilities. A major, although small, gain was realized through this advocacy with the establishment of the Bureau for Education of the Handicapped within the Office of Education which took as its focus the development of training programs for special education teachers and initiated research programs on how to effectively teach children with disabilities (Percy, 1989). It would, however, ultimately be the courts to conclude that the state educational systems in America had failed to provide an education for children with disabilities (Tucker and Goldstein, 1992).

Two court cases, in particular, provided the foundation for the creation of PL 94-142: Pennsylvania Association for Retarded Citizens v. Commonwealth of Pennsylvania (343 F. Supp. 279, 1972) and Mills v.

Board of Education of the District of Columbia (348 F. Supp. 866, 1972). In the *PARC* case, children who were labeled as mentally retarded ". . . sued the state claiming that they were denied the right to a public education . . . (on the basis of) . . . three claims: (1) a violation of due process because there was no notice or hearing provided before retarded [*sic*] children were excluded from public school or their educational assignments were changed; (2) a violation of equal protection due to the lack of a rational basis for assuming that mentally retarded [*sic*] children were uneducable and untrainable; and (3) a violation of due process because it was arbitrary and capricious to deny mentally retarded [*sic*] children a right to the education guaranteed by state law" (Tucker and Goldstein, 1992, p. 2:14). The *Mills* case, similarly, centered on the denial of a publicly supported education and involved not only children labeled as mentally retarded but children with other disabilities as well. Both the *PARC* and *Mills* cases demonstrated (*PARC* through a consent agreement and *Mills* through a summary judgment) that children with disabilities were entitled to a free and suitable public education based on the constitutional rights extended by the Due Process and Equal Protection clauses of the Fourteenth Amendment (Tucker & Goldstein, 1992).

The Education for All Handicapped Children Act was passed and signed into law by President Gerald Ford in 1975 and regulations were finalized less than two years later. PL 94-142 mandated that each child with a disability be provided with a "free, appropriate public education" (FAPE).

The concept of a "free appropriate public education" was welcomed, in particular, by parents of children with disabilities–who could deny the inherent worth and value of the principles upon which this concept was formed? Free appropriate public education from a parental perspective means the best educational situation for any child to succeed. However, this was not exactly the meaning of free appropriate education as ultimately noted by the Supreme Court. Amy Rowley, a young girl who had minimal hearing, was an excellent speech reader. She was in the first grade and had been provided with a hearing aid and was receiving speech therapy and had a tutor for the deaf. Academically, Amy was doing well in her studies (upper half of her class) and passing from grade to grade. However, Amy's parents, who were deaf, felt that she was missing too much classroom instruction and requested that the school provide Amy with a sign language interpreter. The school refused and an administrative hearing officer and the state upheld the school's decision. The Rowley's filed suit in the federal courts and won at the district court level which was appealed by the school board. The Rowley's again won at the Court of Appeals for the Second Circuit and the school board appealed to the Supreme Court. The Supreme Court in its decision in Board of Education of the Henrick Hudson Central School District v. Rowley (458 U.S. 176, 102 S. Ct. 3034, 1982) found for the school board. The Supreme Court concluded that since Amy had access to and was benefitting from her educational program, this met the intent of free appropriate public education. In other words, it did not matter that she may achieve more with the provision of a sign language interpreter. Tucker and Goldstein (1992, pp. 16-5 and 6) noted that:

> Thus the Supreme Court in *Rowley* set forth a two-prong test, one procedural and one somewhat substantive, for courts to apply in determining whether children with disabilities have been provided a FAPE. The Court indicated that the individual needs of the child, as determined by an IEP, are the appropriate focus. Furthermore, the Court held that children with disabilities do not have an enforceable right to achieve their maximum potential, but rather are entitled only to receive some educational benefit, the sufficiency of which is to be left to a case by case analysis.

Amendments in 1986 to the Education for All Handicapped Act (PL 99-457) authorized early intervention programs for preschool age children with disabilities. In 1990, the Act was amended and titled the Individuals with Disabilities Education Act (IDEA) of 1990. In addition to changing the title of the Act, IDEA represented a shift in thinking about children/youth with disabilities. IDEA abandoned the use of the terminology "handicap," "handicapped" to describe children and youth with disabilities and adopted person first language—a much sought after change which had the potential to reduce negative attitudes or stereotypes of what, mostly, children with disabilities cannot do. Children and youth with disabilities are, however, still labeled with such negative terms as educable mentally retarded, trainable mentally retarded, emotionally disturbed, severely and profoundly handicapped, or disabled among others. IDEA also required the development of an individual transition plan (ITP) for each student with a disability that would facilitate transition from school to post-school activities (e.g., work, training, further schooling, independent living, and so forth). Rehabilitation professionals have a significant role to play in this transition. Hayes, Bain, and Batshaw (1997) have noted that the provisions of the IEP should require:

1. the process to be outcome oriented,

2. students to be meaningfully involved in the process,

3. students' needs to be projected beyond one year,

4. schools to work with external agencies responsible for the provision of services or funding, and

5. schools to provide extensive community-based instruction.

Moreover, Hayes et al. (1997, p. 762) observed that not all school systems are providing these services because ". . . educators believe that these requirements go well beyond the school's responsibilities or capabilities." The potential effect or reality is that some youth will not receive transition services and may likely "fall through the cracks" and end up at home watching television while awaiting services from unknown agencies.

Other Significant Legislation Passed in the 1980s

The 1986 amendments to the 1973 Rehabilitation Act emphasized the use of rehabilitation engineering services, supported employment services for persons with severe disabilities, and mandated a gradual reduction in federal financial assistance to the state programs from the, then, 80 percent to an anticipated 75 percent matching ratio in 1993 (Rubin & Roessler, 1995).

The Technology-Related Assistance for Individuals with Disabilities Act of 1988 (PL 100-407) had as its purpose to improve access to technology devices and services for individuals with disabilities. Kurtz and Harryman (1997, p. 719) noted that the Tech Act was to ". . . support not only the purchase or lease of equipment but also a range of services to ensure success with their use. . . . [Moreover] . . . [t]hese [services] include (1) evaluation of the child's technological needs, (2) maintenance and repair of equipment, (3) training in the use of the devices, and (4) coordination of technology with other therapy services." The

Tech Act encouraged the states to engage in a competitive grant process that would allow the development of a consumer responsive system of technology services that would be accessible.

The importance of assistive technology cannot be understated. Assistive technology has the capacity to lessen or reduce the effects of disability which then allows for participation in education, employment, and activities of daily living; that is, participation in the work and play of American society. It is the great equalizer for persons with disabilities. Technology is available but not always financially accessible. Wallace (1994, p. 79) noted that ". . . the funding of assistive technology continues to be the area of greatest need identified through consumer surveys across the country."

Americans with Disabilities Act

In 1986, the National Council on Disability issued its report *Toward Independence* which set the stage for the development of the Americans with Disabilities Act (ADA). Frank Bowe (1992, p. 3) credits the enactment of the ADA to the efforts of Justin W. Dart, Jr., and noted that:

> . . . for three years . . . Dart chaired a private sector body created by Rep. Major R. Owens (D-NY), chairman of the Select Education Subcommittee in the House. Dart's U. S. House of Representatives' Task Force on the Human Rights and Empowerment of Americans with Disabilities brought several hundred thousand adults and children with disabilities from all 50 states into the ADA "movement." The Task Force was an entirely voluntary effort: no one was paid nor were any expenses covered by Congress. Dart himself traveled to every one of the states, at his own expense, holding hearings to solicit the input of people with disabilities, parents, employers, educators, and local government officials.

For Senator Tom Harkin, an early legislative leader and supporter for the passage of the Americans with Disabilities Act, the potential impact of ADA meant:

> . . . inclusion, integration, and empowerment. For business, it means more customers, increased profits and additional qualified workers. For labor, it means greater protection from arbitrary action for members. And for government, it means more taxpayers and fewer persons on welfare, social security, and other social programs. (Harkins, 1994, p. 939)

Dart (1995) has noted that the substantive requirements of the ADA were based on Section 504 of the 1973 Rehabilitation Act and that the procedural requirements were based on Title VII of the 1964 Civil Rights Act. The ADA as envisioned by Dart (National Council on Disability and its staff and consultants) observed that Sections 501, 503, and 504 of the 1973 Rehabilitation Act were useful but did not extend to the vast private sector of the American economy (Bowe, 1992). The creation of the ADA's five Titles were developed with this perspective:

Title I–Employment

Prohibits discrimination on the basis of disability with regard to job application procedures, hiring, advancement, discharge, compensation, training, and other privileges of employment.

Title II–Public Services

Prohibits discrimination on the basis of disability with regard to services and programs of local and state government including accessibility of such activities and programs. Public transient systems (operated by governmental agencies) accessibility are covered by this title.

Title III–Public Accommodations

Prohibits discrimination on the basis of disability with regard to accessibility of public transportation services operated by the private sector. Cover restaurants, banks, hotels, and others regarding

	accessibility or exclusion. Set standards for the accessibility in existing and new buildings.
Title IV—Telecommunications	Prohibits discrimination on the basis of disability with regard to persons with speech and hearing impediments. Required the establishment of 24-hour relay services.
Title V—Miscellaneous	Prohibits retaliation.

The effectiveness of the ADA has been the basis for many television news reports and has been studied by the various constituents who have been affected by its provisions. Professor Blanck (1994) in a comprehensive empirical study of the impact of the ADA investigated 1,100 persons with mental retardation in Oklahoma over a period of three years (1990-1993) vis-a-vis Title I of the act. Blanck's findings revealed modest gains in integrated employment, wages, and independent living. Senator Bob Dole, an ardent supporter of the ADA, commented that Blanck's study focused on the correct issues for assessing progress; that is, employment and economic well being but if employment was the major goal sought, then the results were not that encouraging. Dole (1994, p. 928) speaking from a national perspective noted "(u)nfortunately, the news isn't so good. In 1986, 33 percent of disabled [*sic*] Americans worked; in 1994, this figure is 31 percent." The 1998 Lou Harris Poll revealed that this percentage had declined to 29 percent.

West (1994) reported in The Milbank Memorial Fund's report, *Federal Implementation of the Americans with Disabilities Act, 1991-1994*, that no federal agency had plans to survey consumers regarding changes brought about as a result of the ADA; that only minimal funding for evaluation studies to determine effectiveness had been allocated; and that neither studies nor data collection activities to determine effectiveness of ADA related tax code provisions had been planned. Nevertheless, this report did recommend that Congress:

1. Retain the current statute without amendment.
2. Establish minimal enforcement standards, including timeliness for complaint processing and closure. Adequate resources should be allocated to EEOC, DOJ, and DOT to enable them to comply with these standards.
3. Appropriate funds to the Civil Rights Division of DOJ for a comprehensive ADA public awareness/education campaign. This campaign should be developed and coordinated with EEOC, DOT, FCC, Access Board, NIDRR, NCD, PCEPD, and other relevant agencies.
4. Designate an internal ADA coordinator for each body and provide for an independent assessment of progress (pp. x-xi).

In assessing the public accessibility titles of the ADA, McMahon noted that ". . . implementation has been more successful." Moreover, "(a)rchitectural and especially communication barriers are being torn down on or ahead of schedule, access to goods and services through technology is greater, complaint and litigation levels are well below predicted levels, and compliance is high because competitive American businesses are eager to tap into the purchasing power of 54 million Americans with disabilities."

It is obvious that more success has been achieved in the area of public accessibility than employment for persons with disabilities. From a historical perspective, the overall effectiveness of the ADA has been somewhat mixed; however, only a brief moment of time has elapsed since the enactment of this most significant and compelling legislation. McMahon, as well, has noted that this ". . . is a short period of time for such an ambitious statute . . . (and) . . . in the long term ADA will change the way we live and do business in America."

1992 Amendments to the 1973 Rehabilitation Act

The 1992 amendments to the 1973 Rehabilitation Act continued the strong emphasis toward provision of services to persons with severe disabilities, even introducing a new category of "most severe disability"; a continuing emphasis on employment outcomes introducing a career perspective; increased consumer choice and control in the rehabilitation process; broadened eligibility to denote that a consumer need only to "benefit" from provision of services; and increased consumer control through the establishment of Statewide Rehabilitation Advisory Councils and Statewide Independent Living Councils. The declaratory statement for vocational rehabilitation services contained in the 1992 amendments stressed the importance of work and of its centrality in American society and recounted the barriers to achievement of this goal.

Eligibility criteria for receipt of vocational rehabilitation services changed as noted below:

An individual is eligible for vocational rehabilitation services when:

1. He/she has a physical or mental impairment which constitutes or results in a substantial impediment to employment,
2. the individual can benefit in terms of an employment outcome from VR services, and
3. the individual requires vocational rehabilitation services to prepare for, enter, engage in, or retain employment.

This broadened definition of eligibility allowed for increased flexibility in working with clients or customers with severe and most severe disabilities since it incorporated the qualifier "benefit" although the interpretation of this word often did not mean the same thing for a person with a disability as it did for the VR agency. This definition of eligibility also allowed counselors to work with persons in a preventive manner regarding retention of employment. Other provisions related to the establishment of time limits for the determination of eligibility (60 day limit) however some consumers complained that they were put in a waiting status before being allowed to apply for rehabilitation services. Use of existing data, particularly from educational agencies as well as from the person with a disability and his or her family was encouraged. The VR agency was mandated to conduct an extended evaluation if a person's disability was considered too severe to serve. In this same vein, the agency was required to specify the reasons for a determination of ineligibility and concurrently advise the person of the availability of the services of the Client Assistance Program.

The Individual Written Rehabilitation Program (IWRP) continued to emphasize the importance of the planning process between the client or customer and the counselor. The IWRP was to be jointly developed and reflect the unique strengths, resources, abilities, and concerns of the person with a disability in terms of the vocational objective selected. The vocational objective was to have a career focus with job placement in an integrated setting. A statement of specific services to be provided and the data and duration of such services were to be specified. An assessment of the need for post-employment services was, as well, to be included in the IWRP. Each client or customer was to receive a copy of the IWRP and, in case of a disagreement regarding the plan or anticipated services, the person was to be informed of the availability of the Client Assistance Program (as well as how to access these services). The IWRP was to be reviewed at least annually allowing for changes and the development of revisions or amendments to the IWRP.

The 1992 amendments also provided that federal support of the VR program be increased from 75 percent to 78.7 percent beginning in 1993. An emphasis on minority recruitment to the field of rehabilitation was to be developed through supports to college and university programs that had minority enrollments of 50 percent or greater (Rubin & Roessler, 1995).

The 1998 Amendments to the 1973 Rehabilitation Act

The Rehabilitation Act amendments of 1998 were signed into law by President William Jefferson Clinton on August 7, l998 as a part of the Workforce Investment Act of 1998. The 1998 amendments continued and expanded emphasis on consumer involvement and choice. Fredric K. Schroeder, Commissioner of the Rehabilitation Services Administration, released an information memorandum which detailed the following areas of emphasis contained in the 1998 amendments (1998, p. 2):

expanding the exercise of informed choice by individuals with disabilities;

streamlining administrative procedures to improve program efficiency and access to services;

increasing opportunities for high quality employment outcomes; ensuring due process; and

linking the VR program to a State's workforce investment system.

State VR agencies and the State Rehabilitation Councils (formally the Statewide Rehabilitation Advisory Councils) were to develop policies and procedures that would insure informed choice regarding eligibility determination, selection of vocational or employment goals, and the selection of services and service providers. The Individual Written Rehabilitation Plan (IWRP) was renamed the Individualized Plan for Employment (IPE) to emphasize the expanded role of the person with a disability vis-a-vis informed choice. The IPE continued the existent requirement for comparable benefits, post-employment services, and due process procedures.

Administratively, the amendments eliminated the strategic plan requirements and supported the expansion of the VR services to persons with the most significant disabilities (a change in terminology from the qualifier "severe" to "significant"). Presumptively, persons receiving Social Security Disability Insurance (SSDI) and Supplemental Security Insurance (SSI) benefits who desire an employment outcome are eligible to receive VR services without going through an eligibility process. Employment outcomes characterized as "high quality" meaning the expansion of job opportunities in such areas as telecommuting, self-employment including small business operation are emphasized in the development of the IPE. The requirement for extended evaluation (when or if ineligibility is being assessed for persons with the most significant disabilities) was replaced with a requirement of trial work experience.

Due process requirements were enhanced for persons with disabilities who disagreed with decisions regarding eligibility, services, or case closure. Mediation is an option that is to be offered a client; the outcome, however, is not binding and cannot be used to delay or deny an impartial hearing. Decisions of the Impartial Hearing Officer, as a result of these new due process provisions, will no longer be reviewed by the state VR director.

Linkages to the state workforce investment system (a consolidation of employment and training programs into a unified statewide system) were contemplated to lead to better coordination and cooperation among the various agencies regarding job opportunities for persons with disabilities.

Future Directions

The disability movement, as witnessed by the historic events of the preceding three decades, has come a long way toward the ideal of rehabilitation as expressed by the National Council on Rehabilitation in 1942 to the passage of the 1973 Rehabilitation Act to the passage of Americans with Disabilities Act in 1990. But, in reality, we have only come a small distance when persons with significant disabilities are still being institutionalized because our society cannot or will not expend money for community options even in the light of economic gain. It costs less to provide services in the community than it does in an institutional setting. The legislative agenda for persons with disabilities has increasingly become more consumer or customer centered and directed and less process oriented. This is a most positive trend which holds great promise for the future not only for people with disabilities but for all people.

The National Council on Disability in its recent report *Achieving Independence: The Challenge for the 21st Century* assessed disability policy of the recent past and concluded:

> Disability policy has made steady progress in the last decade in empowering people with disabilities; however, this progress is threatened, compromised, and often undermined by lack of understanding and support in the Congress and among particular segments of society.
>
> Most public policy affecting people with disabilities does not yet promote the goals of ADA–equality of opportunity, full participation, independent living, and economic self-sufficiency.
> Most Americans with disabilities remain outside the economic and social mainstream of American life. (pp. 3-4)

The National Council on Disability also offered these recommendations:

1. Existing laws should be more vigorously enforced.
2. People with disabilities should direct policy and decision making when they are affected by the outcome.
3. Outreach and awareness campaigns must be launched to educate the public about the human and societal benefits of achieving independence for people with disabilities and the important role that civil rights and community-based supports play in promoting independence.
4. Incentives for the inclusion of people with disabilities in all aspects of society must be further developed and implemented.
5. Principles of universal design should be universally applied.

6. Systems, services, and supports for people with disabilities must be further developed as a part of the mainstream of community life.
7. Accurate data about people with disabilities should be regularly collected, analyzed, and reported. (pp. 5-6)

Recent events and present-day trends in rehabilitation indicate that programs have become much larger and more complex. Because of the increasing size, its recognition by other professionals in the delivery of rehabilitation-related services and most significantly, the emerging importance of a strong alliance between the client or customer and the rehabilitation counselor or other professional personnel, the rehabilitation movement demonstrates a positive growth during the past three decades.

While the Independent Living program is in need of additional financial assistance from the federal government, this movement and its pioneering program development have the potential of becoming the comprehensive rehabilitation program for the future. Centers for Independent Living now provide services of increased scope ranging from assistance with housing, to food preparation, to vocational training and placement.

In spite of the phenomenal growth in the independent living field, thousands of people remain unnecessarily institutionalized and over-protected. Many of these individuals have not chosen the style of life they lead; they are awaiting the opportunity to acquire information and skills that they need in order to become independent; they are awaiting resources in their communities such as accessible housing, transportation, and attendant care; they are awaiting the continued growth of the independent living movement and new independent living programs that this growth will bring.

With this comparatively new awareness of persons with significant disabilities as capable of living independently and with the recognition of accompanying advantages of increased quality of life, frequently with economic benefit, a thrust toward an emphasis on independent living in rehabilitation settings is on the increase. Professionals providing services focusing on skills for living independently are practicing from various disciplines: rehabilitation counseling, occupational therapy, therapeutic recreation, social work, psychology, rehabilitation nursing, special education, and others. With the firm establishment of the Independent Living movement and the new and increasing emphasis on support, encouragement, and skill development for living independently, it is expected that rehabilitation professionals of the future will have a heavy investment in the area of independent living.

REFERENCES

Americans with Disabilities Act of 1990. Public Law 101-336.

Batshaw, M. L. (Ed.). (1997). *Children with disabilities* (4th ed.). Baltimore: Paul Brooks.

Berkowitz, E. D. (1987). *Disabled policy: America's programs for the handicapped.* New York: Twentieth Century Fund Report.

Blanck, P. (1994). Employment integration, economic opportunity and the Americans with disabilities act: Empirical study from 1990-1993. *Iowa Law Review*, 79 (4), 853-923.

Board of Education of the Henrick Hudson Central School District v. Rowley. 458 U.S. 176, S. Ct. 3034, 1982.

Bowe, F. F. (1992). Development of the ADA. In N. Hablutzel & B. T. McMahon (Eds.), *The Americans with disabilities act: Access and accommodations.* Orlando: Paul M. Deutsch.

Braddock, D., Hemp, R., Parish, S., & Westrich, J. (1998). *The state of the states on developmental disabilities.* Washington, D.C.: American Association on Mental Retardation.

Dart, J. , & West, J. (1995). Americans with disabilities act. In A. E. Dell Orto & Marinelli R. P. (Eds.), *Encyclopedia of disability and rehabilitation.* New York: Simon & Schuster Macmillan.

Davis v. Southeastern Community College. 442 U.S. 397, 1979.

Dejong, G. (1979). *Report of the National Conference on Independent Living Service Rehabilitation per P.L. 95-602, March 7-8, 1979.* Boston: Medical Rehabilitation and Research Training Center No. 7, Tufts New England Medical Center.

Developmental Disabilities Services and Facilities Construction Act. Public Law 91-517.

Dole, R. (1994). Are we keeping America's promises to people with disabilities? Commentary on Blanck. *Iowa Law Review,* 79 (4), 925-939.

Education for All Handicapped Children Act of 1975. Public Law 94-142.

Hablutzel, N., & McMahon, B. T. (Eds.). (1992). T*he Americans with disabilities act: Access and accommodations.* Orlando: Paul M. Deutsch.

Harkin, T. (1994). The Americans with disabilities act: Four years later Commentary on Blanck. *Iowa Law Review,* 79 (4), 935-939.

Kurtz, L. A., & Harryman, S. E. (1997). Rehabilitation interventions: Physical therapy and occupational therapy. In M. L. Batshaw (Ed.), *Children with disabilities* (4th ed., p.). Baltimore: Paul Brooks.

Lou Harris and Associates. (1998). *NOD/Harris survey of Americans with disabilities.* New York: Author.

Lou Harris and Associates. (1995). *NOD/Harris survey on employment of people with disabilities.* New York: Author.

Lou Harris and Associates. (1986). *Harris survey on employment of people with disabilities.* New York: Author.

Lou Harris and Associates. (1986). *ICD survey of Americans with disabilities.* New York: Author.

Lou Harris and Associates. (1994). *NOD/Harris survey of Americans with disabilities.* New York: Author.

McMahon, B.T. Personal Communication, October 14, 1998.

Mills v. Board of Education of the District of Columbia. 348 F. Supp. 866, 1972.

National Council on Disability. (1996). *Achieving independence: The challenge for the 21st century.* Washington: Author.

National Council on Disability. (1986). *Toward independence: An assessment of federal laws and programs affecting people with disabilities with legislative recommendations.* Washington: Author.

New York State Association for Retarded Children v. Rockefeller. 357 F. Supp. 752, 1973.

Pennsylvania Association of Retarded Children v. Commonwealth of Pennsylvania. 334 F. Supp. 1257, 1971.

Percy, S.L. (1989). *Disability, civil rights, and public policy.* Tuscaloosa: The University of Alabama Press.

President's Committee on Employment of People with Disabilities (1990). ADA: A special issue. *Worklife*, 3(3), pp 1-48.

Rehabilitation Act of 1973. Public Law 93-112.

Rehabilitation Act Amendments of 1974. Public Law 93-651.

Rehabilitation Act Amendments of 1978. Public Law 95-602.

Rehabilitation Act Amendments of 1984. Public Law 98-221.

Rehabilitation Act Amendments of 1986. Public Law 99-506.

Rehabilitation Act Amendments of 1992. Public Law 102-569.

Rehabilitation Act Amendments of 1993. Public Law 103-73.

Rubin, S. E., & Roessler, R. T. (1995). *Foundations of the vocational rehabilitation process* (4th ed.). Austin: PRO-ED.

Schroeder, F. K. (1998). The rehabilitation act amendments of 1998. *Information Memorandum, RSA-IM-98-20.* Washington, D.C.: Rehabilitation Services Administration, United Stated Department of Education.

Scotch, R. K. (1984). *From good will to civil rights: Transforming federal disability policy.* Philadelphia: Temple University Press.

The Technology-Related Assistance Act for Individuals with Disabilities Act of 1988. Public Law 100-407.

Tucker, B. P., & Goldstein, B. A. (1992). *Legal rights of persons with disabilities: An analysis of federal law* (Volumes I & II ed.). Horsham, PA: LRP Publications.

Wallace, J. F. (1994). *A policy analysis of national loan financing practices: Strategies for the development for the loan programs for the acquisition of assistive technology.* Unpublished doctoral dissertation, Virginia Commonwealth University.

West, J. (1994). *Federal implementation of the Americans with disability act, 1991-1994.* New York: The Milbank Memorial Fund.

Wyatt v. Stickney, 344F. Supp. 752, 1973.

Part 2

PORTRAITS OF LEADERSHIP

Chapter 5

PATRICK'S METAMORPHOSIS

J. Dewey Brown and Patricia Johnson Brown

ONE OF THE GREATEST JOYS IN LIFE is learning that one is going to become a parent. We can recall 23 years ago our anticipation of becoming parents. We had reached a point in our lives where we were solidly engaged in our own careers. We were supposedly well educated, financially stable, and had traveled extensively. We were ready to accept the responsibilities of a child. We had a house in suburbia, a large backyard, a new car, and a pet—all the amenities to offer that special one who would soon be a part of our lives.

The prospective mom followed all the rules: no alcohol, proper diet, exercise, and regular check-ups by the doctor. We were told everything was perfect as we prepared for the arrival. All the necessary preparations were made including a well appointed nursery, toys, clothes, and all the necessities, including a cuisinart to prepare homemade foods. We were both very excited; our families were excited. We were eagerly awaiting the arrival of a new individual into our lives.

The day arrived about a month early. The excitement was still there. Natural childbirth was the way to do this we read and were told; however, heavy breathing during a 36-hour time frame was not necessarily what either of us needed: hyperventilation resulted.

A baby boy was born. We named him Patrick. Having worked in and around the medical profession for a number of years, we recognized that our baby was somewhat small and experienced some difficulty breathing initially, but these symptoms were not extremely unusual for a premature infant. We were instructed by the hospital staff to get some rest and we both gladly obliged.

Four hours after the birth we were approached by a pediatrician who just happened to be on duty that day and one whom we had never met. We, at this time, had never been able to see or even hold our baby. The doctor was a rather impersonal, matter-of-fact type of person who proceeded to describe everything that was wrong with our baby starting from the top of his head down to his toes. The pediatrician pointed out that he had a small head, epicanthal fold, narrow eye sockets, short neck, heart murmur, and abnormal hands and feet. We were devastated. "Is there anything right?" we asked. There was no response from the doctor. There was absolutely no positive reinforcement at that moment. One can only imagine how we felt. All this news was totally unexpected. Our hopes, aspirations, and dreams were totally exterminated with the news the doctor delivered to us.

After regaining our senses, we began to ask questions. We wanted all possible medical advice available and to find doctors that would work with us and attempt to be empathetic toward our situation and to us. Batteries of tests and genetic screening yielded no new information. There was no definite diagnosis. The heart murmur persisted and Patrick could not nurse because of weak facial and lip muscles. He had to be gavaged fed by inserting a tube through the nose and down the esophagus. He was slow to gain weight and all his responses as well. We never gave up. We developed the attitude that if we only had a diagnosis; if we could only find out what was missing and fix it. We loved our baby and were willing to do everything possible to help him. We came to the realization that we could not wallow in self-pity. The earlier we began interventions, the earlier we would see positive results, we thought. We constantly searched for ways to help Patrick.

At age five months, Patrick was diagnosed as having cerebral palsy (CP) by the Georgetown University Child Development Center in Washington, DC. This diagnosis precipitated an array of tests ranging from developmental level, speech, hearing, and sight. Of course, all these tests were scheduled on different days by all the various professionals who were totally insensitive to our time schedules or convenience. The tests revealed that our child did not measure up to the norm of children his age. This was no revelation to us. We reached this conclusion for ourselves several months earlier, but the tests were necessary for receiving therapy, which had not yet begun.

After all the testing and diagnostic workups, the actual job of finding help for him was still ours. We contacted many agencies: mental health departments, social services, and school systems. We finally located a therapist that would work with Patrick in an early intervention program. To our surprise, this therapist would work with him at a time convenient to our work schedules, even at 6:00 A.M. before our workday began. The therapist not only worked directly with Patrick, but also taught us how to support and reinforce what she was doing.

The task of locating child care was difficult. We had to work to maintain insurance coverage and to pay the rapidly growing medical bills. Patricia spent the first two months caring for him which was very intense and demanding. Dewey was able to spend the next few months with Patrick as he was employed as a teacher. Dewey was the main child care provider during these months. At the end of the summer we needed child care assistance. Finding a provider that was willing to accept the responsibilities of a special child was very difficult. We wanted Patrick to have interaction with "normal kids" whatever or however that is defined. After several negative experiences, we located a mother of a preschooler who agreed to provide child care for Patrick. In this environment he was exposed to "normal" peers.

Patrick's development was very, very slow. He learned to sit up alone by 13 months. This event was a milestone and we were overjoyed. It was at this time that we decided to make our move from the Washington, DC suburbs to Richmond, Virginia, and guess what? The whole process began again.

The move to Richmond provided challenges for us in locating child care providers, therapy, educational services, and of major importance, the necessity of maintaining medical insurance coverage. Dewey was a teacher in a large school district in Maryland and Patricia had just assumed a new job as a college professor at a state university in Richmond. Patrick had a pre-existing medical condition that would not be covered by Patricia's new insurance. Patrick was however fully insured under the terms of Dewey's policy. One can quickly see that a commuter marriage had unfolded. This commuter marriage lasted approximately 22 years. Dewey would work in Maryland during the week and return to Richmond on Friday. He would have to leave either very early on Monday morning or late on Sunday evening to return to Maryland. Patricia was the primary caregiver during the week. The decision to maintain Dewey's insurance was a wise one since there had been three major surgeries, many minor surgical procedures requiring hospitalization, and much therapy which amounted to more than $1 million in medical expenses.

In Richmond, the location of a child care provider proved to be less stressful than locating appropriate educational programs. Early in our search for educational services it was determined that Patrick did not have CP. The game began again. In order to receive educational services Patrick must be labeled. Now that he had no label, no services could be provided.

Patrick's heart problem had been diagnosed as Tetralogy of Fallot. The physical aspects of this heart anomaly could be corrected by surgery provided his weight was thirty pounds or he was five years old. This was a major challenge, but at age five Patrick was 28 pounds which was close enough, so off we went to Georgetown University Hospital. We had to go to the DC area because Dewey's insurance was with a Health Maintenance Organization (HMO) and we had to use doctors and facilities within their area of service. The HMO had no facilities or doctors in the Richmond area. Patrick's surgery was completed and after a month of intensive care he was discharged. His weak body was slow to recover from such a traumatic experience, but he gradually began to show some signs of improvement. During this time, we sought and did receive much encouragement and actual help from grandparents, concerned neighbors, friends, and many professionals. Shortly after his recovery from this experience, a miracle happens: he begins to walk. What encouragement for us! The advancements were slow to come, but advancements did happen.

Patrick's physical and mental development was still severely impaired. We continued to search for a genetic basis for his disability and after years of searching by the National Institutes of Health, and Yale University, a diagnosis finally emerged: Cri-du-Chat Syndrome, the researcher indicated to us. This syndrome is a hairline fracture on the short arm of the fifth chromosome. Prior to this time, there was no known procedure to definitely identify the syndrome, but now there is a procedure. We had been searching for a diagnosis for eight years.

Finding the cause of his disability seemed like a milestone, but after all these years of searching the reality hit us that there was no cure. Patrick could not be given some missing substance or a miracle drug to make him well. Again, we had to remind ourselves that we could not wallow in self-pity. We had to remain proactive and seek ways to help Patrick develop to the greatest potential possible.

By this time we were approaching the age of 40, and well beyond what doctors considered being the safe childbearing years. We wanted to have other children, but we were afraid of having another child with the same disability. At that time we did not know that Patrick's disability was an accident in the nature of a chromosome and not a trait that either of us possessed (and would not pass the trait to successive children). We were also concerned about Down Syndrome because of our age.

Luck was with us. We had a wonderful opportunity to adopt a baby boy. This was a watershed event in our lives. We started the adoption procedure, which was long and exhaustive; but we were able to adopt a baby two days following his birth. This addition to our family was wonderful. Patrick loved the new baby, and as this baby grew and developed, he reciprocated his brother's love. A very special bond developed between these two siblings.

Because of our unique living situation, our lives have been complicated: the demands of work, maintaining two households, furthering our education, and finding child care providers to accommodate work and study were powerful stressors for both of us. This lifestyle has been extremely difficult for Patricia (she was like a single parent most of this time). Dewey was available only weekends and the summers when he was not teaching. We did manage to fight many battles with the school system together. We discovered that the Richmond, Virginia educational system was not designed in the late 1970s to deal with children with special needs. This system was in a state of flux and reorganization as result of an annexation suit, and ensued many parents to move to the suburbs and/or placed their children into private schools. Private schools, at this time, did not exist for children with special needs. We were dependent upon the public educational system to provide the services Patrick needed. Public Law 94-142 was beginning to be implemented in school systems. With the help of an attorney, a special education class was established not only for Patrick, but for 27 other children in the city. It happened that his first teacher was wonderful; she was a caring, well-trained professional in the field of special education and early childhood development. The preschool situation was great; however, through the elementary years we ran into many problems with teachers not being well trained. Many professionals who maintained jobs as directors and administrators of special educational programs did not know how to manage and deal with this specialized and very demanding population within their educational system. We must give credit to those teachers and administrators who did not fall into this mold. There were some that did the best they could to integrate our child into programs with "normal" peers.

Patrick's experience in middle school was somewhat positive as he remained in the same school and with the same teacher throughout the middle school years. The teacher was nurturing, kind, and tried to do all she could do to integrate Patrick in regular classes. The problem was that he was in a self-contained classroom with others some with more severe disabilities, and had, for the most part, no role models from whom to learn positive social behaviors.

The move to a high school setting was one transition that we dreaded. We were always fearful of change. The high school that he would be attending was large and located in the inner city. Again, the system provided a self-contained classroom situation with a teacher and two aides. There was very little opportunity for integration into regular classes, except for homeroom. We met with the teachers to encourage the development of peer groups with regular students in a community service project that would be oriented toward recreational activities. This type of interaction never occurred even though we spent many hours trying to make it happen.

Patrick was well liked and nurtured by the students at his high school. He went to the school prom. He was allowed to participate in the school choir. Even though he could not sing the words of the songs, he would clap and proved to be an integral part of this group as they sang not only at school, but in the larger community. This choir experience was the closest he ever came to being totally integrated into any type of activity at the high school level. His choir peers adopted him and helped him in every way possible during their community outings.

He was given the opportunity during his high school days to work in various capacities under the supervision of his teacher. He would go to various locations and work separating clothes for washing, polishing silver, collating papers, and stuffing envelopes. All these experiences were helpful in learning some specific skills for employment later on.

Graduation day did arrive. What a wonderful moment it was when the entire senior class stood when Patrick was presented with his diploma. He gave a high five to the choir director who just happened to be on stage. The local newspaper wrote a story about his accomplishments which is reprinted in part (Reprinted with permission from *The Richmond Times Dispatch*, Bill Lohmann, July 28, 1999):

> His classmates at Huguenot High stood and cheered when Patrick Brown, with the help of an aide, walked across the stage to receive his diploma.
>
> It was a powerful moment, and a telling one.
>
> Patrick wasn't the smartest among them. He never mastered chemistry or calculus; learning the alphabet and counting to 10 presented great challenges for him. He is small and awkward and has the language skills of a preschooler.
>
> In some ways, though, Patrick was one of the best teachers they will ever have.
>
> Patrick is severely disabled, physically and mentally. He was born with cri du chat syndrome–a rare chromosomal disorder–and cerebral palsy. One doctor told his family early on that Patrick would be nothing more than a burden. He didn't walk until he was 6. He underwent open-heart surgery. He spent days in a coma. A steel rod was implanted to straighten his crooked spine. He still needs help doing things most of us take for granted such as bathing and dressing. He is 22 years old.
>
> Yet, he was sunshine in the hallways of Huguenot. He greeted everyone. He sang in the choir. He looked sharp in his concert tux. He became a symbol of pluck and mettle and heart.
>
> "When we're out in the community, people will come up and give Patrick high-fives," said Patrick's mother, Dr. Patricia Johnson Brown. "We don't know them, but Patrick does."
>
> And so, as Patrick picked up his special diploma last month during Huguenot's commencement at the Landmark Theater, he heard the cheers.
>
> It was a momentous occasion.
>
> "He's had to overcome a lot," said his mom, who invited teachers, therapists and caregivers, as well as family and friends to his graduation party. "It was a team to get Patrick though."
>
> Which brings us to this:

Now what?

What's out there for a young adult with as many strikes against him as Patrick? It's taken all of the skill and patience, love and encouragement the Browns and others have been able to muster to help Patrick reach this monumental moment. It is a terrific achievement. But the question won't go away.

What next?

Patrick has received vocational training. He learned how to do simple things such as sort laundry and polish silver trays. He's working in a sheltered workshop. The long-term goal is for Patrick to hold a job—he will always need close supervision—and to live as independently as possible. But that goal might be a reach.

One of the first things you hear about when talking to families like the Browns is a story about waiting lists. That's the way the game is played. The Browns are on long waiting lists for all kinds of services Patrick could desperately use, including the opportunity to live in a group home. He has been on some lists for years. It seems fairly hopeless. And ridiculous.

Patricia Brown, who has become a strong advocate for people like Patrick and families like hers, said, "The people who need the most help have the least ability to advocate for themselves. You just sort of do what you have to do."

The Browns—Patricia, father Dewey and younger brother Christopher—have been doing what they've had to do for years.

When Patrick was still a baby, Patricia moved to Richmond to take a job at Virginia Commonwealth University. The academic setting allowed her greater flexibility to care for Patrick. However, Dewey, a science teacher and school administrator, stayed behind in Maryland, because the medical insurance coverage provided by his school system was superior to what was available here.

That's a significant consideration considering Patrick's medical bills—including four major surgeries during his life—have totaled in the neighborhood of $1 million. For 20 years, the Browns have lived a commuter marriage. Dewey would be home on weekends, holidays and vacations. That separation will end this fall when Dewey retires.

"That's going to be really terrific," said Patricia, now associate dean in the

School of Continuing Studies at the University of Richmond. "It'll be an adjustment."

As Dewey and Patricia grow older, they look back and celebrate the small milestones achieved by Patrick and the big ones. They marvel at how far he has come. They also wonder and worry about Patrick's future. They take things, as they always have, a day at a time. Life has not been easy with Patrick, but they cannot imagine it without him.

"I've become more humble. I've become more patient. I've become a lot of things because of him," said Patricia Brown. "We wouldn't have these passions if we didn't have a kid like Patrick."

One of the more frustrating situations involving a person with a disability and having only one parent at home monitoring the situation is dependable transportation. During the summers and after Patrick graduated from high school, he worked at a sheltered workshop about ten miles from home. In order for Patrick to experience work, we had to employ a transportation company to transport him to and from our house each day. Keep in mind, Patricia is the one getting up, feeding, and dressing Patrick and putting him on the van for transport to work each day. Patricia also has a demanding job and has to be at work at a certain time. Many days the van just didn't show up or would come very late. Very frequently, Patricia would have to drive Patrick to work and both were late. Afternoons were a nightmare as well. On many occasions we would receive a call that Patrick had not been picked up from work or that he had been delivered to a neighbor or to a former caregivers' residence. In order to save money, the van companies would (many times) place him on the van about 2:00 pm and then drive him and other passengers to a location to wait for a client to have a 2-3 hour dialysis treatment.

In 1992, Patrick was approved to receive services through a Medicaid Waiver program which provided funding for in-home and community integration programs. This program was not dependent upon family income and was designed to offer assistance to families so the family could more adequately care for the person at home instead of an institutional placement. Money was appropriated to provide a certain number of hours per day and for occasional Saturdays. Various contractors in the area could bid on the contract to provide this service. Patrick received about four hours of service per day and about six hours of service on one Saturday per month. This assistance was a great help to us, especially during the week when Patricia was the parent with the responsibility for Patrick's care. Caregivers would arrive each day to get Patrick from the school bus, give him a snack, help him with the toilet, and to work with Patrick on pre-set goals. These goals ranged from emptying the dishwasher, making his bed, putting clothes away, going shopping, and also going out to eat. Emphasis was placed on improvement of socialization skills within the community. Many afternoons were spent going to parks, zoos, museums, and athletic events.

At first we had some stability in the caregivers' longevity, but because of the low pay and for the most part, young people, primarily women, completing their education and moving on to higher paying employment, caregivers were constantly in a state of flux. Sometimes we might have a different caregiver each day. This constant change not only created confusion for Patrick but also meant added work for us, as we had to constantly provide training for these people coming into our home.

There was a time when we had a male caregiver for a period of almost 2 years without interruption. This situation and relationship was ideal. This caregiver really cared about Patrick—they bonded and became best buddies. This caregiver also worked well with our other son, Christopher, and often all three would participate in activities together. This ideal situation came to an end when the caregiver had children of his own and had to give up the low paying job that he thoroughly enjoyed. To this day, he and our son have wonderful affection and frequent association with each other.

Following this rather positive experience with caregivers, we had a period of time with disrupted service. Since pay was so low, no one really wanted to work for the company, which, it seemed, was benefitting financially. There were no benefits for caregivers. There were absolutely no incentives to be dependable and to do a good job. We became so frustrated we changed from one contractor to another. Guess What? We had the same result. The new care providers were no different from the previous contractor.

Finally, after 17 years of being on a waiting list for a group home, Patrick, at age 22, was now on the active list for immediate placement. We had very little lead-time and frantically began looking for available and suitable homes. Patrick had always had a local case manager assigned to him because of his placement into the Medicaid Waiver Program and this manager was very helpful to us in providing direction. We were given a list of possible homes within the City of Richmond. We interviewed them and they interviewed Patrick and us. We wanted him to be in a location near us. We found one rather quickly. The location was in a good neighborhood where people with disabilities were accepted and not shunned. This was indeed a good sign. A clean, well-maintained, and well-staffed home was also a must. This house appeared to meet all of our requirements. Patrick had dinner with the three clients who were already residents of the home. We went along and observed the interaction between Patrick and the other residents. Patrick also went on a community outing and spent a weekend with his soon-to-be new family before we made our final decision.

In January, 2000, Patrick was accepted into this group home and from all appearances he seems to be doing well. He has 24 hour/day care. He continues to work each day at a sheltered workshop improving his skills for possibly more gainful employment in the future.

We are very happy with the housing situation. Of course when we go by for a visit, we as parents, can always find something that we don't like such as his clothes not always being just as we would dress him or his hair not combed as we would like it, but he is happy and adjusting to his new home environment extremely well. He comes to our house for visits on holidays and weekends. Patrick will continue to go to Camp Easter Seal for special weekends and at least one week of camp during the summer that has always been a favorite activity since he was very young. These are his friends and he is adamant about having "his friends" around him.

Conclusions and Implications for Systems Change

Patrick has gained system changes and services through much effort on the part of his parents. His parents had to play the pivotal role in making sure their child received the services he was entitled to receive. Patrick could not practice total self-advocacy and needed much assistance.

All citizens with disabilities deserve equal opportunity for self-determination, family, and equal access to recreation, school, vocational and technical training, housing, and medical care. If one takes a look at the funds allocated annually for the support of these citizens, one quickly learns that those with disabilities, particularly significant disabilities, have not always been included.

In Virginia, more funds have been allocated to those who have committed crimes against society and are in prison than are funds allocated for people with disabilities. Prisoners are afforded better housing conditions, medical care, food, and amenities such as recreational activities, movies, and TV than we afford persons who have done nothing more than being born with a disability.

Money must be appropriated well above what has been appropriated in the past to take care of the needs of this special population. The number of people needing special services continues to grow each year. These citizens deserve the right to learn some useful employment skills and they must be afforded the right to living arrangements within the community. This is certainly more cost-effective than an institution that is poorly staffed and that is clearly inadequate with regard to community inclusion. Human warehousing is not community inclusion no matter how adequately staffed and nice an institution may appear.

People with disabilities have the right to live a normal life in a home setting with people who love and respect them as fellow human beings. One of the most poignant observations we have made recently is observing a local church community reaching out and embracing Patrick and the other residents in his group home. This church community has created a Sunday School Class called the Rainbow Class. They have welcomed Patrick and the others into their congregation and encouraged them to participate in choir and in social events at the church. Recently we were invited to attend a very special worship service at the church as they celebrated Disability Awareness Sunday. The Rainbow Class, composed totally of people with disabilities, presented the featured music. This church community is educating everyone about special needs and how to treat people with the same dignity that is expected by all people. For years we tried to find churches that would accept our son, but were told there were no provisions for "people like him."

There is a definite need for parents to educate their children, and for adults to educate themselves to understand that all people are not created physically and mentally equal. We are all different but we all deserve to be treated with respect. Our younger son became very upset several years ago and addressed his concerns about how his brother was looked upon and treated by other people, especially children, to a counselor. The counselor suggested that he write about his concerns. Christopher's essay was later published in *The Exceptional Parent.* Below the article is included in its entirety and contains a message that we all should pass on to our children and our adult peers as well (Reprinted with permission from *The Exceptional Parent,* Christopher Brown, December, 1995):

A Really Neat Brother

My name is Christopher Brown and I am nine years old. I have a brother named Patrick, who has bright red hair and is 17 years old. Patrick likes to watch TV, listen to music, dance and play games with me. He can't run very well, but he walks fast. He has trouble talking, but he has a great smile. He has a disability called cri-du-chat syndrome.

When we go out into the community, people stare at Patrick because he sometimes acts differently. This makes me feel sad because he is a really neat brother. I admit that he sometimes gets on my nerves, and I wish he didn't have to act the way he does. But Patrick is a very sensitive brother—he knows when people are looking at him strangely and making fun of him.

I wish everyone would love my brother like I love him. I wish all other kids would like him also. People need to be taught how to act with others who are different from them. We need to teach others that people with disabilities are good people, too. If each of us would just show one other person that people with disabilities have many abilities, what a great world this could be.

We have learned many lessons from our leadership and advocacy efforts on behalf of our son. We have learned that raising a person with a disability is a partnership effort between the individual with the disability, therapists, other family members, the schools, community agencies, medical staff, friends, family, neighbors, and colleagues. We have learned that this partnership needs to always be person-centered.

Our experience throughout the years has taught us that empowering people with disabilities is not easy. The tasks are challenging, require commitment, a lot of energy, and persistence but success comes with:

Facilitating locally needed changes.

Helping others value inclusive communities.

Communicating needs to politicians, educators and urging them to
   make necessary changes.
Establishing friendships within the community.
Empowering and organizing people with disabilities to become
   advocates.
Working with the media to influence change and to communicate
   success stories.
Building networks.
Promoting collaboration.
Increasing awareness of the person's abilities.

We have learned over the years that all people belong to a community. As parents, educators, and neighbors, we need to empower people with disabilities to exercise greater control over their own lives. We need to assist them by accessing resources in the community and by making our own personal commitments to equalizing opportunities and including people with disabilities into society and community. As an ancient African Proverb notes:

> When there is a thorn in the foot, the whole body has to pluck it out. The tribe needs to take responsibility for the whole child.

All people belong together. We need to empower and help people to move toward a goal or dream, to help people make choices, and to act on those choices. A friend once reminded us that we, like Native Americans, need to be dream catchers. We need to capture wonderful dreams and let the bad dreams escape. She said, "together we can make things happen but alone the task is impossible."

REFERENCES

Brown, C. My brother. *The Exceptional Parent.* December, 1995.
Lohmann, B. Brotherly love of a special kind. *The Richmond Times-Dispatch.*
   July 28, 1999.

Chapter 6

HOW I GOT HERE

John P. Coates

REACHING OUT FOR HELP in resisting a crippling disability requires a major extension of one's ego. Normal socialization, after all, instills within most of us the belief that the support system surrounding us when we enter the world can be trusted to shield us from whatever harm may come our way, if only we are loyal, work hard, and respect authority. While these are wonderful traits, anyone who has lived long with a disability knows their limitations where recovering anything resembling normal independence is concerned. That requires a gritty love of life and involvement with others that will not be denied.

I first learned something about recovery when I finished second grade and turned eight years old. As had previously occurred at the end of kindergarten and first grade, my teacher told my parents in my presence that I was capable but so lazy that, among other acquired deficits, I still could not really read. I did not realize at the time that I had been diagnosed with a learning disability but could not get professional help because the private school I attended considered such ideas absurd—as most people did in the early 1950s—and threatened to dismiss me from school unless I stopped the tutoring and started working.

All I knew was that, if I wanted to read—which I did—I would have to do it for myself, because both my parents had tried and failed to get it through to me.

I stepped forth with the blithe confidence of the uninformed in the full expectation that I would not only succeed but succeed before school resumed in September. Amazingly enough, I was correct on both counts. The experience taught me a lesson that I hope to carry with me for the rest of my life. A genuinely enthusiastic person can rarely be kept down for long because his passion will see him over, under, around, and through almost any obstacle he may face. Not long thereafter, I began showing early signs of Charcot-Marie-Tooth disease. For years, I did not know what was going on as I first experienced reduced sensation in my fingertips and the soles of my feet at about age nine or ten, and then experienced a gradual broadening of both sensory and motor loss throughout my adolescence. My feet were both paralyzed by the time I was 16, and by the time I was 19, I had severely burned or otherwise injured my feet and ankles repeatedly. As had been the case with reading, I learned slowly, but I eventually got the point.

Enthusiasm alone will not carry the day. Success follows focused understanding that is enthusiastically lived. But understanding of what? How many people discover a task worthy of their best efforts and throw themselves into it, only to lose interest or become discouraged when the hill looks too steep to climb or the slight too humiliating to be set aside? Yet perseverance, the magic quality, can be nurtured even among those to whom it does not come naturally. The first step is to set appropriate goals.

Goal-setting, while important for everyone, is essential for the person with a significant disability because of the narrowed range of their physical capacities and their stamina. The amount of time that the average teenager or other person in the workplace with normal physical or mental abilities "wastes" in a given day may not necessarily be inappropriate, given the surplus of energy that most people have and their consequent ability to make up for lost time, not to mention the fact that they may have no interest in what they are doing anyway. If they lose the job, the impact is often negligible because of their ability to find another with ease.

For the student or worker with a disability, though, life is different. The range of jobs available to him or her is intrinsically smaller, because the physical requirements simply exceed the person's capabilities. Many jobs, now theoretically open because of the Americans with Disabilities Act (ADA), still may be beyond the person's reach if approached in the same relatively passive and thoughtless way as many applicants. The person with a disability needs to generate interest and enthusiasm in the would-be employer by coming to the job interview with goals: How can I set things up to accommodate my needs with a minimum of fuss for others? Once I am hired, how can I consistently meet or exceed my job's requirements?

I realized by the late 1980s that my neurological situation was deteriorating beyond the point that I could continue to operate like any other teacher. As an English and history teacher, I continuously handle lots of paper. In order to keep up with my disciplines, I must read constantly. In order to keep up with my students, I must assign, read, and grade their writing on an almost endless basis. My hands have both been without feeling since the early to mid-1960s, but my fine motor control and strength remained at a gradually declining but still acceptable level until shortly after my older daughter was born, in 1986. At that time, the quality of my anesthesia changed: it became noticeably deeper as my digital movement first slowed and then disappeared altogether by about 1990. Life looked awfully bleak to me at that point. At 44 years of age and with a wife and two small children to support, I faced the prospect of financial collapse. Networking was a primary reason that my worst fears did not come true.

I had read some years earlier of preliminary breakthroughs in voice-recognition technology for computers, and had made a mental note to remember it in case I should ever need it. Total functional paralysis in each hand struck me as a sign that the time had come to move, but how? I did not know, but I was confident that if I spoke to everyone I knew, I would find someone who did. Eventually, my faith proved justified: perhaps 18 months after beginning my quest for access to voice recognition technology, after talking with everyone at my school about it, after talking with an acquaintance at the state level about possible financing should the technology actually be available, I began to hit pay dirt during a chance phone conversation with an old friend, Ronne Jacobs.

When Ronne asked me how I was doing physically, I swallowed hard on my pride and told her. Frankly, my hopes were dim that anything would come of it, but I figured I had nothing to lose. Imagine my surprise when I found that she was a close friend of Susan Urofsky, then head of the Virginia Department of Rehabilitative Services (DRS). When Ronne called her on my behalf, Susan put me in touch with Ken Knorr, who runs the assistive technology section at DRS, and with Susan Green, who heads the Chesterfield County (where I live) office of DRS. Both turned out to be lifesavers.

Ken immediately told me about Dennis Brink, at that time a systems analyst with IBM and a pioneer in bringing technology to people with disabilities. Dennis immediately leaped in with both feet. While Ken arranged an evaluation for me at Woodrow Wilson State Rehabilitation Center with Bob Crawford, Dennis was working with me to find out what was available from IBM's VoiceType system.

Once Bob's recommendation that I get the system came through, all that remained was to find the money necessary to purchase it. As I recall, the cost of the computer was about $3000 and VoiceType was another $2000. With Susan Green's help, and my own resources, I raised most of the money, but I was still short. I needn't have worried, though, because my school lent me the rest. I was on my way!

"On my way" and "out of the woods" are two different things, of course. Life tends to be demanding for those without disabilities, and proportionately more so for those with them. Today, the good news is that I have a third child and have retained all the professional responsibilities I had ten years ago. The bad news is that my neuromuscular weakness is significantly worse than it was seven years ago when I took possession of my first voice-activated computer. I walk very shakily when I walk at all, I drive a specially equipped van with an expensive electric wheelchair inside, and I take pain medication throughout the day.

Occasionally, parents and colleagues comment that they don't see how I do it. The answer is the same now as it has always been: my love of what I do has enabled me to create dynamic working relationships with my students and their families; my past and present division heads at The Collegiate School, Bill Reeves and Charlie Blair, as well as my other colleagues there, especially Weldon Bradshaw, Bob Sedivey, "Schnookie" McCabe, Joan Shepherd, and Sally Chambers; my doctors, Warren Vaughn, Jane Wootten, Albert Jones, and Bob Leshner, who have not only encouraged me but have worked with Collegiate to help the school create a better "fit" for me within the overall community. Special friends, such as Jim and Barbara Sellman, and all the parents they mobilized to buy that expensive wheelchair I now use, seem to come forth like manna from heaven when the need is greater than the apparent resources that are available to meet it.

My greatest and most dynamic relationships, though, are obviously those I share with my wife, Lucy, our three children, Marie, Jack, and

Chloe, and with our two dogs and a cat, especially Little Bit, who graciously allows me to attach his leash to my wheelchair and walk with me for a mile or so at least once most days of the week. Together and separately, the members of my family work every day to remind me that they love me, that I am important, and that, no matter how bleak the outlook may be at a given moment, they know that I can find a way to make things happen.

Surround yourself with people who love you, radiate that love outward toward everyone you meet, and pursue your goals relentlessly. Few people can fail to be drawn to those who will not be beaten. Allow those who can to help you and you cannot be beaten.

God bless you, and Good Luck!

Chapter 7

A VOICE TO HEED

ANN TUCKER DURDEN

As I WRITE THIS, I am waiting for the newest of my arsenal of drugs to take effect. Until it does, my senses are so heightened that my fingers tremble and hitting the correct key on the keyboard is a game of chance. For three years I have controlled my disability, or rather I should say, an antidepressant controlled my disability until it was no longer effective. I was left 40 pounds heavier and suicidal. If you haven't already guessed, I have clinical depression and as of recently, I was diagnosed with Generalized Anxiety Disorder. Together the two disabilities make life very interesting and at the same time very, very painful. To the undiscerning eye, I was a twenty-something woman who lived in a large beautiful house, had lots of money, a budding acting career, a supportive husband, and appeared to have her stuff together. A well-trained clinical eye would have seen beyond my persona to see a person who always walked with her head down and shoulders slightly stooped. The clinician would have probably detected a certain unkempt look about this girl—her makeup a little too uneven and her clothes somewhat sloppy. The clinician may have also noticed her constantly clinched jaw as if she hurt all the time, her sporadic work record, her extreme mood swings—going from the pits of despair to flights of fancy as Virginia Woolf referred to her highs—and of course, her highly addictive behaviors.

As a preteen, when my disability came into being, a typical day consisted of waking up, getting ready for school, and going to classes until mid-afternoon, which left me, abnormally exhausted mentally and physically (depression). When I got home I would jog in place in my room for at least three hours. I would only stop when mom or dad absolutely made me and even then I'd go into my closet and secretly jog. I now understand that the jogging was a way to medicate my anxiety. To the trained clinician I have what is commonly called "hidden disabilities"–not readily viewable like someone who has an amputated limb or some other physical disability. My disabilities really were hidden because not only had I worked very hard to hide them from the outside world, but I had worked just as hard to hide them from myself. After years of ignoring my mental illnesses, my behavior became unusual and quite dangerous.

In order to survive my psychic pain, I shifted my focus away from my own self-awareness onto other things. *The Dictionary of Medicine, Nursing, and Allied Health* notes that:

> ". . . addiction is the state of giving up to some habit or compulsion." And a compulsion ". . . is a repetitive and stereotyped action that is performed to ward off some untoward event, although the patient recognizes that it does not do so in any realistic way. A compulsion serves as a defensive substitute for unacceptable unconscious ideas or impulses."

Some would argue the difference between an addiction and compulsion is that addictions have a physical dependence and withdrawal component and compulsions do not. Either way, addictions and compulsions ward off deep emotional pain. For purposes of describing my disability, I use the terms synonymously. My self-destruction began with ignoring the warning signs and a deep desire to "fit in" that manifested itself in seemingly innocent behaviors like weight loss, shopping, and exercising. In college, I subsisted only on diet cokes and chocolate chip cookies for weeks at a time, all the while exercising two to three hours a day. My weight normally was 135 pounds and ultimately dropped to 104 pounds. At a fraternity party someone snapped a picture of me waist up with a drink in my hand; my elbows were considerably larger than my biceps. The type of comments people made to me usually involved how terrific I looked because of the weight loss. Their comments just enabled my starving. I often wonder if it was a case of *The Emperor's New Clothes*? Today, I realize how sallow my features were and that my skin color was a strange shade of gray. Why didn't anyone say anything? They must have known that I was not well. Also, it was in college that I developed my love/hate relationship with shopping. I loved the rush that came with the actual purchasing of things, but I hated the thousands of dollars of debt I would accumulate each time this urge to "buy" overcame me.

I used money, weight, and strangely enough relationships to hide from the painful feelings of inadequacy that were simply symptoms of my depression and anxiety. Unfortunately, at the time, I had little to no knowledge of mental illness. Mental illness, in my family, meant it was something that caused people to be locked away in asylums. I may not have known anything about mental illness, but I certainly didn't want to learn for fear of being locked away. My great-grandfather started a mental hospital that, ". . . locked people away because they were crazy" according to my extended family. Visions of people screaming and drooling while a "Nurse Ratchet" character administered needles filled with tranquilizers to people strapped to beds in padded rooms filled my head. There was NO way I was ever going to admit that I needed help of a psychiatric nature. No, I strove to appear normal and to be a good little girl so I wouldn't be locked away. Obviously, no one in my immediate family or otherwise really discussed mental illness or for that matter any type of disability. I thought this was strange because my aunt had albinism and was legally blind, and my grandfather had alcoholism. With my grandfather, the word alcoholic was neither used nor was the fact that he attempted suicide on numerous occasions ever mentioned. The word suicide was not even used when my great uncle did commit suicide at the age of thirty-six; to the family he simply died–nothing more, nothing less. My mother's constant handwashing and erratic sleeping habits (i.e., up at two and three in the morning and taking long naps in the afternoon) was never pointed out. I am not saying that my mother, my aunt, or my grandfather should have been put under a microscope and dissected. I am simply giving examples of other family members who ignored their disabilities and have suffered because of it.

One of the situations affected most severely and profoundly by my disability was my education. Once in the eighth grade Mrs. Cunningham, my math teacher, looked at me and smilingly stated that, ". . . you're such an unusual student. Your grades go like this . . . ." and with that she made a gesture with her hand that outlined the ups and downs of a roller coaster ride. Unfortunately, neither she, my other teachers, or my parents questioned the strange inconsistency in my grades. One grading period I would be top of the class; the next, flunking out as result of my lows. Each time I took a test my mind would virtually go blank even though I knew that the material was in my head; I just could not produce it for the test. If I had to write a paper I was OK, but test taking was a different situation (that was the anxiety aspect of my illness). I still wonder how I actually got into college. In graduate school I was prescribed an antidepressant and my performance level began to reflect my true intellect.

I always wanted to be financially independent. No woman in my family had ever achieved financial independence on her own. My work history was at best sporadic. Because I could not sustain employment and not wanting to live with mom and dad for the rest of my life, I married a man who had the means to financially support me. Consequently, this arrangement was like making a pact with the devil. If you think that having a mental illness is crippling, try living with a man whom you don't love, particularly if you feel you must in order to survive, is beyond devastating. I was living a completely dishonest life. His money enabled me to hide from myself and allowed me the luxury of not having to confront my mental illness. During this time, my physical health began to decline. I developed eczema. I would scratch my face so forcefully that my pillow on occasion would be covered in blood. I started to lose my hair; clumps would fall out every time I took a shower. I developed what I thought were food allergies. Every time I ate sugar, white flour, eggs, cheese, and a host of other similar foods, I would immediately have severe headaches. For years I thought these were allergies but were, in reality, psychosomatic symptoms of depression. By the end of the marriage my mind and health were in a state of chaos. I attempted suicide at this very low point in my life. At this time a strange voice came into my head and changed my life: "You have a choice," this stern yet soothing voice said. To this day I'm not certain where or how this came into my head. Maybe the voice was a hallucination, or God, or a tiny piece of lost humanity, or maybe I was just listening to me for the first time since I was eight years old. Whatever it was, it saved my life.

Conclusions and Implications for Systems Change

And here I sit today, writing a chapter about my adaptation and cohabitation with these disabilities. While pursuing a Masters degree in Rehabilitation Counseling, I learned that a disability is not something you suffer from, battle, or try to get rid of, it is just a part of you like your heart or brain. It took intense studying and a Masters degree to learn this simple truth about disabilities, especially hidden disabilities. Many magazine articles and news programs note that mental illnesses are treatable and not hopeless. Even though great strides in research and awareness relating to mental illnesses have been made, there, unfortunately, still exists a great stigma regarding mental illness. While interviewing an incarcerated woman (who has served 9 years on a 70-year sentence), she told me that she was a recovering heroin addict and was to soon appear before the parole board. I was developing a pre-release plan for her to present to the board in the hope she would be given the chance to start over in the community. I asked her if she was on any drugs. She emphatically stated "No!" Her record however revealed that she had been admitted to numerous psychiatric institutions, taken lithium for many years, and had also been addicted to cocaine. She had been diagnosed with bipolar disorder. When questioned about this, she quite freely admitted that yes, indeed she had episodes of manic-depression. When I asked her why she had stopped taking her prescribed medication, which she acknowledged had helped her greatly, she replied: "The parole board won't grant parole to anyone on drugs for mental illness because they'll think you're crazy and should stay locked up." Her reply, unfortunately, was not that unusual. In fact, it is quite typical. Most incarcerated women that I have interviewed believe the same. Educating the public is one way I hope to change the negative myths that shroud having a mental disability. Educating the public on the virtues of having a disability however is a lot like teaching people the benefits of not smoking—much remains to be done.

Today the only real hassle I face as a result of my disability is from health insurance companies. Most believe that all drugs are the same and therefore they will only pay for the least expensive ones. Not all antidepressants are the same. For example, I work well with Prozac® but it is one of the more expensive antidepressants. My insurance company offered an alternative–Paxil®. Because Paxil® has a sedative side effect and Prozac® has an activating side effect, for someone like me who gained forty pounds on a similar antidepressant, Paxil® would make me look like a horse. Luckily, I have a doctor who is aggressive and cares. I am constantly studying and educating myself in every way possible about my mental illness and I would encourage others in similar circumstances to do the same. In this way I can advocate to my physician and others regarding the best pharmacological alternatives for my particular mental disability.

Educational and medical institutions provided little, if any, assistance in helping me detect and openly deal with my disabilities. I attended a private school where counseling services were not readily available. No one seemed to understand the meaning of my inconsistent grades. My physician did not notice or perhaps did not comment on my weight fluctuation nor my uncommonly high blood pressure. Even the institution of marriage failed. Marriage was a huge vacuum in which I could hide with relative ease; I could shop and exercise to my heart's content because I was married and he "could afford it." Marriage safely cloaked my out-of-control behavior. Even when our marriage was hitting rock bottom, no one questioned my behavior, they were more concerned about the visibility of the marriage.

Interestingly, the one system that enabled my disabilities was also the one that also facilitated a halt to my self-destruction. Actually, there were two systems that saved my life: my family and my faith in God. My family provided me with a threshold of stability from which I was able to begin healing. Religion, which I had taken for granted, provided stability when my life was full of chaos.

Based on my experiences, I believe it is vital that professionals approach a client not simply as a problem, but as a person. Professionals must determine what motivates a person through the eyes of that person in order to foster stability. Stability facilitates growth and development that allows the person the opportunity to build a meaningful life.

Chapter 8

I'M BLIND: WHAT ABOUT IT!

Robin Fischer Hoerber

On November 14, 1953, I arrived into this world three and a half months early. Being premature, I was placed in an incubator to assist my breathing. Unfortunately, the oxygen which sustained my life, damaged my optic nerves to the point of irreversible damage. As a consequence, I have been blind all of my life. I do, however, have some light perception that allows me to see shadows. It helps me to avoid running into things–but it's not always reliable.

I grew up like any other child. During the summers I would go to camp (for the blind). I was expected to do chores around the house. I was expected to behave appropriately. And I was expected to achieve high grades in school. Luckily for me, I lived in the state of New Jersey. New Jersey, California, and Washington, at that time, were the only states that permitted blind children to go to public school. The New Jersey Commission for the Blind would pay for all supplies needed for my schooling. From kindergarten to high school graduation, I had a counselor from the New Jersey Commission for the Blind who would come to the school and help me with reading and writing as well as grading my work. She drove two hours each way just to come and assist me.

In kindergarten, I learned Braille by shaped pegs and by third grade I was typing Braille. The school system had my books put into Braille by volunteers. In the first grade my parents made me learn the state capitals and states and where they were in relation to each other. They bought me a puzzle map and I was expected to learn how to put it together. That is how I learned geography. I was placed in regular reading groups along with my peers. Books were provided for me and worksheets were put into Braille. The New Jersey Commission for the Blind also provided me with a reader throughout my school years who assisted me with research, writing papers, and reading textbooks.

In the seventh grade I was given a white cane. Elementary school is when cane travel should have been taught to me. I went ballistic! I had never used a cane before, so why did I need one now? I was determined not to stick out. I hadn't been viewed any differently growing up and I wasn't about to now. I hung the cane in my locker and only used it when I had a mobility lesson—which was once a month. The mobility instructor tried to teach me the north, south, east, and west method of mobility, and to this day, I still don't understand it. I knew basically where to go in school and was permitted to leave class early to get to the next class. Looking back now, I wouldn't have had a problem using the white cane. But at that time, it was symbolic of being different.

Dating for me didn't begin until I went to college. In high school, the boys did not think I was dateable. My parents would not permit me to date at that point anyway. However, I wasn't the only one that didn't date. I had plenty of friends, who as well, did not date.

I remember going to church with my parents and sisters. My church experience, however, as a child was not a pleasant one. A lot of parents made it difficult for my family and myself so we decided to go to another church. At our new church, I became the "token blind girl." In the youth group I was not accepted and was not included in any projects. I was isolated because of my disability. I hated it and started to question my belief in God. What kind of God would put me in this kind of situation? One would think that church groups would be more inclusive, understanding, and more accepting, but that was not the case. Nowadays, people are more aware of the ability in disability. The church I presently attend accepts me for the person I am.

Seton Hall University had a program for blind youngsters who wanted to go to college. When I was a junior in high school, I was selected to attend this program. I took classes in typing (i.e., how to type a business letter), learned homemaking skills (i.e., doing laundry and ironing), and I learned how to take care of my finances (i.e., what a check looks like and how to sign it). Since I already knew a lot of these skills, I began teaching them. Once I completed this program, I enrolled in Dickinson University. The New Jersey Commission for the

Blind paid for my college education; they bought my books, provided readers for me, and paid my tuition, room and board.

At Dickinson University, there was no resident Rehabilitation Counselor and there were no student support services for persons with disabilities. I had to learn the campus on my own as well as how to interact with my professors. I had to be assertive enough to ask for an accommodation. Sadly, most of the blind students who were attending Dickinson at that time, could not or did not know how to ask for accommodations and eventually dropped out. In my sophomore year, I decided that I wanted to become a Rehabilitation Counselor. I wanted to make a difference in helping people with disabilities. After graduating with a major in psychology, I applied to and was accepted to a graduate program in Rehabilitation Counseling at East Carolina University.

Dr. Sheldon Downs was the chairman of the Department of Rehabilitation Counseling at East Carolina University. He was a very supportive person. Dr. Downs didn't give me any leeway and I didn't expect him too. After completing my masters program I took a job in the Women's Studies Department at UNC in Charlotte. Following that position, I accepted a job as a Rehabilitation Counselor with the state of North Carolina. Because of an inability to get drivers and readers, I only held this job for a few months. I, then, worked at an Independent Living Center for several years.

In college, I was involved with a young man for three years. He proposed to me and I turned him down. I was not sure how his parents felt about their son dating a blind person and I wanted their approval. Well, his parents did not approve and when it came to either his parents or me, he chose his parents. Luckily, that was a blessing in disguise. Soon afterward I met a wonderful man whom today is my husband. His parents as well, were not too excited about their son wanting to marry a person with a disability. Nevertheless, he told his parents that he loved me and that he did not need their approval. We got married. Several years later I became pregnant with my son Chris. Being a mother has been an amazing and wonderful experience. I was just like any other mother. I taught my son numbers, words, shapes, and even colors! I would have Chris' books put into Braille and I was able to assist him with his homework. Today, we have a wonderful 18-year-old son who is currently preparing for a career in youth and pastoral counseling at East Carolina University.

My husband's work took us to New York State in the mid 1980s. While there, I worked in a program for the homeless. In the late 1980s, my husband was transferred to Virginia where we are presently.

In Virginia, I have been actively involved in advocacy. I currently chair the Disability Services Board for my locality and have been involved with this board for the past nine years.

I was appointed by our Governor to the Statewide Independent Living Council and to the Statewide Rehabilitation Council (for the Department for the Visually Handicapped where I have been actively involved in the design of independent living services and rehabilitation services for the past six years). I have thoroughly enjoyed my service and feel that I have made a contribution to the lives of people with disabilities.

Conclusions and Recommendations for System Change

The agencies that provide services to persons with disabilities need to take more of a holistic perspective; that is, we as clients, customers, consumers (all labels which I do not particularly care for—person with disability is preferable *when* a label is needed) are not something that needs to be fixed. We need a hand up, not a hand out.

Technology is the great equalizer for persons who are blind, but this technology needs to be available and accessible both at a work site and in one's home.

Transportation that is available, accessible, and dependable is a must for people who have visual impairments or who are blind. I don't need or want an alternate system that costs more and is not reliable.

Recreational opportunities need to be more inclusive; that is, to be a regular part of the community and not just on an exceptional basis.

There is a great need for mentors and more employer awareness regarding the abilities of persons with disabilities. Policies that relate to the receipt of Social Security Disability benefits and the amount of money that may be earned must be realistic and provide incentives, not disincentives to working. It's better to pay some taxes than not to pay any taxes.

Finally, the general public needs to be educated about disability. Stereotypical thinking that is based on limiting characteristics of a particular medical condition results in false myths. We need to make people more aware of the ability that resides in disability; that is, what people can do, not what they cannot do.

Chapter 9

RICHARD'S JOURNEY

Ruth Mackey Martin & E. Davis Martin, Jr.

"**H**e's a throwaway." "I beg your pardon?" Did we hear him correctly? This seemingly nice middle-aged, balding, and overweight pediatric neurologist who came highly recommended by our family pediatrician uttered words which just did not make sense to us. This was our second visit to this physician and we were anxiously awaiting a diagnosis that would tell us what to do for our six-year-old son, Richard. Richard had these staring spells which lasted briefly where he was nonresponsive. He, as well, had been a little slow in meeting developmental milestones. We suspected that something was wrong. His pediatrician reassured us that children, particularly boys, often mature at latter times–that there was great latitude in develop-ment. In short, he said "Stop worrying!" The pediatrician's words were exactly what we wanted to hear but we were not reassured. The neurologist, we were convinced, was going to give Richard a pill that would cure him or he would tell us what we could do to help Richard.

Richard was our firstborn child. He survived a difficult labor and, even though he was bloody and dazed when the OB brought him in to us, it was a joy to be able to hold him and see him. Ruth had been anesthetized just prior to his birth as he had turned and was trying to come into this world feet first. The OB had to turn him around. So we were both seeing him for the first time. Ruth was still a little dazed. Dave asked the OB "Are they okay?" He replied "Oh, yes! They're both just fine. They just need some time to overcome the difficultness of the birth. They will be fine tomorrow." Dave left the hospital feel-ing relieved yet still a little worried. He called our respective parents and grandparents with the happy news—Ruth and the baby were fine.

"I don't mean that he is a *throwaway* in the way you are thinking," the neurologist said, ". . . it's just that he will not achieve educationally or career-wise what you have." We were not really certain what he meant, but, for sure, we didn't like the way in which it was said. He then referred us to the Child Study clinic for a comprehensive medical, psychological, and educational evaluation and recommendations. The people at this clinic were, for the most part, cold and aloof, who poked and prodded Richard while asking us a multitude of questions. About one month after the evaluation, we were asked to come in for the results. The director of the clinic, a small woman with petite features, spoke to us without looking at us and said "Richard is moderately retarded; he has brain damage. He will never be normal. He will never experience life in the way you have. He will always have problems. He will live with you or be dependent on your support for his entire life. You may want to think about a residential placement for him. Do you have other children?"

What we expected to hear was "Yes, Richard has some cognitive problems, but with work he will be able to be independent and have a job and have a good life. It will be a long haul, but it can be done. He does have some abilities." The Director left us with little hope; every question we asked was responded to in a negative way or was prefaced with "No, he will not be able to do that. Not that either. No, no, no." At the very least, she could have said "He has beautiful dark brown eyes (or curly dark hair)". . . or "He is a well behaved child". . . or something positive. We felt alone and depressed. Our next stop was to speak with the educational specialist.

Just a few months earlier, the Education for All Handicapped Children legislation (PL 94-142) had been passed by Congress and signed into law by President Gerald Ford. The principles upon which this law rested were worthy and gave us hope that the public education system would take Richard to his highest possible level of achievement. The educational specialist was less optimistic than we were about the ultimate outcome of PL 94-142 and steered us to a placement in the private sector. The private school that we visited was within commuting distance (the others were residential placements), and, aside from its cost, did not do much more than babysit its charges—at least that was our impression from several visits and talks with other parents. And we were not going to have Richard live in an institution.

We visited the public school and were told about the virtues of PL 94-142 and how Richard would undoubtably thrive under this new approach to the education of the "retarded"–to be educated in "the least restrictive environment." We opted for the public school system–how could anybody not do so after reading the principles upon which PL 94-142 were built.

Richard had been in private school prior to his comprehensive evaluation. Ruth was convinced that the sensorial method of learning was exactly what Richard needed in order to succeed. The Montessori method was our goal for Richard. The Montessori method is not typically designed for children with cognitive disabilities although Montessori developed this model based on this population of children. Getting him into Montessori school however, was a feat in and of itself. But that is exactly what Ruth did. Richard passed his interview with the teacher, was accepted for the preschool class and attended the first year of elementary school there before falling behind the other children. To this day, Richard's experience at Montessori school provided him with a sense of belonging and of inclusion that he would not again experience until he exited the public school system. At Montessori, he was included in all aspects of the school. When the children put on a play for the parents, *all* of the children were in the play–whether you were the lead character or a tree who stood tall and silent–both were valued and both had importance. Unfortunately, Richard would not experience inclusion or importance while in the public school system.

Richard's transition to the public school system–to what we thought would be in the least restrictive environment, was a self-contained classroom that separated children labeled as Educable Mentally Retarded (EMR) or Trainable Mentally Retarded (TMR) from little, if any, contact with the rest of the student body. While in the public school system both of these labels at various times were affixed to Richard. The Individualized Education Plan (IEP), another of the cornerstones of PL 94-142, turned out to be less than we hoped for and expected. We arrived for our first IEP meeting expecting that we (the teacher, principal, special education coordinator, social worker, psychologist, occupational therapist, and parents) as a team would develop the best educational program for Richard. When handed a mimeographed listing of goals and asked to sign as the IEP for that school year, our reaction was less than sanguine. Dave asked "What

is individualized about a mimeograph sheet of predetermined goals?"
Apparently this was an out-of-bounds question and all members
focused their attention on the principal to respond. She began *slowly*
explaining to us that Richard is "retarded" and "retards" learn in just
about the same way as other "retarded" children, so the goals are the
same. But we could propose to them (we were now *us* and *them*, no
longer a team) additional goals that *may be considered.* What was to
have been a collaborative meeting ended on an adversarial note. We
requested a future meeting once we had an opportunity to review the
pre-determined goals and given time to formulate our goals. What we
learned from this first IEP meeting (and we later discovered this meeting was not atypical) was threefold: (1) You need an advocate to prepare you for these meetings or to go with you to these meetings particularly when the goals or services you seek exceed the authority or
expertness of the teacher (e.g., a request for related services–OT, PT,
Speech, Supported Employment, etc.). (2) You need to know and
understand the laws that control the process (PL 94-142, Section 504
of the 1973 Rehabilitation Act, etc.) at least as well as school personnel, hopefully better, and (3) you need to be polite but firm in your
request for service(s) and not be swayed by factors such as limited
school budgets or to be reasonable because all children need help not
just your child or some variation on this theme.

As Richard moved on to middle school, we thought he would be
integrated more with his peers rather than maintained in a self-contained class. At the parents orientation to middle school, the principal
told us that she did not want any of "those special ed kids" and that
she had no plans to mainstream "those children," nor did she have a
budget for that sort of "nonsense." What an introduction! Then Dave
asked to review Richard's records. You would have thought that he
had asked to see the most confidential information ever recorded:
"Why do you want to see his records?" Because I do. "If you insist
on reviewing his records, you must wait five days." Why? Dave asked.
"Because you would not understand these records and we must provide someone to interpret them for you." Again, not an atypical incident although it seemed that we were the only parents who had ever
asked to review their child's academic records.

While in middle school Richard's physical education teacher who
was certified as an adaptive physical education teacher established a
goal for him to learn how to ride a bicycle. This was one of the goals

set forth on the IEP. Richard had told her that he could ride a bike and did so with his dad several times a week. Actually he learned this psychomotor skill without much trouble and in a relatively short period of time. For a child who was very awkward this seemed to be amazing. Nevertheless the adaptive PE teacher chose not to believe Richard and here we were in the IEP meeting telling the PE teacher "Yes, he can ride a bike and has for the past several years. And he is very safety conscious. He doesn't need that as a goal."

The PE teacher professed great amazement and responded "Really?" She went on to say she felt this was an appropriate goal and that she would work with him on it. We proposed that he needed occupational therapy in the context of a fun activity that would enhance his eye, hand, and foot coordination. This was rejected and we were told that we would have to take it to a hearing if we still disagreed.

In high school, Richard was placed in a self-contained classroom with others labeled as Educable Mentally Retarded. This class of about 12–15 children was the only special education class in that particular high school. The special education kids were targeted by a minority of the others and teased, taunted, and called names (e.g., "retard," the same term used by the special education coordinator who considered this scientific language). It was at this time Richard experienced his first bout of depression. We requested that he be placed in another school that was more accepting and tolerant. He was and that school had a special education population of approximately 20 percent. His label was changed to "Trainable Mentally Retarded" and, of course, with such a label expectations were lowered. This new program was to be more vocationally oriented–he would learn to wash tables and clean toilets. There is nothing wrong with these activities if that is what you want to do and what you are capable of doing. Also there was a class to learn how to count money, wrap silverware, staple, and other similar tasks. The money used was paper coins. There was very little transferability to the real world. Actually, this was training to learn how to work in a "sheltered workshop." Because of the lowered expectations, there was less stress and pressure, yet not much learning was occurring. In fact, we were told that we really should not expect too much (and the unsaid words were "He's retarded, what do you expect?"). Our expectations were for him to get the most he could out of school but to this point mostly what we got or what Richard got was a place to go and spend six hours a day. In our experience with Special Education we found it to contain very little education and it certainly was not very special. We found Richard's teachers to be well intentioned and meaning but ill-trained and unable to advocate for their charges.

Toward the end of Richard's stay in high school, a new concept called "supported employment" was beginning to emerge. We had read about the successes attained with young people with significant disabilities who were able to learn and hold employment in the competitive labor market. This was like a ray of sunshine for us; we began to advocate for our school system to incorporate this activity. We spoke to the Special Education Advisory Committee who, in turn, advocated for supported employment to the School Board, to parent groups, and to state committees, boards, and commissions not to mention legislators. Within our school system, one special education teacher (who had training in supported employment) was released from the classroom to function as a job coach. This young woman could only work with about 3–5 students per year. As a job coach, the person works one-on-one with the student in the actual employment situation to learn the tasks associated with the job and stays with the person until they can perform the job without supervision or assistance. It is very labor intensive and one job coach did not meet the need for our school system. It quickly became a money issue. We were convinced that supported employment was the answer for Richard. We began to advocate at IEP meetings that this was the only service we desired from the school system. We got supported employment listed as his IEP goal. About a year or so after we began to advocate for this service, Richard was interviewed by the job coach regarding the type of job he wanted. He selected a job as a "bagger" at a grocery store about one half mile from our house. The job coach stayed with him for eight or so weeks full-time and over the course of the next few months began to gradually fade out. Contact was made with the local Community Services Board (CSB) with an eye toward Richard's transition from school to receipt of services from the CSB (i.e., job coach, case management, residential services, etc.). Richard graduated or more precisely exited the secondary school system at the end of that year. He began to receive follow along employment services, placed on a waiting list for a residential option (living in a supervised apartment), and case management services from the CSB. He continued his job at the grocery store and seemed to enjoy it for the most part. In this job Richard experienced success and the knowledge that he was a competent human being. He truly recognized this when one of his co-workers called and asked Richard to take his shift. He had finally achieved a sense of equality. What he longed for however was a sense of equality in being a fully accepted person in a social manner.

In the interim, his name came up on the waiting list for a supervised apartment. He was to live in an apartment with one other person. After a few months, this placement was not working; Richard was isolating himself in his bedroom and wanted no interaction with his roommate. His roommate was about 10 years older than Richard and had previously been living in a group home. His roommate did not like this arrangement either but had difficulty letting others know how he felt as he was nonverbal. They had nothing in common and were in the process making each other miserable. Richard wanted an apartment by himself; the policy was not to have a "consumer" in an apartment by himself. A very courageous supervisor advocated for Richard and the policy was changed. He would be approved to live in an apartment by himself.

Richard stayed with this job for approximately five years and then began to advocate for another job–his dream job was to be an office clerk. No one felt that Richard could do the clerk's job except his new job coach; she felt he should, at the least, have the opportunity to try. He tried but could not achieve competency on all the job tasks. Another site was located where he would operate collating machines and would load and unload mail. He did not like this job as it required a two-hour ride (mostly waiting while other consumers were picked up and delivered to various work sites) in the morning and a two-hour ride in the afternoon. He was forgotten by drivers on several occasions and after repeated calls sometimes was picked up but more often than not we would go and get him and deliver him to his apartment. Richard hurt his back on this job and that effectively ended that employment. Richard had lost his confidence and his next job was in a supervised enclave of consumers working in a book/video distribution center (a vocational regression). He was making significantly less money on this job than any of his previous jobs. That bothered him too. This was to be a temporary situation that lasted for more than two years. He was making, according to this job coach, the maximum; consumers were paid according to their productivity. He complained that he wanted another job for more than one year but was put off by the employment specialist saying that there were no other jobs available. We, as well, were advocating for another job more in line with Richard's desires. Richard had always come home on the weekends but now did not want to quite as frequently. He was complaining about work; would refuse to go to work; would miss the van; would not answer the door if it was a CSB employee; and was becoming increasingly more depressed and withdrawn. We were unaware of his actions regarding work and interactions with his case manager. Because Richard was an adult, the CSB workers felt that they could not contact us about these problems due to confidentiality rules–even though Richard had signed a waiver allowing CSB employees to speak with us. The CSB workers interpreted the confidentiality rule to mean that Richard would have to sign a waiver for each time they communicated to us about an incident.

We knew he did not like his present situation and we were asking him to be patient. We all underestimated his sense of despair and desolation. He became suicidal and had formulated a plan to kill himself. We brought him home. He began to have hallucinations and to withdraw from reality. We had to hospitalize him as we were afraid that he might hurt himself. He was hospitalized for a week and then released to us. His psychiatrist was treating him very aggressively with antipsychotic medications but Richard was not getting any better. In fact, he was getting worse. Each new medication was taking him further away from us. He was no longer talking to us. He was actively hallucinating. He would sleep for most of a 24-hour period. He stopped eating. He lost about 40 pounds and became extremely emaciated. He looked like the pictures of a Nazi concentration prisoner. Nothing held his interest.

We were losing hope. Richard was slipping away and we were afraid we would not be able to get him back. We had lost faith in his present psychiatrist. We sought out other practitioners who were more familiar with drugs, particularly with a person who had brain damage. After an exhaustive search and several false starts we finally located a psychiatrist who was able to help Richard. At the very first meeting with Richard and us, the doctor was able to get Richard to respond–something that we could not accomplish. Richard had not spoken to us or anybody for almost a month and very little for several months prior to that. Our sense of hope was restored. We knew, as bad off as Richard was at that moment, he was going to get better. And that he did. The doctor got Richard on the right mix of medications and he slowly but surely began to become the Richard that we so desperately missed and loved. It was good to have him back.

Ten months after experiencing this second episode of major depression, Richard was ready to move into his new apartment and to start a new job. Richard decided that he wanted to be a courtesy clerk (bagger) at a particular store and that was his goal. With assistance through the Community Services Board and the Department of Rehabilitative Services, a job coach was assigned to Richard to begin the process of reacquiring the skills he had once had. It had been more than five years since Richard had worked as a bagger. This particular store, a local family owned and operated chain of grocery stores, placed great emphasis on each position within a store and provided training in customer relations. The philosophy of the owners is very customer oriented and as well as employee oriented.

It was an ideal work environment. Richard gained competence in the tasks of this position within a few months and has subsequently earned the respect of his fellow workers and supervisors. He has been on this job for almost two years, enjoys his work, and looks forward to each new day.

No, he is no throwaway!

Conclusions and Implications for Systems Change

Our experience with the various agencies and professionals who have provided services to Richard over the years can be characterized in one word: inconsistent. This is not to say Richard has received poor services or had been denied services; quite to the contrary, he has, at times, had dedicated, caring, and passionate workers as well as workers who were cold and aloof that treated him with little respect or regard. Fortunately, he has had more of the former than the latter. However, those professionals who had a positive influence on his life were, all too frequently, in his life for only a relatively brief period of time. Salaries for human service workers are much too low and, as such, create little stability in job tenure; workers tend to job-hop for similar jobs that pay only slightly more. This results in inconsistency and delays in service delivery and much too frequently denial of services. Jobs in the human services must be perceived by potential professionals as a career and must be recognized, rewarded, and regarded as such by those who manage and operate the service delivery agencies and institutions (e.g., schools, community based mental health and mental retardation organizations, state human service agencies, and so forth). These managers must provide continuing education and training opportunities that foster commitment and stability which allow professionals to embrace a holistic perspective of persons with disabilities. Professionals must know and appreciate those that they work with and hold expectations for their success and be messengers of hope for their charges and their families.

Individuals who aspire or who work in the human services must commit to the ideals of independence (choice and control over one's life), productivity (real money for real work), and inclusion (to be a part of the work and play of the community). If a person cannot commit to these values then they must opt out of education or training programs or work situations as they are impeding the lives of people who need services to be delivered by caring and competent persons.

Advocacy efforts on behalf of persons with disabilities as well as encouragement and facilitation of advocacy efforts of people with disabilities must be a mandatory aspect of every human service worker's job. Professionals as well as parents and persons with disabilities must encourage access to and *real* inclusion in the most integrated settings in our school systems, work and leisure environments, health care institutions, and transportation systems.

Several years ago Richard was asked to speak at a public hearing advocating the state legislature to allocate more funds for community based services. This was Richard's first experience in speaking in front of a large number of people and to a panel of officials. His remarks were simple, quite elegant and to the point. In part, he said:

> People need real jobs, not make-believe jobs.
>
> People need to live in their own apartments. And to choose their roommate or choose not to have a roommate.
>
> People need to have their own money and pay for the things you need to live.
>
> People need to have friends, not just friends with disabilities or county workers.

Embodied in these four statements are the values of independence, productivity, and inclusion.

Whether you are or aspire to be a rehabilitation counselor, psychologist, social worker, occupational therapist, physical therapist, recreation specialist, or a teacher, know and understand that your actions *can* and *will* have a tremendous impact on the lives of those you counsel, provide services to, or teach. The nature of that impact may be subtle and, perhaps, imperceptible to you at any specific point in time. Nevertheless, you can choose to be positive or negative, growth enhancing or retarding, encouraging or discouraging, or ego building or deflating. Choose wisely what the nature of your impact will be—it is life altering!

Chapter 10

MY BIG BROTHER

MICHELE MARTIN MURMER

IDO NOT REMEMBER the exact moment when I knew my brother was different. He was just my older brother. We were like any other "normal" siblings: we fought, we laughed, we played. I always felt that we were the typical American family.

I knew my brother's abilities were lower than mine. I was his younger sister who could do higher math, could read better, who seemed to excel faster than he. I took advantage of that. I admit I would manipulate Richard into doing tasks for me that I did not want to do. I knew I could get away with it. At that time, I did not feel guilty for what I was doing. However, as an adult, I wish I could take back a lot of the unsavory nonsense that I put him through. It surprises me that average adults still take advantage of Richard. Sales people can be particularly malicious. As soon as they speak with him and see that his mental abilities are lower than average, they know they can get away with selling him the most expensive product. Richard does not realize that he is being exploited. So he pays for his product and leaves. Restaurants also have conned Richard out of money that he wouldn't have spent. Female servers especially note that Richard is developmentally slower than "normal." They can get any amount of money they wish for a tip. They can just tell him that he is suppose to leave a twenty for a tip and Richard will trust her and do as she says.

His transportation to and from work has always been unstable. He is in a program that provides transportation for people with delayed cognitive development. There have been times when he was left at work because they forgot to pick him up. He has also been left at home all day because the transportation neglected to pick him up. At these times, I become so outraged that an organization (whose only duty is to pick up and drop off people) forget their profession. My assumption why this occurs is because they know they can get away with it. They certainly believe that these "retarded" people will not say anything. So they get to spend their day however they wish.

I always felt that I was the oldest child. I would constantly try to protect Richard. When someone would make fun of him or look at him as if he was some sort of "circus freak," I would stare at them the way they stared at Richard. I would make fun of them the way they made fun of Richard. Why not? I wanted them to feel the exact pain that he was feeling. I remember when I was a child, Richard would refuse to go to school because of the torture he experienced there. He would run away from the house in the morning to escape from getting on the short school bus. He was embarrassed to get on that bus. Automatically people knew that something was wrong with you if you had to ride on the short school bus. So once again he became labeled and this permitted the student body to ridicule him.

Richard has gone through various jobs. Some he enjoyed and others he didn't. Right now he works for a local family-owned grocery store. This is the happiest I have ever seen him. His fellow employees treat him as if he is "one of the guys." He feels accepted there. Both the younger employees as well as the older employees see him as who he really is–Richard.

My earliest recollection of knowing that Richard was different was when I entered middle school. I learned how cruel kids could be to others who do not look "perfect," act "perfect," dress "perfect," and who do not fit into their "perfect" lives. The "special ed" children seemed to be one of the larger groups to be ridiculed. I did not understand this. I knew Richard was in a "special" classroom. I thought "So what? They are people too. They just need more time to learn." My friends had never been around anyone who was mentally handicapped. This was a new experience for them to see that the "special ed" children were just like everyone else. They had a heart and a soul just like they did. I soon learned who my real friends were. If any of my friends used the word "retarded" derogatorily or called Richard any names, they were removed from my buddy list. I hate to hear people say that someone is retarded and use it to mean stupid. My brother is not stupid. My brother is a very special person who just happens to need more time to learn. There is nothing stupid about that.

When I was a child, I would fantasize about my future husband. He would be tall, dark, handsome, loving, and accepting. He would not only love me, but love my family as well. It was very important to me to find someone who did not treat Richard like an outcast and ignore him. My husband Steve is a dream come true. He doesn't think of Richard as mentally retarded. He sees Richard as if he is "normal" because Richard is normal. Richard, like a lot of people, has a disability; it is a part of who he is, not what he is. Steve talks to Richard exactly how he talks with his buddies. He sees Richard as a person who is no different than anybody else. Steve's family all love Richard. Every time they go to the grocery store that he works at, they will request Richard to bag their groceries. They have even screamed in the store that "Richard is the best bagger!" I feel so fortunate to have found such a loving and nonjudgmental family. It's hard to find those qualities in one person let alone the entire family.

I often feel bad that I am "normal." Richard sees me, his baby sister, doing things that he wishes he could (and hopefully will) do: drive a car; go to prom; go out with friends on a Friday night; get married. Approximately a month after my wedding, my brother fell into a deep depression. He lost a considerable amount of weight, gradually began to abstain from talking, walked around like he was a zombie, and continually said that he wanted to die. He was institutionalized for a week or so and eventually my mom and dad found the right psychiatrist who was able to reach him. Since that incident, I have felt guilty for being a "typical" adult. I believe that my wedding was the straw that broke the camel's back. Even though I have been told that it was not my fault and I know that, I shall always feel guilty for Richard entering into that horrible depression.

I wonder what Richard would have been like if he had not sustained brain damage at birth. Would he be married? Would he have a family? Would he have been there to protect me? Would he have been the older brother who warned my dates to not break my heart? Would I be an aunt already? Despite not having all of these, I have learned a lot from my brother and feel blessed to have him in my life. I have learned to have an open heart and an open mind. These are the gifts Richard has given me.

Chapter 11

MY INVISIBLE DISABILITY: CHRONIC PAIN

Michael D. Payne

I T WAS A BEAUTIFUL SUNNY DAY in Boston; I was on top of the world. I had just completed the largest business deal of my professional life–this was a career maker. My career had always taken first priority and this was another mark to measure my success. As I stepped from the curb at Quincy Market, I felt an electrical shock shooting from my neck to the end of my fingertips. A sudden weakness overwhelmed me and I dropped my attaché case. The papers contained in the case were caught by the wind and sailed across the square as I fell to the ground. As a consequence of this fall, I began a series of tests that eventually determined that I had structural difficulties at multiple levels in my cervical spine. Surgery was necessary and the recommended cervical fusions (5, 6, and 7) failed, leaving me with significant impediments that included atrophy, sleeping difficulties, and, most significantly, chronic pain. Since that moment more than seven years ago, I have been engaged in a seemingly endless process of searching for healing and the hope for, at the least, adequate pain management. This quest for a cure or the hope of pain relief has proven to be highly elusive.

My surgery was to be routine or that is what I was told. The doctor said he would remove a bone from my pelvis and fuse C5, 6, and 7. An incision was made to the front of my throat just beneath my Adam's apple. The esophagus was moved to the side to provide clear access to the spinal column. A routine two-hour surgical procedure was scheduled but unanticipated complications extended the time by five hours. Recovery was slow necessitating extra time in the hospital and a period of recuperation at home. After three months it became evident that something was wrong; the fusion was not successful. The pain was unbearable. My doctor prescribed physical therapy and narcotics that gave me only temporary relief. I tried to return to work, but each two-day work trial was followed by nine or ten days of bed rest. This cycle repeated itself until I decided to apply for long-term disability from my company and Social Security Disability benefits.

I am convinced that the application process for disability insurance is one of the most humiliating events a person can experience. It seemed that once this process was initiated, I exchanged my dignity and independence for a road full of potholes and detours. If by chance, this happens to you, hopefully you will have enough savings to survive the two years of medical exams, caseworker visits, and Social Security disability appeals. All total, I was subjected to three Independent Medical Examinations, my medical history sent to and shared with anyone remotely connected to my case, three caseworker visits to my house, a strenuous two-day Residual Functional Capacity (RFC) examination, two Social Security appeals and a hearing with a Social Security Administrative Law Judge. One claims supervisor told me that many people lose their house during this process. This person's callousness, I later learned, was typical of many professionals who process disability cases.

Since my neck problem resulted in chronic pain, the medical exams always proved to be inconclusive. Repeated MRIs showed scar tissue and an incomplete union at C6–7. Pain is not something that science can objectively measure therefore it holds little weight in a disability decision. Insurance professionals and doctors alike, for the most part, have not been schooled in the disease of pain and consider chronic pain to be psychosomatic at best and malingering at worst. Either way, I began to get the message that they thought the problem was in my head. It became clear that these so-called professionals were adversaries and not caregivers. Applying for disability is a legal process not a medical process. So, do not take it personally or you will not survive the ordeal.

Anxiety caused me to seek a therapeutic counselor that I could trust. Her wisdom introduced me to the idea of taking classes in Rehabilitation Counseling. During one of my first classes, the concept of adaptation was introduced. The notion of focusing on what you can do and not on what you cannot do was a significant insight for me. It was hard for me, the hard charging investment sales person, not to measure myself against my peers. My personal identity had always depended on where I ranked. The vocational counselors for the insurance carrier recognized this and played on my fear of falling behind and challenged me to return me to work prematurely. Taking this challenge exacerbated the pain in my cervical spine and delayed or permanently impeded my recovery. However they did their job. I never saw them again–thankfully. The next two years were spent at home in bed or on the couch.

The first independent medical exam ordered by the insurance company was extremely embarrassing. The appointment was scheduled with a top neurosurgeon that had obviously hardened to patients who complained of pain–a doctor, in essence, who believed all pain is psychogenic. I believe you can tell a doctor's orientation by the type of magazines found in the waiting room–all of his were yachting or gourmet food magazines. His demeanor was arrogant and his manner rough; my wife who accompanied me to the examination confirmed these feelings. He pushed me to move in a manner that was painful and asked questions that implied that I was motivated by secondary gain. Ultimately, the doctor's report to the insurance company was ambiguous. From that moment, I have lived with a constant fear that the insurance for which I had paid premiums could be taken away on the basis of a cursory physical exam by a professional who could care less about me or my family.

While private insurance was difficult, the process of applying for Social Security Disability benefits proved to be a seemingly endless maze of filings and appeals that would last for three years. It was clear that the only way for my case to advance was with professional representation. A new term was introduced by my long-term disability carrier called "social security integration." Simply stated what this meant was that any payment that I would receive from the Social Security Administration (SSA) would be used to reduce my long-term disability payments by a similar amount. The insurance company hired an attorney to help because it would be to their benefit, not mine. At least I had some help. Many people never seek advice and do not know how to obtain proper benefits once they are denied. A majority of cases are denied on the initial determination and reconsideration appeal. However if you have a solid case, many are approved at the Administrative Law Judge hearing level. The Social Security

Administration in the early 1990s finalized the first ruling related to chronic pain. This ruling is strict and relies on the Administrative Law Judge's assessment of the claimant's credibility provided there is a reasonable medical basis to expect pain. My experience was that professional representation, particularly where pain was alleged as the major disability, was the best way to deal with the Social Security system.

The functional capacity evaluation was the most exasperating of all the examinations I had to endure. For two days I was subjected to lifting, bending, stretching, endurance and other tests of strength, while being photographed by a physical therapist. This evaluation merely demonstrates what a person can do on any given day, not every day. The basic premise was that if you could lift 10 pounds, you were qualified for sedentary work regardless whether you could lift it more than once. This report was used to badger my physicians to send me back to work. As a person who experienced chronic pain secondary to spinal cord disease, the functional capacity exam was not a fair measure of what I may be able to do in a work environment over a period of days, weeks, or months. Over the course of the last seven years I have attempted to work or volunteer 22 times only to find that two days of repetitive stress on the spinal cord results in my being homebound for weeks at a time. One day of examination is not a valid measure for a person who experiences chronic pain. Increasingly, more medical professionals are beginning to recognize this fact. Ultimately my disability claim was finally approved. To this date, I still dread any communication from the insurance company or from the Social Security Administration.

Chronic pain is an invisible impairment that affects the entire family. I have three sons that I have not been able to take fishing, to play golf, or to simply toss a baseball around with. My wife understands, but does not understand. As a consequence a short separation occurred while the family adapted. Family and individual counseling was essential for our adaptation. Our family attended 20 counseling sessions over a period of a year and ultimately we grew together as a team. I am thankful because I know this is not the outcome for many persons who experience chronic pain. Adaptation is a lifelong process. In many ways I feel blessed because I have experienced what is an eventuality for all of us. This experience has given me an appreciation for everyday miracles.

Conclusions and Implications for Systems Change

I believe that self-care and self-education for people with chronic pain is essential, otherwise the usual scenario is running from doctor to doctor wandering in what I call the "diagnosis desert." For the past three years I had been engaged in the study of Rehabilitation Counseling that resulted in the award of a Master of Science degree. More importantly this educational experience enabled me to establish a multidisciplinary approach to pain management that I feel has implications for professionals and persons who experience chronic pain. My team includes a physical medicine and rehabilitation physician, physical therapist, medical social worker, dietician, neurosurgeon, herbal pharmacist, lawyer, and a vocational rehabilitation counselor. This team has provided me with functional relief through an organized treatment plan. Specialization and territorial protection among professionals has kept most individuals who experience chronic pain from receiving the benefit of this kind of care. It is essential for me to ask for my treatment notes so that I can function as the case manager. In this way each team member has the complete picture regarding treatment modalities and options. If one does not take responsibility for self-care, the current system will fail the person who experiences chronic pain.

Professionals who believe they have seen it all, have not seen anything yet. The age of genetic research will demonstrate that there is a fair amount of biochemical diversity and that the commonly held convictions about pain management will only be partially true. Advances in the understanding of nutrition, genetics, and the role of neurotransmitters will bring relief to many who experience chronic pain. I have already experienced great benefits by using vitamin supplements and good nutrition planning to develop stronger cellular health (i.e., use of vitamin B-complex, vitamins C and E, and minerals such as calcium, potassium, and magnesium). Certain mind-body techniques such as meditation and autogenic training have been helpful as well. Massage, chiropractic, and acupuncture have had little effect on the reduction of pain for me but may be of use to others.

From an allopathic standpoint, I have tried many of the pharmaceutical protocols and had adverse reactions to almost all them. My physician has been very proactive in her usage and combinations of various drugs. These included narcotics that for me caused upper GI disturbances. The usage of NSAIDs caused similar problems as well. Another standard protocol for pain patients is the use of antidepressants for sleep. Some people have paradoxical reactions to these drugs and actually become overstimulated. I belong to that group.

After many months of trying different combinations of drugs, I think we have finally got the right one. This combination relaxes the strap muscles around my neck and allows me to sleep. In conjunction with physical therapy, I have been able to regain the minimal activities of daily living that I had lost over the past several years. I still cannot sleep on a flat bed nor can I sit or stand for more than an hour. Walking in sand or on inclines exacerbates my pain. I only drive on off hours because the range of motion in my neck is restricted. But life is once again manageable.

I have entered into this discussion to demonstrate the need for case management for individuals trying to find their way in the "diagnosis desert." This service should be extended not only to people with catastrophic injury but to all persons and families that experience disability. An effective case manager could find the right care providers, reduce anxiety related to benefits, and assist an individual in returning to a productive life on an acceptable timetable. From my experience, I believe that integrated case management for persons who experience chronic pain would provide effective care, save millions of healthcare dollars, and increase the quality of daily living.

I recently received a notice from the SSA to report for a Residual Functional Capacity Examination; my case is being reviewed for continuing eligibility to receive benefits. A recently completed MRI revealed problems with the fusion in my cervical spine. A second surgery may be required. It seems as if this process never ends, but this time I am more prepared for the SSA and I won't take it so personally—after all, it is just a legal process.

Chapter 12

LEADERSHIP AND ADVOCACY:
A POLITICAL PRIMER

James A. Rothrock

As I PUT PEN TO PAPER or should I say fingertips to keyboard, the 2000 session of the Virginia General Assembly has ended. For the 15th time in the last 16 years, I have spent numerous hours involved in my state's legislative process advocating for expanded supports and opportunities for Virginians with disabilities. The successes and failures I have experienced have taught me a great deal about the legislative process. This chapter will address several issues regarding these efforts and keys to success for persons with disabilities, in particular, and others who wish to participate in the legislative process to improve policy and funding for disability-related issues.

Justin W. Dart, Jr., a major force behind the development of the Americans with Disabilities Act (ADA), often relates a story about the advice given to him by his father, who often provided guidance and counsel to President Ronald Reagan. Justin's father told him to get in politics as if his life depended on it because it does! Well, for more than three decades, courageous leaders have taken Mr. Dart's advice and persons with disabilities have benefitted. Frank Bowe, Bob Kafka, Wade Blank, Ed Roberts, Evan Kemp, Judith Heumann, Patrisha Wright, Maureen Hollowell, and Theresa Preda to name a few, have demonstrated that success in the legislative arena can be realized. BUT, as we begin this new millennium, it is essential that more persons with disabilities and other advocates participate in legislative process at the local, state, and federal levels.

Many Americans have a certain level of political malaise. Voter turnout is at an all time low. Political leaders are not necessarily revered and ofttimes held in contempt rather than as role models. Moreover, many individuals do not wish to participate in the legislative and political process. John McCain in his unsuccessful campaign for the Republican presidential nomination in 2000, had as one goal an initiative to make public service and individual involvement a more desirable career or personal aspiration for more Americans—"to inspire young Americans to devote themselves to causes greater than their own self-interest."

People with disabilities, in order to sustain the progress initiated by the heroes previously referenced, must become more involved and active. It is not that difficult to become active. In fact, Woody Allen, a noted actor and movie producer/director, once opined that the most important key to being successful in any activity is to show up. Well, now is the time for all persons with disabilities to show up and make a difference.

Advocacy is the central theme to any and all efforts. Ed Roberts, who before his untimely death, founded much of what our nation's Independent Living movement is based on, was once asked what are the three most important functions of a Center for Independent Living (CIL). He quickly responded:

> **advocacy, advocacy,** and **advocacy,** but not necessarily in that order.
> (NCIL Newsletter, Summer, 1995)

Some people think of advocacy in a negative light almost as if it were a "dirty" word. It is essential, however, that we see advocacy as the key to any success we may have, and I offer the following to underscore the value of advocacy.

The Four-Letter WORDS of Advocacy

To be successful we must remember the importance of the following four-letter words:

Put a "Face" on the Issues

First and foremost is the ability of a person with a disability to become part of the political process. It is critical for success to get real live consumers of services involved in advocacy for the desired services. This is not a revolutionary concept. The National Organization of Women (NOW) is led by women. The National Rifle Association (NRA) is led by people who own and use guns and rifles. And the list goes on and on. BUT, the history of disability advocacy begins with many persons without disabilities in the forefront of advocacy. Only in the 1960s and 1970s did we see the emergence of significant leadership provided by those directly impacted progressing to the significant strides being made at this time. As a person who has used a wheelchair for mobility since experiencing a spinal cord injury in 1965, I have an identity that is useful. In all honesty, I may not have the strong consumer orientation of others who have been recently involved in a service delivery system, but I do have and use the credibility of a consumer during my advocacy efforts. I also try to stay in touch with consumers to be sure I am aware of current issues.

I hope to convince the reader that this *consumer centered orientation* is an automatic asset that many persons with disabilities can seize if they choose. Nothing makes a statement better than a room full of wheelchairs, a few assistance animals, a sign language interpreter, and four or five consumers serving as a receiving line going into the committee room. I genuinely hope that someday this will be routine, however, this is not a regular occurrence. It, nevertheless, does get folks' attention!

Politicians at all levels usually have to deal with large figures and broad concepts. They seldom have time, and ofttimes more sadly do not have the disposition to see the real impact of their actions. There is no better advocate than an informed and committed person with a disability advocating on something that directly impacts him or her. Political decisions, good or bad, are easy to live with when dealing with an abstract item, but when the politician looks at the *FACE* that the item has a direct impact on, it takes on a real life. The success of most advocates has been based on their connection with the issue–they need an accommodation, they need accessible transportation, and they want to live in the community rather than an institution. They are genuinely invested in the legislative action.

"Care" About What You Do

Here is where persons with disabilities have another natural asset.

Every time I have been with groups of consumers with disabilities, I am made aware of the genuine *CARE* they have, not only for their own lives, but also for all others with similar disability issues. Years ago, I wrote on the process through which persons go through to adjust to their disabilities. This behavioral process engenders in many cases anger, a desire to join a group of others, or other motivating factors that can naturally feed the ranks of advocates. When this level of caring is combined with a basic understanding of the issue (e.g., emphasis on serving persons with the most significant disability, Independent Living, personal assistance services sponsored by Medicaid, etc.), the success potential of the advocate is substantial. In fact, this could be cited as one of the greatest assets in the disability movement. A zealous informed advocate can bring about real change.

Make "Time" to Make a Difference

In this, the twenty-first century, many Americans complain about being too busy. Ofttimes that is true, but it is critical to find the time for our advocacy. Those heroes earlier referenced found the time–no, made the time–to become active in the advocacy movement. Showing up at public hearings, committee meetings, and regular sessions of local, state, and federal government is mandatory. Offering comments on regulations and policies that are out for comment must be an activity of each person, not just the paid staff who represent different human service agencies.

TIME is the most important resource we have and we should manage it well.

Beyond that we must understand that many things in life are not within our realm of control, but we all do have the ability to manage our time and choose how we invest this resource. If the ADA, Individuals with Disabilities Act (IDEA), and other important legislation are to continue to positively evolve, we as disability advocates must make the time to make a difference.

"Vote" for Candidates Who Support You

Substantial progress needs to be made in the voting habits of persons with disabilities. Recent polls note that one of the life activities not fully participated in by persons with disabilities is voting. There continues to be barriers in many precincts. If not barriers to the physical entrance of the precinct, problems with equipment or lack of supports to assist persons with the most significant disabilities, prevent many from voting and exercising the most basic right of citizenship. This is an endowed right and responsibility that we need to assure persons with disabilities have an opportunity to exercise. Regardless of the success of recent voter registration efforts, I, nevertheless, note the importance of such efforts. Moreover, persons with disabilities need to become vested in the political process. Although disability cannot be allowed to become a partisan issue—where only one party assumes responsibility for disability issues—party activity is critical. During a recent statewide election in Virginia, both the Republican and Democratic parties had some form of a disability caucus. But even with this success, we were not able to see significant involvement of persons with disabilities in the day-to-day operation of phone banks, envelope stuffing, sign distribution, etc.–the kind of person power that campaigns rely on. Without this day-to-day level of contribution, candidates will never learn the importance of having a TTY for their offices, or assuring that public events are held in accessible sites with sign language interpreters. Contributions of money must also be made. Money is the mother's milk of politics. Even with campaign financing laws, there are ways to raise funds and to let the candidate know where they came from. Legislators know the value of responding to people who vote for them and who have the potential to keep on voting for them, and this is not to be overlooked. BUT it is not rocket science to understand that the cash contribution gets the desired access and attention.

Effective Legislative Advocacy

It is hoped that by now, the reader—especially if the reader is a person with a disability–is ready to become active. Over the years, I have seen the importance of the following *rules* for successful advocacy and offer them to guide future political action.

Rule 1: The First Priority of Any Politician is to Get Elected

Within this first rule lies the POWER a person with a disability needs to encompass in order to have an impact on the political process. When a person, any person, decides he or she wishes to enter politics, the first priority is to figure out a way to get more votes than the other people who may run for the desired office. The best way to accomplish this—again not rocket science—is to connect with more voters than the opposition. Talking to voters, learning about what they want, and convincing them that IF elected they will act in a certain way on certain issues, is the key to election. With this in mind, the disability advocate can begin to establish a relationship with the candidate. An elected official is never more open to a constituent's ideas than during an election. The disability advocate can use this, at a minimum, to voice concerns and share ideas. Immediate success may not be guaranteed but getting the attention of the candidate is the first step.

Rule 2: The Second Priority of Any Politician is to Get Re-elected

As a natural extension of Rule 1, staying in office is even more important than getting in office the first time. The successful elected official stays in touch with those who voted him or her into office and continues to build a broader voter base. In most cases, this base is increased when the politician is responsive to the concerns and requests of constituents. A relationship can be developed where the elected official knows that he or she can count on the constituent and the constituent can then begin to keep the official accountable. It is interesting to watch elected officials mature. Some do well and keep connected, but each year, one does not have to look far to identify an official who is out of touch with constituents. The name given to these individuals is "ex" senator, delegate, and so on.

Rule 3: All Politics Are Local

"Tip" O'Neill, former member of the United States Congress and Speaker of the House, is usually credited with this basic premise, that continues to hold true. Coupled with the two preceding rules, the disability advocate can build a solid strategy using this axiom. Elected officials are continually charged with looking at bills and budget initiatives and asking the basic question: "What will it do for my folks back home?" The disability advocate must let the politician know that there are real folks back home–who vote–that are interested in some particular service, program, or initiative that will benefit the community. Letting the official know what you want and illustrating the benefit of the program is critical. Chambers of Commerce, road builders, physicians, and other groups are expert at illustrating the value of certain actions with value being defined by "how it benefits folks back home." It has been interesting to observe, that as we expand our disability efforts, the community at large has benefitted by the inclusion of persons with disabilities in the work and play of our towns and cities.

Most persons are aware of the social injustices remedied by the Americans with Disabilities Act. This landmark legislation was more easily "sold" by noting to each member of Congress the positive attributes of the bill for all of their constituents: the economic impact of getting persons with disabilities to work; the increased income generated from purchasing technology to assist persons with disabilities; and the many jobs that will be created in communities across our nation as a result of increasing access for all persons. When any initiative is contoured in a way that is focused on how people back home will benefit, the likelihood of gaining a favorable vote is greatly enhanced.

Rule 4: The Art of Politics is Compromise

Almost as frustrating as the slow pace of the political process is the realization that compromise is a required component of politics. Seldom is the disability advocate satisfied with the results. BUT, like the song performed by Rolling Stones said:

> You can't always get what you want, but if you try sometimes, you just might find, you get what you need. (Jaggar & Richards, 1969)

The legislative process is based on trying to satisfy all sides–even when there may be polar opposites, which often is the case. It takes time to identify all sides of an issue, go over it time and time again to find common ground, and when there is none, how to build it by facilitating a consensus. Anyone involved in politics lives by the motto "a half a loaf is better than no loaf at all." Understanding this axiom and planning long-term strategies where everyone is a winner is another asset the disability advocate must develop.

Rule 5: Never Burn Bridges. Your Opponent Today May be Your Bedfellow Tomorrow

The political process requires a winner and a loser. We all enjoy winning more than losing, but we need to remember that advocacy is a long-term process and the person we defeat today may need to be counted on for assistance in the future. One aspect of the political process the casual observer may see and find different is the institutional politeness that is found on the floor of any legislative body. There is a good reason that people are referred to as the "Gentleman from Henry County" or the "Gentlelady from Sussex."   Moreover, there are rules about attacking an individual; only comments can be made in the context of the bill or the resolution and not the person. This forced genteelness focuses attention to the issues not the persons involved. You can disagree or fight about an issue and come back tomorrow and work with the person with whom you disagreed. The disability advocate needs to mirror this. Always respecting the position the official occupies, even if the respect for the person is not very high. With this protocol fully in place, officials can work together over the long haul on the myriad of issues they must deal with and form the partnerships that are required to make progress. Being able to connect with different officials over time and getting them on the "disability team" is a major goal for the disability advocate.

This is not to say that gentility must be a constant for all advocacy. For legislative advocacy yes, but for other forms of consumer advocacy, there is room for a sharper edge. The historic civil disobedience actions of ADAPT to the recent protests surrounding the *Olmstead* case, advocacy that attacks officials and institutions has proven successful especially when more reserved and subdued measures do not work. BUT, within the legislative process, decorum and protocol should always be sustained. There is room for both forms of advocacy. Malcolm X and Martin Luther King could not have been as successful alone as they were in a complimentary fashion. The successful disability advocate will know what style to adopt for the particular situation they are trying to impact.

Rule 6: Anything That Does Happen is the Result of More Than One Factor

Understanding this is critical to advocacy successes. There is a political axiom that notes that "timing is most important in sex and politics." An effective disability advocate must be able to scan the environment for all factors and then build a strategy recognizing all of these factors. Timing is key. It makes little sense to ask for and expect to receive increased funding during an economic downturn.

Knowing the background of officials is vital. In Virginia, we had a senator several years ago who was incredibly supportive of all measures that would expand services for persons with a brain injury. It was not obvious what his motivations were, but after a bit of research, it was found that his wife had a brain injury, although minor, as a result of a car accident. Being aware of the potential opposition an official may face can also give the disability advocate a competitive edge in inviting an official to be a supporter. Personal connections are always important. When identifying officials to be patrons for disability measures, successful advocates must be able to identify the official's:

past voting record;

personal connections to disability based on relatives, neighbors;

prior experiences;

future aspirations;

party affiliation; and

capacity to be a leader within the process.

By understanding the implications of these variables, the disability advocate may not be able to guarantee success, but can certainly increase the likelihood of success of the issue or initiative that is being advocated.

Rule 7: Real Success is the Product of Hard Work, During Hot Weather

In Virginia, we have an unusual process wherein our legislature meets from 45 to 60 days during the winter season. The disability advocate is involved on a daily basis during the legislative session, although the best time to educate officials, get to know them, support their campaigns, and build political capital is in the spring and summer. Inviting legislators to come and tour programs, to participate in local advisory groups, and, in general, to educate them on important topics is as important as being there in January, February, and March. This is a powerful avenue through which a face may be imprinted on the issue. No one can ever fully appreciate the value of a Center for Independent Living unless they actually visit one. To actually see a person with a significant disability work can best be done by touring a community rehabilitation program.

It is also critically important to thank those legislators who have contributed to the advance of the disability rights agenda. It is amazing how often this is overlooked. Legislators are people too, and all of us like to be appreciated. For those who have gone the extra mile, some form of formal appreciation can be very helpful; giving a tangible award for good work is a fine idea. I have never been into a politician's office that did not have a wall of plaques and certificates. These awards indicate that they are still connected with the people who put them in office and is a reminder of who gave them these awards.

Rule 8: It's Not a Sprint, It's a Marathon

One of the most disappointing aspects of the legislative process is that it takes time. After a person with a disability gets fired up and involved, there is an expectation to get results—get results now! But in most cases, it does not work that way. By design, the political process takes time. Time to allow issues to be understood and fully examined from every perspective. Time to allow all voices to be heard. Time to allow the politics of an issue germinate and fully blossom. The successful disability advocate must understand this and not be discouraged. It takes time to build relationships with legislators, but every minute invested in this process is time well invested.

In conclusion, we are on the cusp of some exciting changes within our society. Technology is helping many persons find employment and attitudes are changing slowly but changing nonetheless. A booming economy is creating more jobs than workers and this dynamic should create opportunities for workers with disabilities. BUT, sustained advocacy in the streets, at the state and national capitals, and within the legislative halls is the essential ingredient to realizing the promise of the ADA and subsequently finding Americans with significant disabilities fully integrated into the mainstream of American life.

REFERENCES

Jagger, Mick & Richards, Keith (1969). You can't always get what you want. *Let it bleed.* London, England: London Records.

Roth, Helen (Summer 1995). Advocacy ! Advocacy ! Advocacy ! *NCIL Newsletter.* National Council on Independent Living. Arlington, VA.

Wallace, David Foster (April 13, 2000). The weasel, twelve monkeys, and the shrub. *Rolling Stone.* New York, New York.

Chapter 13

ADAPTATION TO DISABILITY

Justin S. Rybacki

Sometime back in my relationship with Sondra (my personal services assistant), she asked me why I thought I had gotten Multiple Sclerosis (MS). I answered her with the only answer that has ever come to mind as my simple reasoning behind the cause for this insidious disease:

> "Because," I said, "I must have really 'pissed' God off."
> "Oh, how's that?", she asked.
> "I don't know, maybe being lazy, never finished my schooling and Mom and Dad had borrowed money for that–knowing that I was a big disappointment to them. I really was not much of a husband to my wife–in the beginning she earned the most money. So, I became a workaholic and took on the challenge and was not at home much in the process. You know, I've spent hours trying to find a reason for my disease and this is the only answer I can come up with. I just really 'pissed' Him off and this was my punishment."

After all, there is the basic biblical belief that God gives people what they deserve, that misdeeds cause our misfortunes, which, of course, is both a neat and attractive solution to the problem of evil or bad deeds at many levels. You know, "What goes around, comes around." So I must have done something really bad that displeased God. I mean, why else would I have been stricken with MS? In Harold Kushner's book *When Bad Things Happen to Good People* he wrote that victims of misfortune try to console themselves with the idea that God has His

186

reasons for making bad things happen to them, reasons that they are not in a position to judge. After all, look at Job, a good man, one of the best, and read what happened to him. Satan enters into the picture and challenges God saying that "You have bestowed everything good and prosperous on Job–take that away and Job will turn on you." God accepts the challenge. As a result, and to prove a point, Job loses his entire family, possessions, and is stricken with bodily infections. Job remains true and in the end regains his wealth, a new family, and his health. A just reward for his faithfulness. So, imagine my surprise when reading Kushner, who posits his interpretation of why bad things happen as randomization, rather than the direct hand of God. That, as the bumper sticker is written "Sh*t Happens." Regardless of our sex, race, national origin, religion, accident, disease, untimely death, and so on, bad things "just happen." The person just happens to be in the wrong place at the wrong time.

To take causality and justification from God and to reassess the entire thought process, thinking anew, that God does not cause the bad things that happen to us was something I stumbled with in my process of adaptation. Instead of God being the cause, God is really there to help one get through and over those "bad" things. This concept was a new, interesting "food for thought" approach to what I, as a person with a disability, and so many more like me are trying desperately to ingest, roll around in our minds, and finally take in or swallow. For so very long we have believed that a past deed, omission, or whatever had caused God so much pain and anger that he needed to punish the perpetrator–that is, one of us. This, then, was indeed a part of my process of adaptation. That process has gone even further in that I now see God as "once again" my friend, my savior who loves me. That, in fact, I have done nothing wrong.

In Kushner's chapter on "God Leaving Us Room to be Human," he asks "Why then, do bad things happen to good people?" Kushner answers that our being human leaves us free to hurt each other, and God can't stop us without taking away the freedom that characterizes our humanness. I interpreted that to mean "choice." For, in reality, life is one choice after another. We choose what we will wear each day, what we will eat, what route we will take to work, how we will respond to our co-workers, family members, and people in general. We can steal, hurt, cheat and Kushner notes that God can look down in pity and compassion on how little we have learned over the ages.

Consequently, bad things do randomly happen to any and many of us. So, if we can rationalize this, then what Kushner is saying makes sense and can be seen realistically—God can't do it all. Neither does He reward or punish each and every living soul. In retrospect, I learned in Catechism that not only does God forgive us, but He also forgets. Imagine if God kept lists, they would be so long that none of us would ever get to Heaven. Prior to Vatican II, we (Roman Catholics) had this holding area called Purgatory. If it were still there, not only would it be full, but it would be overflowing.

On the subject of prayer—that time that we talk to God—Kushner discussed the real meaning of prayer. Often we pray for health (ours or for another), a favorable outcome to an operation, or a cure. If prayer worked the way many people think that it should, no one would ever die since no prayer is ever offered more sincerely than for life, for health, or for recovery from a chronic disease for ourselves or those we love. If granted, we re-avow our commitment to God in faithfulness and piety. But if it is not granted, then, we in essence become "pissed" with God. How could He do this—I am a good person, a faithful person? I deserve to be cured or to be made whole again because of those qualities of piety and faithfulness.

By our own admission, the world is a cold, unfair place in which everything held precious can be destroyed. But instead of giving up on this unfair world and life, instead of looking outward—to churches or nature—for answers, Kushner writes, we must look inward to our own capacities for loving, for caring, for making lemonade out of our lemons. We must persevere and live to our fullest. So, in the final analysis, it is not the question of why bad things happen that is relevant, it is how we will respond now that it has happened. Our process of adaptation must lead us to that ultimate end when we do not question, do not blame God nor ourselves. It has happened and we need to move on, saying not what we can no longer do, but instead, saying what we can still do, enjoy, and participate in.

REFERENCE

Kushner, Harold S. (1983). *When bad things happen to good people.* New York: Avon.

Chapter 14

TO MAKE A DIFFERENCE

CHARLES C. WAKEFIELD, JR.

THE REALITY OF LIVING IN THIS WORLD with a chronic impairment has been my experience for almost 40 years. As a young child, I was treated for flat feet by an orthopaedic surgeon for about two years. When no improvement could be demonstrated, I was examined by another physician for possible symptoms which could be linked to rheumatic fever. Again the findings were negative. What started out as a slight limp in my right foot slowly progressed to severe mobility problems, including moderate to severe stiffness in several joints, especially during the morning. By the time I was correctly diagnosed with juvenile rheumatoid arthritis (RA) at age seven, I was barely able to walk. This, however, was just the beginning of what the next 30 years would manifest.

My early years in school proved to be quite difficult. I remember always being stiff and in pain upon arising in the morning. It would usually take me at least an hour to be able to function on a somewhat normal basis, but the pain, that horrible creaky pain, was always present—a great way to start the day. My arrival at school was usually greeted by kids asking me why I walked funny or some inconsiderate schoolmate calling me names such as "cripple" or "gimpy." In fact, I was subjected to this treatment not only during my early school years, but for much of my life. Words can't begin to describe how difficult it was to go through my daily activities in pain, but to be subjected to verbal abuse and embarrassing questions as well was a bit too much.

Looking back at my experiences between the third and seventh grades does not make me very happy. The pain and ridicule that I endured was, at times, overwhelming. I remember missing a lot of

189

school because I did not want to have to listen to the insults. I was absent for that reason almost as much as the actual physical symptoms associated with RA. I now realize that children can often be cruel and insensitive, often reflecting the attitudes of adults; however, this knowledge does not make that part of my life any easier to digest. I wonder how I ever made it through that difficult period of my life. Surely the love and patience exhibited by my mother was a prime motivator in those trying days. I don't think that I could have endured without her unending compassion to help me, somehow, find a way to carry on.

When I was in the fifth grade, I remember having a great deal of pain and stiffness. I could barely function. I recall hearing my mother discuss my situation with another family member when I was around nine or ten years of age. She told my aunt that the doctor had said there was a strong possibility that I would be in a wheelchair in a few years if the RA could not be controlled. Evidently my treatments were not effective at that time. My mother did not realize that I had overheard her, but she also never knew what hearing the word wheelchair did to my emotions. Beside searing me to the core of my emotions, I believe that hearing that possible scenario actually motivated me. It made me determined that I would fight this disease with every ounce of my soul. Instead of feeling sorry for myself, I got mad. No damn disease was going to take away my ability to walk. I simply would not let it happen.

The medical treatments that I have received during my lifetime have been astronomical. I have endured somewhere between 20 to 30 operations. I really cannot give the exact number. I have had surgery on 8 of my 10 fingers, some more than once. Four of my fingers have been fused, which means the joints have been removed and the other digits have received synovectomies (cleaning out the bad tissue). I have had surgery performed on both knees (synovectomy). My knees, fingers, elbows, wrists, and other joints have been aspirated over 100 times (which means that the particular body part is aspirated in order to draw off excess fluid and then cortisone is usually injected during these procedures). If you can only imagine what it feels like to have needles injected into the small joints of your fingers, then you will have a greater understanding of what the word pain means.

My most serious medical procedures were two major surgeries performed on my face. Because of the disease, I had bones which grew abnormally in my jaw area. I had an unusually small chin which made it appear that my mouth dropped straight back to my neck. You can imagine the insults and psychological trauma that this condition brought into my life. The first operation was preceded by braces, extractions, and orthodontic appliances being required before the surgery could be performed. The operation lasted for nine hours and consisted of surgically breaking my jaw and then grafting bone, which had been removed from my hip area, into my jaw. This procedure was fairly new at the time it was performed. My mouth was wired together for three months and it took almost two months for me to be able to walk without pain in my hip where the graft material had been removed.

The first operation in 1974 was successful and made my life a little more pleasant. However, the bones once again became abnormal and, in 1984, I underwent an incredible 12-hour operation. Grafts were again taken from my hip and placed in my mandible, only this time metal mesh was also included to, hopefully, prevent further relapse of my jaw. My teeth were also rearranged to provide for better alignment. My girlfriend, at the time, told me that when she visited me in Intensive Care after the procedure, my head was purple and the size of a basketball. I remember that horrible tube in my nose and throat and not being able to talk or breathe. I kept getting sick and the nurses had to use suction to remove the fluid. Because my mouth was wired together, vomiting was very dangerous because of the potential for choking. Needless to say, this experience was pure hell.

Rheumatoid Arthritis has required me to consume an endless regimen of medications. I have used just about every drug that has been approved for treatment. In addition to the countless medications, I have also gone through hundreds of tubes of creams, salves, and ointments. I have had hot wax treatments, worn copper bracelets, even tried WD40 and anything else I could think of which gave some hope of relieving the pain. The costs of the over-the-counter products alone have, at times, created an economic hardship for my family and me. I could not begin to put a price tag on how much this disease has cost in terms of dollars and cents. I know that the figure would easily be in the six figure category.

The type of arthritis that I experience is a chronic disease of unknown origin that exhibits its symptoms in the form of recurring inflammation in the synovial tissues of the joints. When the disease is active, the tissues become inflamed, swollen, thickened, warm, and quite painful. The disease is a progressive disorder; however, not all people are affected at the same level of intensity. Some can have severe consequences which can happen over a short period of time, while others who have the disease are able to live fairly normal lives. The disease manifests itself in the form of remissions (lack of symptoms which can last from days to years) and exacerbations (symptoms worsen), which may cause the connective tissue to have severe damage and deformity. Other symptoms include elevated body temperature, irritability, fatigue, loss of weight, and depression. The disease also has the ability to attack other body organs such as the eyes, spleen, heart, lungs, and so on—any place that connective tissue exists has the potential to be affected.

The main treatment for rheumatoid arthritis is to minimize joint damage, maintain existing mobility, and to prevent deformity. Treatments include both oral and injected drugs, surgery, rest, and various forms of exercise depending on the severity of the symptoms. I have noticed that no single drug seems to work for very long. It has been my experience that some drugs will work for a while, then become ineffective. Change is a big part of a person's lifestyle who experiences RA. While medical research can claim no absolute cause for the disease, it is thought that it is associated with the immune system. The body's cells recognize its own tissue as foreign and the immune system attacks these healthy body cells. Early treatment and strict treatment compliance seems to offer the best chance to reduce the potential for negative consequences associated with RA.

Conclusions and Implications for Systems Change

The physical, emotional, financial, social, and psychological problems associated with RA have brought about much hardship in my life. It caused me to give up a possible career in sports. During my teenage years and during a period of remission, I was an excellent baseball player. In fact, my team went to the city championships two years in a row. I was named "Most Valuable Player," quite a feat for someone who was headed for a wheelchair. The remission of my adolescent years gave way to increased symptoms when I reached adulthood. The years from age 20 to 35 were characterized by one operation after another, time missed from work, discriminating employers, the breakup of my marriage and finally, forced retirement from my vocation as a dental technician.

I believe that a significant impediment for people who have RA is the simple fact that those who don't have the disability do not understand what the affected individual is experiencing. My employers never understood how difficult and painful trying to perform my job duties could be, despite the obvious visual deformities. My ex-wife believed that I was using the disease as an excuse to withdraw or escape responsibilities. She never could understand that I could not cut the grass because I could not manipulate the bar that had to be pressed in and out in order for the lawn mower to work. My hands simply would not allow me to perform that type of manipulation. I could recount many other episodes where people were not able to comprehend the restrictions of this disease process. But the bottom line was the disease often prevented me from performing certain tasks. Some people simply do not recognize that reality.

When the associated problems involved with the disease are taken into consideration, the picture of living with a disability becomes much clearer. The progression of RA, for me, has resulted in a financial burden. I missed countless hours from work that caused all kinds of dilemmas for not only me, but my workplace as well. When I was not there, someone else had to perform my job duties. I only received sick pay for a certain number of days, so when these days were exhausted and I still could not work, I would be without wages. Imagine the hardship this created in my already strained lifestyle. Mortgage holders and electric companies do not care if you have arthritis, cancer, AIDS, or whatever—they just want their money at the time payment is due.

Depression is also a major player in the life of a person who has a disability. I cannot count the number of times that I have been so down that I contemplated suicide. Many times I have wondered if death and the afterlife would not be an acceptable alternative to having to exist with the problems that disability had brought about. It took me quite some time to understand how disability had been a part of my life. I had to struggle to realize that despite the pain and emotional suffering, I could use my experience in a positive way. I could channel my efforts and energy into helping others.

I finally understood that my life really did have a purpose. Feeling self-pity and blaming God for my problems was wrong. I made it through four years of college and a graduate degree in counseling and completed nearly half of the requirements for a second masters degree in special education. I am currently employed as an exceptional education teacher at a private school. I hope to use my life experience, education, and compassion for others, to help those who have similar problems to mine, and to give my own life a deep-rooted meaning.

Where would I be now if I had been unable to receive the excellent help that was afforded to me? Financially I would not have been able to achieve the necessary education and training had I not applied for and been granted Social Security disability benefits. I would be worse off physically, because I would not have been able to manage my severe arthritis without medical assistance. Other factors such as transportation, housing, recreation, and social activities would have been problematic to say the least. All of these factors have affected my life and must be considered in any realistic rehabilitation effort. I have been lucky enough (or unlucky) to view the rehabilitation effort from both sides (as a professional and as a client), and I can sincerely relate that you have chosen a difficult profession in which to perform, however, good can develop out of a bad situation. Believe me, my life can attest to the fact that change has been hard. Going back to school is difficult as you approach middle age, especially with significant physical and emotional stressors. Any form of rehabilitation is not easy. Thank God for people like you, who help make the journey just a little more tolerable.

I want to use my own walk through life to motivate others. I feel that I can motivate others by what I have experienced. I would like to mention that I have not written this chapter to draw pity or sympathy. It has been my intention to tell how RA has affected the life of this one person. My life has been characterized by a series of ups and downs. I've laughed, cried, gotten angry, withdrawn, and reached out in order to try and cope with this disease. I have no bitterness in my heart for those who have been unable to realize how RA has affected my life. I admire those who have dedicated their lives by trying to help others with disabilities. Most people who have disabilities do not want pity or handouts, they simply want a fair chance at a decent existence. I hope and pray that I can use the strength that I have gained from my own challenges in life to help others. Only then will I feel that I have made a difference.

Part 3

LEADERSHIP AND SYSTEMS CHANGE

Chapter 15

LESSONS LEARNED: IMPLICATIONS FOR SYSTEMS CHANGE

E. DAVIS MARTIN, JR.

PROGRESS IN THE DEVELOPMENT and implementation of policies that affect people with significant disabilities, particularly when judged by the advances of the past century have not been good. The lack of progress in the resolution of issues (i.e., education, employment, housing, transportation, health care, and leisure) that affect the lives of people with disabilities, their loved ones, and families continues to impede the independence, productivity, and inclusion of persons with significant disabilities in the education, work, and play of our communities. Institutionalization continues to be, for many policymakers, a preferred option to community alternatives even in light of societal economic gain. When people are institutionalized because it is felt to be the best choice for the person or that person's family in terms of care and habilitation/rehabilitation, it would seem that we have not heeded the lessons of the past century regarding the evils of institutions (note in particular the *Wyatt* and *Willowbrook* cases) or even that we are really aware of the abuses that are currently tolerated within institutions.

The changes brought about by the passage of the Americans with Disabilities Act (ADA) currently are being challenged in our courts. The cause of disability rights, for instance, if the *Garrett* case is decided by the U. S. Supreme Court in favor of the "states' rights" argument would render the recent *Olmstead* decision moot and would place the future of the ADA in jeopardy. A recent survey conducted by the

197

American Bar Association (ABA) revealed that employers have prevailed in ADA Title I cases more than 95 percent of the time (President's Committee on the Employment of Persons with Disabilities, 2000). This represents an increase in employer-won suits since the first survey undertaken by the ABA on this topic (completed for the time period 1992-97) when employees won 8.4 percent of their cases. Positive changes, nevertheless, have occurred within our communities, human service agencies, and educational institutions since the passage of this landmark legislation in 1990. There exists a considerable amount of hope within persons with significant disabilities and their families that positive change has occurred and continues to progress. Advances in technology, greater availability of work supports, architectural changes within our physical society, and attitudinal changes occurring in our educational, work, and leisure environments contribute to this sense of hopefulness. Yet, the effects of change, while often dramatic, remain to many persons imperceptible. Variability in the interpretation and implementation of policies that affect persons with significant disabilities often have lead to inconsistency, confusion, and, in some instances, delays in the delivery of services. Witness, for example, the confusion, inconsistency, and delay in implementing the Medicaid Waiver.

Change and the Infrastructure of Human Services

Gerry and Mirsky (1992) proposed five organizing principles for infusing positive change in human service agencies. They noted that these principles were based on the needs of persons with significant disabilities, currently available technology, and the best practices of each of the human service professions (pp. 345–346):

1. Services for people with disabilities should be based on the needs and wishes of the individuals themselves and, as appropriate, their families.

2. Services for people with disabilities must be inclusive to empower consumers and flexible to reflect the differing and changing needs of people with disabilities.

3. Every person with a disability must have a real opportunity to engage in productive employment.

4. Public and private collaborations must be fostered to ensure that people with disabilities have the opportunities and choices that are to be available to all Americans.

5. Social inclusion of people with disabilities in their neighborhoods and communities must be a major focus of the overall effort.

Certainly these principles are most appropriate and encourage growth and development. However, in order for these guiding principles to be effective there must be a foundation or infrastructure that allows for services to be delivered in a consistent manner. First and foremost, this requires that human service workers—whether they are rehabilitation counselors, social workers, psychologists, case managers, educators, or allied health professionals—to be qualified professionals in terms of their education and training. Certification in the professional or occupational designation should be the minimum criterion for eligibility to function as a counselor, social worker, psychologist, occupational therapist, physical therapist, teacher, behavioral specialist, etc. Currently, for example, the Rehabilitation Services Administration has mandated that rehabilitation counselors must hold certification (Certified Rehabilitation Counselor, CRC) in order to function as a *qualified rehabilitation counselor* within the state-federal program of vocational rehabilitation. In order for the various state rehabilitation agencies to comply with this mandate, a Comprehensive System of Personnel Development (CSPD) effort was initiated that will eventually result in counselors obtaining graduate degrees in rehabilitation counseling, or education, or training that will qualify the individual to sit for the CRC certification examination. Other occupational specialities, as well, have certification procedures in order to practice; all occupations within the human services should have minimum standards for entry and practice within the particular occupation or profession. Does certification guarantee that services will be delivered in the best possible manner? No, but it does assure a greater probability that services will be delivered in an ethical and appropriate way. And it assures the existence of a process to censure or correct inappropriate behavior that may be the result of incompetence or lack of education or training. A major advantage for human service workers to have education, training, and certification in their occupational speciality vis-a-vis the person with a disability is the delivery of appropriate services in a timely and efficient manner. The often cited studies regarding rehabilitation counseling (Cook & Bolton, 1992; Szymanski & Danek, 1992; Szymanski & Parker, 1989) outcomes and level of education are particularly relevant and point to the ethical need not only for the establishment of minimal standards of excellence, but the adherence of those standards when hiring persons to function as rehabilitation counselors.

Secondly, not only must assistive technology be readily available, it must be readily accessible. While assistive technology may be the great equalizer for persons with disabilities, it does little good if the person cannot pay for it. The availability of low cost loan funds is a significant and positive advance but does little for those whose functional limitations are such that, even with assistive technology, full-time work is not feasible. This is not intended to mean that all assistive technology should be given to persons without regard to financial consideration. Policies that take into account the financial ability of a person to repay the loan and also to access the American Dream must be developed. What good does it do for a person to live a marginal existence with great debt? Incentives must be developed that foster the ability to access the American Dream and all that comes with it—decent housing (as well as the ability to purchase one's own home); transportation that is available and accessible comparable to existing public transportation systems, not just alternative systems that often do not maintain a consistent schedule or costs more; accessible health care; and accessible leisure opportunities. Policies affecting work must provide incentives for persons to return to employment or to engage in work activity in the first instance. Persons who are receiving Social Security Disability benefits (inclusive of medical benefits) must be assured that benefits will not be terminated prematurely. The Ticket to Work and Work Incentives Improvement Act of 1999 (TWWIIA) holds great promise for persons with significant disabilities that are currently receiving Social Security Disability benefits. Under this initiative choice or selection of a service provider will be within the control of the consumer or customer. In using The Ticket to Work, it is felt, a person may select a service provider that will yield the best possible training or education opportunities.

Third, educational systems must be inclusive. Children and youth that are educated in segregated school systems are at a disadvantage that extends into adulthood and throughout one's lifetime.

Segregation from one's peers—other children and youth—creates a situation where difference becomes a defining attribute rather than recognized as an ordinary part of diversity. Because of difference and the general devaluation that often accompanies a particular characteristic, a lowering of expectations often results. This *Guardian Angel Attitude* is often expressed by those in authority positions by requiring little of the child or young person because of the perceived severity of the disability. Isolation from one's peers—other children—often perpetuates stereotypical thinking and what a person cannot do, not what a person can do. Segregated classrooms or self-contained classrooms coupled with stereotypical thinking lead to segregated living, work, and play arrangements once the person exits the school situation. For the most part, this has nothing to do with severity but with the perception of severity of the disability. Self-contained classrooms are often defended on the basis that it is the "least restrictive environment" (LRE). The phrase itself implies restriction and or that separation is required. When the intent of this phrase is stated in a positive way such as "most integrated environment" it connotes integration and inclusion. Moreover, from a conceptual perspective this type of language allows for the achievement of greater expectations. The language that we use to describe persons and the learning environments a child is placed in sets certain performance expectations; the more limiting the language (e.g., trainable mentally retarded, emotionally disturbed, disabled, etc.) the lower the expectations are for that person. Language which is more neutral and less limiting or stigmatizing allows for growth and heighten expectations more in line with the capacities of the person.

Recommendations for Change: Personal Perspectives

The effects of disability may vary considerably among persons with disabilities, their loved ones, and families; for some it is a bump in the road of life and for others it may be a devastating experience. For most, it lies somewhere between these two extremes. Disability does not have to be a negative and limiting experience; it may very well be growth enhancing. Carolyn Vash (1981, p. 130) in discussing her disability noted:

> Sometimes I'm not sure what my disability is. Is it being paralyzed, or does that add a laughably small increment to the primordial handicap of being

mortal human? The core of psychological development is realistic acceptance of one's limitations–be they physical, intellectual, spiritual, or of some
other realm. We are not perfect; we are never what we would hope to be–
however beautiful, good, gifted, serene, or strong we appear. These imper-
fections must be accepted without rancor before we can get on with the real
and simple business of psychological development–do the best we can with
whatever we've got. (Vash, 1976, pp. 2-3)

Adaptation to the effects of disability is a highly individualized
process as illustrated in the following memoirs: *Moving Violations: War
Zones, Wheelchairs, and Declarations of Independence* (1995) by John
Hockenberry; *Still Me* by Christopher Reeve (1998); *The Body Silent*
(1987) by Robert Murphy; *A Whole New Life* (1982) by Reynolds Price;
I Raise My Eyes to Say Yes (1989) by Ruth Sienkiewicz-Mercer; *Flying
Without Wings* (1989) by Arnold Beisser; *Thinking in Pictures and Other
Reports from my Life with Autism* (1995) by Temple Grandin; *An Unquiet
Mind* (1995) by Kay Redfield Jamison; *Undercurrents: A Life Beneath the
Surface* (1994) by Martha Manning; *Waist-High in the World* (1996) by
Nancy Mairs; *Prozac Nation* (1994) by Elizabeth Wurtzel among many
others. In each of these memoirs and the memoirs contained in the
second part of this text, "Portraits of Leadership," the reader is lead to
a truth that was revealed in Harold Kushner's widely read *When Bad
Things Happen to Good People* (1981); that is, the counterproductive
effects of focusing on the why questions that are often asked when disability occurs. Justin Rybacki (Chapter 13, p. 188) best expressed the
resolution of this often characteristic behavior when he noted that:

> . . . in the final analysis, it is not the question of why bad things happen that
> is relevant, it is how we will respond now that it has happened. Our process
> of adaptation must lead us to that ultimate end when we do not question, do
> not blame God nor ourselves. It has happened and we need to move on,
> saying not what we can no longer do, but instead, saying what we can still
> do, enjoy, and participate in.

Michael Payne expressed this same thought in this way (Chapter 11, p.
172–3):

> Adaptation is a lifelong process. In many ways I feel blessed because I have
> experienced what is an eventuality for all of us. This experience has given
> me an appreciation for everyday miracles.

Michele Murmer (Chapter 10, p. 168) spoke of the impact of her brother's disability and its meaning for her:

> Richard, like a lot of people, has a disability; it is a part of who he is, not what he is. . . . I have learned a lot from my brother and feel blessed to have him in my life. I have learned to have an open heart and an open mind. These are the gifts Richard has given me.

The centrality and significance of work in our lives must not be underestimated. Recent legislation, particularly during the decade of the 1990s (e.g., ADA, amendments to the 1973 Rehabilitation Act, TWWIIA) supports the basic thesis that meaningful work presents the mechanism and means truly to be a part of the life of the community. Persons with significant disabilities need to set goals, as do all persons, regarding work. John Coates best illustrates this point in his chapter (Chapter 6, pp. 140–41):

> For the student or worker with a disability, though, life is different. The range of jobs available to him or her is intrinsically smaller, because the physical (or cognitive, sensory, mental) requirements simply exceed the person's capabilities. Many jobs, now theoretically open because of the Americans with Disabilities Act (ADA), still may be beyond the person's reach if approached in the same passive and thoughtless way as many applicants. The person with a disability needs to generate interest and enthusiasm in the would-be employer by coming to the job interview with goals: 'How can I set things up to accommodate my needs with a minimum of fuss for others? Once I am hired, how can I consistently meet or exceed my job's requirements?'

Coates continues:

> Enthusiasm alone will not carry the day. Success follows focused understanding that is enthusiastically lived. But understanding of what? How many people discover a task worthy of their best efforts and throw themselves into it, only to lose interest or become discouraged when the hill looks too steep to climb or the slight to humiliating to be set aside? Yet, perseverance, the magic quality, can be nurtured even among those to it does not come naturally. (p. 140)

On the subject of rehabilitation, Charles Wakefield (Chapter 14, p. 194) noted the factors that have the ability to encourage success or to impede one's efforts:

Where would I be now if I had been unable to receive the excellent help that was afforded to me? Financially I would not have been able to achieve the necessary education and training had not I applied for and been granted Social Security Disability benefits. . . . Other factors such as transportation, housing, recreation, and social activities would have been problematic to say the least. All of these factors have affected my life and must be considered in any realistic rehabilitation effort. . . . Going back to school is difficult as you approach middle age, especially with significant physical and emotional stressors. Any form of rehabilitation is not easy.

In any rehabilitation effort, the relationship that is established between the person with a disability and the professional is key to the outcome of that effort. Ann Durden (Chapter 7, p. 149) has noted that the responsibility of the professional must go beyond merely viewing the client as a problem-solving experience that only needs this or that service to be successful. Durden's admonishment reflects the notion of a holistic perspective:

I believe that it is vital that professionals approach a client not simply as a problem, but as a person. Professionals must determine what motivates a person through the eyes of that person in order to foster stability. Stability facilitates growth and development that allows the person the opportunity to build a meaningful life.

On the same topic, Robin Hoerber (Chapter 8, p. 153) reminds professionals that:

The agencies that provide services to persons with disabilities need to take more of a holistic perspective; that is, we as clients, customers, consumers, (all labels which I do not particularly care for–person with disability is preferable when a label is needed) are not something that needs to be fixed. We need a hand up, not a hand out.

The vocational rehabilitation system, in particular, but also community service boards, agencies, and educational systems must through their human service workers or teachers offer to their clients or students meaningful education or training that will allow entry into the primary labor market–that is, a job that pays at least minimum wage, benefits, and offers a career ladder. What good does it do to place persons into jobs that lead to a marginal existence? Is that rehabilitation or habilitation? Some persons may never be able to enter the primary labor market because of the limitations associated with their disability. Does that mean they should be placed in sheltered employment activities and denied the opportunity to access the competitive labor market? No, with the advent of work supports, most notably the supported employment model, persons who were thought to be unemployable have achieved success (Wehman, Revell, & Kregel, 1998). Many, however, may never gain total entry into the primary labor market and in those instances, our policies relating to the receipt of Social Security Disability benefits and the amount of money that can be earned through work activity, needs to be sufficient to access more than just a marginal existence. Richard Martin (Chapter 9, p. 164–65) noted that:

> People need real jobs, not make believe jobs.

> People need to have their own money and pay for things you need to live.

Dewey and Pat Brown (Chapter 5, p. 138) expressed this sentiment in the following manner:

> All people belong together. We need to empower and help people make choices, and to act on those choices.

To facilitate change and to empower persons with significant disabilities, we–persons with disabilities, family members, loved ones, and professionals–must become effective advocates. James Rothrock's chapter on leadership and advocacy illustrates the need for all of us to become actively involved in the political process within our communities and beyond. Change in a democracy comes about through the actions of an enlightened citizenry. Advocacy is the first step in bringing about change but, in the words of Rothrock (p. 184–85):

> . . . sustained advocacy in the streets, at the state and national capitals, and within the legislative halls is the essential ingredient to realizing the promise of the ADA and subsequently finding Americans with significant disabilities fully integrated into the mainstream of American life.

To make a difference in the lives of those we work with, within ourselves, or those we may not personally know but, nonetheless, advocate on their behalf for change we should heed the advice of Ruth and Dave Martin (Chapter 9, p. 165):

> . . . know and understand that your actions *can* and *will* have a tremendous impact on the lives of those you interact with, counsel, provide services to, or teach. The nature of that impact may be subtle and, perhaps, imperceptible to you at any specific point in time. Nevertheless, you can choose to be positive or negative, growth enhancing or retarding, encouraging or discouraging, or ego building or deflating. Choose wisely what the nature of your impact will be—it is life altering!

SUMMARY AND CONCLUSIONS

The ideal of living, working, and playing in the community is on the surface a simple one. It is for most persons. For those persons whose disability has become, for whatever reasons, the defining attribute of their existence, this simple reality is often beyond their grasp or, at best, highly elusive. Jan Nisbet (p. 2) has noted that our current service delivery systems:

> . . . approaches a person with disabilities not as a unique individual, but rather as discrete sets of problems to be fixed, needs to be met, and issues to be addressed. Not recognized as a "whole" human being, the individual is excluded from making the decisions that affect the very quality and direction of his or her life.

The purpose and goals of policies that affect the lives of persons with disabilities beginning with the 1973 Rehabilitation Act (as amended) through the passage of the Americans with Disabilities Act in 1990 have been to develop human service systems that are consumer centered and that are empowering. The intent or the spirit of these policies has been directed in this manner; however, human service decision makers have not always recognized this focus when implementing or enforcing these policies. Inconsistencies and delays in the delivery of services, variability in the education and professional training of human service workers, lack of knowledge or belief in the advantages of assistive technology, work supports, social supports, and a general lack of knowledge of the subtle effects of attitudes that surround the lives of people with disabilities, are the major issues that currently confront human service professionals. The inability to gain closure on these issues results in a parallel existence of shadow for many persons with significant disabilities.

Institutionalization or a variation on this model, segregated schools or self-contained classrooms, and a societal response that, at best, is characterized by a lack of awareness of the impediments that are faced by persons with disabilities has been the predominate response for much of the past century. Is this situation changing? Do we, as Americans, want change? Do we, as a culture, aspire to a diverse and inclusive society? Do we, as a people, want everyone to access the American Dream? Answers to these questions depend not so much on the words that we respond with, but rather the actions that we undertake. The voices of those who call for change, as noted throughout this text among others, are our guides in this journey. We *must* listen.

REFERENCES

Americans with Disabilities Act of 1990. Public Law 101-336.

Beisser, A. E. (1990). *Flying without wings.* Bantam: New York.

Cook, D. W., & Bolton, B. (1992). Rehabilitation counselor education and care performance: An independent replication. *Rehabilitation Counseling Bulletin, 56* (1), 37-43.

Gerry, M. H., & Mirsky, A. S. (1992). Guiding principles for public policy on national supports in Nisbet, J. (1992). *National supports in school, at work, and in the community for people with severe disabilities.* Baltimore: Paul H. Brooks Publishing Company.

Gradin, T. (1995). *Thinking in pictures and other reports from my life with autism.* New York: Doubleday.

Hockenberry, J. (1995). *Moving violations: War games, wheelchairs, and declarations of independence.* New York: Hyperion.

Jamison, K. R. (1995). *An unquiet mind.* New York: Vintage Books.

Kushner, H. S. (1981). *When bad things happen to good people.* New York: Avon.

Mairs, N. (1996). *Waist-high in the world: A life among the non-disabled.* Boston: Beacon Press.

Manning, M. (1994). *Undercurrents: A life beneath the surface.* San Francisco: Harper.

Murphy, R. (1987). The body silent. New York: W. W. Norton.

Nisbet, J. (1992). *Natural supports in school, at work, and in the community for people with severe disabilities.* Baltimore: Paul H. Brookes Publishing.

Price, R. (1992). *A whole new life.* New York: Atheneum.

Reeve, C. (1998). *Still me.* New York: Random House.

Rehabilitation Act of 1993. Public Law 93-112.

Sienkiewicz-Mercer, R., & Kaplan, S. B. (1989). *I raise my eyes to say yes.* West

Hartford CT: Whole Health Books.

Szymanski, E. M., & Danek, M. M. (1992). The relationships rehabilitation counselor education to rehabilitation client outcome: A replication and extension. *Journal of Rehabilitation*, 58, 45-56.

Szymanski, E. M., & Parker, R. M. (1989). Relationships of rehabilitation client outcome to level of rehabilitation counselor education. *Journal of Rehabilitation*, 55, 32-36.

The Ticket to Work and Work Incentives Improvement Act of 1999.

Vash. C. L. (1981). *The psychology of disability.* New York: Springer.

Wehman, P., Revell, G., & Kregel, J. (1998). Supported employment: A decade of rapid growth and impact. *American Rehabilitation*, 31-42.

Wurtzel, E. (1994). *Prozac nation: Young and depressed in America.* Boston: Houghton Mifflin Company.

NAME INDEX

SUBJECT INDEX

A

Accessibility
  ADA requirements, 90, 103, 113
Accommodation
  ADA requirements, 90, 113
  Sec. 504 reasonable accommodations, 56,
    86–87
Advocacy, political primer, 175–85
  issues
    care about topics, 178
    face of disabled, 177
    time investment, 178
    voter advocacy, 179
  rules for political advocacy, 180–85
    compromise, 181–82
    election and reelection power, 180
    lobbying and mutual support, 183–84
    long-haul efforts, 184–85
    opponent today, collaborator tomorrow,
      182
    politics are local, 180–81
    results, cumulative factors, timing, 183
AFSCME
  campaign against deinstitutionalization,
    74–75
Almshouses, 18
  (*see also* Workhouses; poorhouses)
  Dix, Dorothea, campaign for change, 20–
    21
  eighteenth century development, 18
  proliferation, 19
  state development, 19
American Association on Mental Deficiency,
    31, 33, 35
  20th century position on elimination of
    defectives, 33–34

American Breeders Association, 28
  categories of socially unfit persons, 28
American Coalition of Citizens With
    Disabilities, 40
American Institute for the Deaf and Dumb,
    20
Americans With Disabilities Act, 14, 90–91,
    106, 110–13, 197–98
  accessibility vs. employment gains, 113
  Act Titles: provisions and prohibitions,
    111–12
  effectiveness measurements, recommenda-
    tions, 112–13
  employer litigation successes, 198
  mandates, 97, 111–12
  private sector economic implications, 90–
    91, 97
  state government compliance, 90–91
  Supreme Court narrowing range of appli-
    cability, 90
Annulment of marriage
  mental retardation, 32
Arc, 40, 84, 88
Architectural and Transportation Barriers
    Compliance Board, 103
Asexualization, 30–31
Assistive technology, 110, 141–43, 200
  case history, 139–43
Association for Children With Learning
    Disabilities, 40
Association for Persons With Severe
    Handicaps, 84, 88
Asylums, Erving Goffman, 44
Asylums
  (*see also* State institutions)
  colonial era home care, 18
  deterioration of caliber, 22

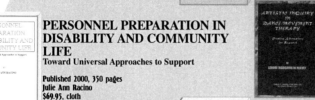